COMPUTER BASICS
FOR MANAGERS
*a practical guide to
profitable computing*

COMPUTER BASICS FOR MANAGERS
a practical guide to profitable computing

RALPH MORRIS

BUSINESS BOOKS
London Melbourne Sydney Auckland Johannesburg

Business Books Ltd
An imprint of the Hutchinson Publishing Group
24 Highbury Crescent, London N5 1RX

Hutchinson Group (Australia) Pty Ltd
30-32 Cremorne Street, Richmond South, Victoria 3121
PO Box 151, Broadway, New South Wales 2007

Hutchinson Group (NZ) Ltd
32-34 View Road, PO Box 40-086, Glenfield, Auckland 10

Hutchinson Group (SA) (Pty) Ltd
PO Box 337, Bergvlei 2012, South Africa

First published 1980
Reprinted 1981
Reprinted 1981 (twice)
© RALPH MORRIS, 1980

Photoset in 11 on 12 point Times.

Printed in Great Britain by The Anchor Press Ltd.
and bound by Wm Brendon & Son Ltd.
both of Tiptree, Essex

British Library Cataloguing in Publication Data

Morris, Ralph
   Computer basics for managers, a practical guide
   to profitable computing.
   1. Business — Data processing
   I. Title
   658'.05'4044   HF5548.2
ISBN 0 09 141570 5

CONTENTS

Preface ix

Chapter 1 **FINANCIAL ASPECTS OF COMPUTING** 1
   1.1 Introduction 3
   1.2 Hardware 3
   1.3 Software 6
   1.4 People 7

Chapter 2 **APPLICATIONS** 11
   2.1 General 11
   2.2 Sales order processing/sales ledger 13
   2.3 Electronic engineering 15
   2.4 Stock control on multiple sites 16
   2.5 Miscellaneous on-line examples 18

Chapter 3 **COMPUTERS AND PEOPLE** 23
   3.1 Introduction 23
   3.2 Social implications 24
   3.3 Specialists 25
   3.4 Users 34

Chapter 4 **SECURITY** 45
    4.1 Introduction 45
    4.2 Threats to data processing installations 46
    4.3 Is data processing security adequate? 51
    4.4 Additional threats posed by computer bureaux 53
    4.5 Providing protection 54

Chapter 5 **OPERATING CONFIGURATIONS** 65
    5.1 Batch 65
    5.2 Remote job entry 68
    5.3 Multiprogramming 69
    5.4 Teleprocessing 72
    5.5 Time sharing 74
    5.6 A comprehensive system 76
    5.7 Real time 76
    5.8 Summary 77

Chapter 6 **SOFTWARE** 79
    6.1 Introduction 79
    6.2 Languages 79
    6.3 Operating software 83
    6.4 Applications software 88
    6.5 Database software 93

Chapter 7 **HARDWARE** 101
    7.1 A brief history 101
    7.2 Elements of a computer system 103
    7.3 Central processing unit 105
    7.4 Peripherals 113

Chapter 8 **SMALL BUSINESS SYSTEMS (SBS)** 121
    8.1 Introduction 121
    8.2 SBS hardware 123
    8.3 SBS software 125
    8.4 Applications software 131
    8.5 Physical requirements 134
    8.6 Suppliers 134

Chapter 9 **SELECTION OF A COMPUTER SYSTEM** 137
    9.1 Identifying the need 138

9.2	Feasibility study	140
9.3	Tenders	144
9.4	Proposal evaluation	147
9.5	Detailed design	148

Chapter 10 **IMPLEMENTATION OF A COMPUTER SYSTEM** — 151

10.1	Communications	152
10.2	Planning and scheduling	152
10.3	Organisation	155
10.4	The changeover	156
10.5	Evaluation	157

Chapter 11 **INTRODUCING MICROCOMPUTERS** — 161

11.1	Background	161
11.2	Features	162
11.3	What makes microcomputers different?	163
11.4	Producing a chip	165
11.5	The developing microprocessor	166
11.6	Applications	168
11.7	Business applications	173
11.8	Sources of help	174

Appendix 1 **THE BASIC LANGUAGE** — 177

A1.1	Introduction	177
A1.2	Statements and expressions	178
A1.3	Designing simple programs	197
A1.4	Further BASIC commands	206
A1.5	Test facilities	212
A1.6	Cost/benefit of user programming	214

Appendix 2 **UK SOURCES OF INFORMATION** — 215

Appendix 3 **COMPUTER MANUFACTURERS** — 217

Appendix 4 **GUIDE TO UK MICROCOMPUTERS** — 220

Appendix 5	**GLOSSARY**	226
Appendix 6	**BIBLIOGRAPHY**	234
Index		237

PREFACE

Whilst it is hardly good practice for the blind to lead the blind — someone who has suffered probably has a better than average chance of helping others. As a user turned 'specialist' in the computer field, I frequently find myself talking to managers who are suffering from inappropriate computer systems or who run the risk of being subjected to one. The numbers in both categories have recently increased considerably and with the advent of low-cost microcomputers they will no doubt continue to grow.

This book has been written with such managers in mind and will, I hope, help readers to avoid many of the elementary mistakes I so often see. Because, in the last analysis, using a computer is a question of weighing benefits against costs, I have tried to emphasise the financial implications. Where possible I have quoted figures in the belief that an astute reader will be able to make allowances for inflation from the time of writing.

Software in particular represents a growing cost to computer users and I make no apology for dwelling on some of the problems before trying to suggest solutions. As a user first and foremost I have collected the concepts which I have found most useful and ordered them in a way that introduces complexity gently. It is an approach that has worked successfully on innumerable courses and seminars — both in-house and public — and which should allow the reader to 'dip into' the book at random. Where possible, each chapter is self-contained with cross-references to other chapters where they are needed. Specialised computer terminology is defined in the chapter in which it first appears and is then redefined in a Glossary. This was produced by asking someone 'who knows *nothing* about computers' to list the words used in the book which they would like to have explained. It is, therefore, quite lengthy.

The Appendices also contain lists of the presently available mini- and microcomputers together with sources of further information. I am well aware that this information will be out of date before the book is available — I just hope that readers will be able to use it as 'ball park' figures with which they can conjure. Anyone wanting to put Chapters 9 and 10 into practice will have to go to manufacturers, software houses and/or consultants for up-to-the-minute information.

January 1980   RALPH MORRIS

ACKNOWLEDGEMENTS

A book of this nature can only be written if the author is helped by his colleagues at work and his friends in the firms in which he operates. I thank everyone who has assisted me with references, examples and material. In particular I thank Jim Thomas for his continuing support and David Hamilton for allowing me to draw on his considerable experience.

Thanks also to L.W. Garner for the cartoons I have used to try to lighten a very heavy subject — I wish I could thank him personally, but since he produced the cartoons for me some years ago for unpublished papers I have lost contact. Thanks anyway!

Thanks finally to Denise Hill who typed everything except these acknowledgements before flying off to a life of sun and sand in the Channel Islands.

RALPH MORRIS

Chapter One
FINANCIAL ASPECTS OF COMPUTING

1.1 Introduction

The installation of *any* computer system depends on one fundamental equation. Does the cost of installation and operation exceed the value of the benefits? If it does, *then the system should not be installed*.
- Never mind if Joe Bloggs has one and boasts about it at the Golf Club.
- Never mind if the children come home from school saying their classmate's father has one in his front-room.
- Don't be panicked by the media saying that only those who live in the Stone Age don't have computers.

If the firm is not better off with a computer, do not have one!

The overall aim of this book is to explain the *what's, why's, how's* and *where for's* of computers, and this first chapter both sets the financial scene and summarises the financial implications of the rest of the book. Each section in this chapter refers to another chapter (though there is not necessarily a section for every chapter).

Some of the benefits

Unless a computer system can show a 'profit' to its owner, there can be no good reason for installing it. Unfortunately it is not easy to quantify either benefits or costs absolutely and there are always mitigating circumstances which can invalidate an apparently powerful benefit or magnify a cost beyond reason. Chapters 9 and 10 discuss the phases of selecting and installing a computer and outline many of the potential benefits that companies may expect to achieve, whilst Chapter 4 (Security) provides a number of examples of costs which can creep up on unwary users.

It would be nice to be able to provide comparative figures, and the percentage of installations which have either achieved given benefits, or fallen prey to hidden costs, but it is simply not possible. However, it is possible to look at some of the benefits that companies may expect to achieve, leaving the final analysis to the person who has to decide whether *that* benefit could apply to his company.

Dealing with increased volumes of business A reasonably well prepared data processing system should allow any clerk — sales, purchasing, production, accounts — to deal with a significantly greater volume of work. Input (via visual display units) is quicker than via most manual systems, the computer does the arithmetic (infallibly) and reports are produced effortlessly.

The corollary, that fewer clerks can deal with the same amount of data is also true (in theory), but seldom applies in practice.

Better working conditions for staff Computers can take over boring and routine jobs, freeing staff to concentrate on 'other things'.

Better management information Using flexible software in the form of database management systems (DBMS) enables management to look at any information stored on the system's files. They can plot graphs of sales, production costs, etc., they can produce analyses in any way, shape or form that takes their fancy and above all they can project the effect of change on their business. What if inflation goes up by 15%? What if raw materials go short? And so on (see also Chapter 9).

Better control over costs By identifying, through their DBMS, where costs are at variance with budgeted figures, action can be taken much more quickly than was ever possible with a manual system. The costs in question can range through
- Raw materials storage.
- Work-in-progress.
- Overtime.
- Finished product stocks.
- Design costs.
- Headquarters overloads.
- Postage.

Because the computer's memory is (to all intents and purposes) limitless, any number of cost centre variables can be stored and reported. The only danger is that the accountant may get carried away and spend pounds trying to save a few pence, or may forget to apply common sense in his enthusiasm for playing with figures. (One organisation even based 'average' expenses of its field staff on two months' information.)

Faster results Some companies have found that month-end figures take five days to produce once a computer system has been installed where previously it only took three days! Usually such failures result from a poor organisational structure, or buying the wrong computer. Any routine operation, such as producing accounts, should be done more quickly and more accurately by a computer than was ever possible manually.

More rapid and reliable results should also be obtained in the design office, technical services, engineering or any department that has to crunch numbers regularly. For example, costing capital expenditure and DCF calculations which take days to perform manually can be completed in seconds. And weeks can be cut from a major design job. The use of special equipment such as plotters and graphics terminals can also help in the design office, but these are frequently difficult to justify in small firms.

It is possible to go on and on about potential benefits that an intelligent user can gain from his computer, but so often the real pay-off will be in terms of some apparently small issue which is important to a particular company. So no more about benefits for the moment; hopefully more will come to mind as examples and illustrations are given in the succeeding chapters (which need *not* be read sequentially).

1.2 Hardware (Chapters 7, 8 and 11)

Hardware has to be obtained and then maintained before being disposed of. There are financial implications at each of these stages which may be different for different types of computer (just to make things difficult).

Obtaining hardware is perhaps the easiest part of the equation to quantify since manufacturers are always willing to quote purchase prices. However, a complete computer system comprises much more than 'the computer'. It contains input and output devices (terminals and printers, for example), storage facilities (disks) and ancillary requirements (such as air conditioning). Some manufacturers (including some of the larger ones) are not as open as they might be about the costs of these 'peripherals', with the result that 'competitive' quotations can sometimes turn out to be more expensive than the higher priced ones.

Where equipment is going to be bought outright, the responsibility for determining the total cost is relatively easy to account, but where hiring or leasing agreements are entered into, the picture is much less clear. More than one large organisation with 'competent' accounting staff has found itself with agreements for different parts of the system which overlap in time. Thus terminating the entire system would necessitate a period of time when idle equipment was being charged. There are no firm rules about purchase or lease.

Certainly computer technology is advancing at such a rate that no machine should be written off over a greater period than five years. Using present-value tables to compare the annual costs of purchase against lease will allow individual companies to assess the value of one against the other.

Remember, though, that government (UK) assistance may be available in Development Areas for any company installing mainframe- or minicomputers; and there is presently massive support available for anyone installing microcomputer systems for virtually any application. If there is a close decision on technical grounds between a minicomputer system or a microcomputer, government support for the micro might carry the day. Such support extends not only to hardware but also to training of managers, users and technical staff.

One word of warning — be careful about lease agreements which result in eventual purchase of the equipment. It may finish up as a millstone occupying valuable space and contributing nothing, since it will undoubtedly be out-of-date, and probably too small for the business after the five-year lease period.

Many 'small' computer users have been surprised at the rate at which their useful usage has grown after installation. Others have been horrified because they have invested in a system that is far too limited for their needs — but which fitted their capital budget!

It is imperative that computers are bought/hired/leased to a *need* — not to a *budget*. If the budget will not stand the cost, then ask if the benefits are sufficiently significant to merit the installation.

As to costs, mainframes will certainly need a capital budget in excess of £500,000 (about half this, $500,000, in the USA since computing is much cheaper there) and very extensive operating costs involving hardware [there is *always* a need to enhance the system, if only to satisfy the data processing (DP) manager's sense of importance], people and premises.

The capital cost of premises for the installation of a mainframe system will certainly include special ceilings, floors, double-glazing and air-conditioning and at present-day prices £100,000 ($200,000) would not be too large a figure to conjure with.

More attractive to medium and to small companies must be the new range of minicomputers and small business systems which can be bought for between £15,000 ($15,000) and £75,000 ($75,000) yet which do not require any special premises or air-conditioning. Even the peripherals for these machines tend to be less expensive than those for mainframes with cartridge disk drives costing £4,000-£6,000 compared with £15,000 for mainframe disk packs. But the message is still the same: 'Don't spoil the ship for a ha'porth of tar'.

It may be tempting to wait a while and get a microcomputer system for less than £5,000 [it's about that by the time floppy disk drives (£750), printers (£1,000) and other bits and pieces have been added to the basic computer costs £1,000)], but in a DP environment, micros are still very limited, and most organisations would be better advised to look to a small business system (SBS) at £15,000-£20,000.

Having obtained the equipment, it now has to be maintained, a field which can resemble a jungle to the uninitiated. Many manufacturers organise excellent maintenance facilities, but they can be expensive — up to 12 per cent of the capital cost of the equipment.

Independent operators can frequently be found to replace the manufacturer's services, and some manufacturers will *only* operate maintenance agreements through second parties. In fact, some manufacturers will only sell through second parties — known as Original Equipment Manufacturers (OEM) — though why a second-party supplier is called 'manufacturer' is a mystery.]

Maintenance costs cannot normally be offset by government grants.

As with leasing agreements, the main traps to watch for are overlapping agreements and ones that do strange things at the end of a given period. For example, some suppliers become reluctant to service equipment that is more than five years old, whilst others only do so on payment of higher premiums. Talking of which, the hardware will need to be insured against all the normal risks, preferably through a company with experience of providing computer insurance packages. With good physical security (Chapter 4), premiums should not be extortionate, but the influence of high capital replacement costs will nevertheless put the figure well into the thousands for a mainframe installation.

Into the 1980s, we can confidently look to decreasing hardware costs for all parts of a computer system in both actual and real terms, and purchasers of computer systems will increasingly have to concentrate their attention on the less easily quantifiable costs of software.

There are literally hundreds of suppliers of computer hardware, both central processing units and peripherals, many of whom provide excellent local services, but do not attempt to cover the country — and numbers are growing almost weekly. It is therefore impossible to provide an exhaustive list and even Yellow Pages will be out of date, but a representative sample is given in Appendix 3. Publications and organisations do exist which try to keep reasonably up-to-date (see Appendix 2) and for specific information it would be better to contact one of them.

1.3 Software (Chapter 6)

When computer hardware was very expensive (in the 1960s) and people were relatively cheap, the costs of either buying or developing applications programs were frequently written-off in a general overheads figure. Today that is not possible, and software costs now account for 50 per cent or more of any major installation — and the proportion is still rising. Thus as hardware costs have fallen over the past five years, the total cost of a system has remained substantially constant. The indications are that total costs are now rising.

Recently a company wanting a relatively simple SBS was quoted £25,000 for the hardware and £30,000 for software. Since the supplier had written many similar program suites, the component of the development costs in that figure must be high and will include some element related to recovering costs from previous systems. Thus the cost of developing suites of 'business' programs from scratch would be horrifying using this supplier's figures.

To be fair to other suppliers, this one particular software house was five times more expensive than the cheapest quote, which also came from a large company. So, in purchasing software, it is worth 'shopping around' to get a good price. But do make sure that within the price comes a guarantee of some software maintenance. There is always a 'bug' somewhere, and it is the firm that tries to cut costs by avoiding a maintenance agreement which will find it!

So much in the software game depends on the rapport developed between the analyst/programmer and his client, that, where quotes are fairly close, the more personable people should be chosen every time.

It is not only in the field of data processing that software costs determine hardware configurations. In microprocessor-controlled situations, the cost of producing software should always take precedence over marginal differences in hardware costs. A printer costing £1,000 is cheap when compared with a month's wasted effort over a year of operation.

It is very difficult without a detailed knowledge of the application to estimate the time needed to specify and write programs, but software houses estimate that a good programmer will average 20-30 lines of coding a day. Now, that does not mean that he only writes 20 lines each day. During the initial stages he may code 200 lines in a day, but by the time his coding has been entered into the computer, tested and debugged, his average will have reached that figure.

An applications suite will comfortably run to 2,000-5,000 lines of programming, or one man-year of effort. Really complex suites of business programs will run to 10,000-20,000 lines, whilst an interactive program with 2,000 lines of processing may have an additional 10,000 lines to handle the interface with the user.

To reduce the effort in this latter area, many SBSs have very high-level languages which can cut the programming effort by a factor of 10 or more. Some purists argue that such programming does not use the machine efficiently. They are right, but it does not matter. More computer power to deal with inefficient programs is cheaper than manpower.

Many manufacturers, suppliers and software houses do, of course, have pre-packed applications programs, compilers or even operating systems which users may purchase (£300-£10,000) or hire. IBM, for example, refuses to allow people to buy software, or to transfer rented software between installations without prior permission, with the result that the unwary company can be faced with a very high annual overhead. This aspect of software costs must be watched very carefully, for though many suppliers 'bundle' at least an operating system and basic compilers in with the capital costs of the hardware, others charge every piece of software separately. Thus, in a recent survey, computer X 'quoted' at £40,000 turned out to be over £10,000 cheaper than computer Y, 'quoted' at £30,000!

1.4 People (Chapter 3)

Nobody needs telling that people are expensive, and for that reason many small/medium firms try to instal SBSs without 'specialist' staff of any type. By and large, that is not a good policy because the cost in time of non-experienced staff will be far greater than the cost of training existing staff in new skills, or even recruiting a 'computer manager' (at about £10,000 p.a.).

Installation of a computing facility will entail significant training costs for all the staff whose jobs are affected, but it is inevitably money well spent. Disillusionment following a poor implementation will cost more in the long run. And do not expect to save staff through the introduction of DP facilities. It may be possible — it should be possible — to cope with increasing volumes without staff increases, but it is unlikely that staff can be shed.

Where process control or robotic systems (see Chapter 11) are being introduced, then it may well be possible to save staff, though there will be a need for some high-grade technical support which may not have been previously necessary.

The 'people' equations, as everyone knows, are not simple, and cannot readily be translated into financial terms. However, allocating 10 per cent of the total installation costs (hardware and software) to user training is a reasonable rule of thumb, starting with 'Computer Appreciation' courses at £500 for two days for up to twelve people and ending with programming courses for selected users at £600 each (plus expenses).

Where computer specialists are employed, their training bill can be quite frightening. In many DP departments up to 20 per cent of an employee's time can be spent on courses of one sort or another — and these costs cannot be avoided if the company is to keep abreast of developments and/or keep its staff — for the career pattern of a DP professional is often determined by the training he is allowed to receive. Fortunately, for the budget, many manufacturers' courses are 'free', i.e. no tuition fees, but travelling and hotel expenses have still to be found.

1.5 Security (Chapter 4)

Security costs can only be approached from a clear knowledge of the internal security procedures required. Hardware, software and file security within the computer system should be specified in advance and bought as part of the hardware of software package. In some cases it may be necessary to extend security procedures after installation and this can be either cheap and easy, or difficult and expensive. Chapter 4 gives some indication of comparative costs.

Physical security is much easier to deal with and one can be certain that the following will be needed:
1 Fire-fighting equipment, preferably carbon dioxide to avoid unnecessary damage to equipment, with a delay mechanism to reduce the risk of asphyxiation to staff!
2 A fireproof safe, preferably *not* in the computer room, to hold important data.
3 Additional hardware to provide on-line security back-up.

It is not possible to estimate costs, but the total is likely to be well into four figures. Because of the difficulty of separating security costs from the measures themselves, a good deal more is said about costs in Chapter 4.

Chapter Two
APPLICATIONS

2.1 General

Writing about applications in a general sense is always difficult. One can either give a lengthy dissertation on the details and security features of tried and tested applications packages (see Chapter 6 — Software) or boldly state:

'If the rules are known, it can be programmed.'

Just as long as one does not expect a computer system to devise the rules — and some people do — then one can safely say that just about anything can become an application. Of course, it may not be an economically viable proposition, or the rules might be exceedingly tortuous, or they may be difficult to translate into a language the computer can understand (Chapter 6), or it may take longer to program the computer than it would to do a 'one-off' job — but provided the rules are known, it can be done. This is particularly true now that users can be in direct contact with the computer.

Business and finance

The timely and accurate handling of data has become an increasingly complex and important task to managers at all levels of business and finance. Computers help bankers to speed up money transfers and loan applications while cutting down on paperwork and inherent errors. The insurance industry is validating claims more quickly and offering faster turnaround times for policy transactions. Foreign exchanges and the Stock Market make constant use of computers to speed financial settlements, endorse orders and generally administer the myriad daily transactions. In the travel business, computers control seat bookings, airport utilisation and flight plans, whilst in transportation managers are making better use of equipment, cutting inventories and more effectively controlling their costs by improved vehicle routing and packing procedures.

In the warehouse, computer-produced picking lists make more efficient use of the manpower available and in manufacturing of any sort (cars, chemicals, food, heavy engineering), orders are processed and goods despatched more efficiently, at the same time that full records are maintained.

Even in service industries, hotels, retail outlets and restaurants are increasingly using computers to monitor and control their throughput.

Research and development

Pioneered by the PDP series of computers produced by Digital in the 1960s, computers are playing an increasing role in laboratories — car, chemical, food, textile, electronic, public services, etc. Laboratory technicians now carry out routine tasks and solve one-off problems using computers. Nearly all engineering design laboratories from ladies' shoes to nuclear reactors have at least one minicomputer to help with number-crunching or access to a bureau service. Highway engineers study the impact of traffic on the environment, and use microcomputers to control traffic signals; architects store survey data and building specifications: civil engineers analyse soil, establish substrata properties, build bridges and tunnels and shift earth — all with computed data. Graphic displays ease three-dimensional design for any engineer of any discipline. Computers now monitor, control and analyse test results, suggest the statistically most probable solutions, reduce data and cut experimentation time.

Production control

As a topic, production control deserves a book, or at least a chapter of its own. As technology advances, the range of activities committed to computer control increases almost daily, and the 'microprocessor revolution' (See Chapter 11) will — as everyone knows from the news media — change our lives.

From the steel industry to aerospace, from petroleum refineries to sugar, computers are taking over jobs previously handled by people. The difficult bit (apart from the programming) is to make the sensors and telemetry work as reliably as the computer they are feeding since, in this area, the system loops are frequently closed, with no human intervention at input or output stages.

The office

Interactive computing (the user in direct contact with the computer) has opened a whole new field of applications which will reduce the clerical load carried by so many firms. Secretaries use 'word processors' to lay out routine letters which are then typed automatically; mailing lists and envelopes can be produced directly from customer files and analysis of sales representatives' time and expenses can be made routine. Even visit reports can be automated!

With that background to applications in general, the rest of the chapter will be given over to some specific examples showing how some users have applied the technology to their own ends.

2.2 Sales order processing/sales ledger

This case study starts some six years ago, when Company A decided to streamline its sales office by accepting orders over the telephone. Up to that time orders had arrived by letter, had been transcribed to internal order acknowledgement, stock, delivery, etc., notes using self-carboning paper in the usual way. In the move to telephoned orders, the company wanted to improve service acceptance levels by being able to tell the customer if the goods he required were in stock, and wanted to avoid taking on additional staff. (There were three order clerks employed at the time.) It seemed to the management that a computer system using visual display units (VDUs) would meet their physical needs, but could they find a computer that was capable of giving them the speed of response they wanted? At the time (mid-1970s), only the very largest companies and commercial bureaux were able to provide 'real-time' systems on computers, costing over £1 million — and it was not an economic proposition to purchase a machine at that price, especially as they were newly into the computer business and felt sure that they would make some mistakes and need some changes to any system they used. The final decision was to use a 'business package' on a commercial time-sharing bureau (see Chapter 5), and to persuade their friendly local salesman to 'doctor' it to their needs as they changed and developed.

Within two years, their needs had changed and developed to such an extent that they could define their ideal system with some accuracy. At the same time, bureau costs were becoming prohibitively high due both to increasing charges and increased usage. Computer hardware and operating software had by now caught up with their needs, and they decided to invest in a computer, producing their own systems and programs based on their bureau experiences.

Included in their requirements were that:

1. Many terminals could be using the same customer file.
2. Only one terminal at a time could be updating a customer's record, but processing should be so fast that other terminal users should not notice a delay if they wanted to update the same record.
3. Invoice details should be posted to customer records immediately, therefore enquiries made to customer file would reflect entries made seconds earlier.
4. Input of data, via VDUs, should
   - *a* Check postings to non-existent customers.
   - *b* Check totals by reference to manually prepared sub-totals.
   - *c* Confirm credit status.
   - *d* Allow easy entry of new customers.
5. All entries should be verified by the software and highlight errors before any postings are made.
6. All VAT calculations should be carried out at the correct rate and totals carried forward. VAT returns should be produced monthly.
7. Discounts could be posted separately.
8. Cash could be posted to any chosen period.
9. Adjustments must be simple to make, yet thoroughly secure.
10. Invoices should be prepared either immediately or in batches, on request, using the company's pre-printed stationery.
11. Statements should be prepared monthly when the sales ledger is updated, and should provide a variety of formats to allow for duplicate entries, prompt payments, etc.
12. Debtors schedules should be produced to show both aged-balances and exceeded credit limits.
13. A variety of reports should be available as a result of updating the sales ledger (monthly), but they should be requested individually.
14. Despatch notes should be generated interactively. Before printing, a check should be made to ensure that the order has not already been despatched.
15. Delivery instructions could be standard (from customer file) or special (entered via VDU).

16   Picking order and containers to be used must be defined for the warehouse.
17   Immediate interactive check should be available to ensure that products ordered are in stock.
18   Stock shortage reports should be produced daily and include:
    a   Economic order quantities.
    b   Lead-time analyses.
    c   Order quantities.
19   The system should also contain a Bill of Materials facility allowing:
    a   Changes in the cost of bought-out parts.
    b   Labour and overheads as 'child' parts.
    c   Gross requirements listings.
    d   Nett requirements listings.
    e   Automatic allocation of 'child' parts to production schedules.
    f   Automatic issue of materials used on completion of production.
    g   Multilevel structures.
20   Monthly stock reports should include:
    a   Movements, both receipts and issues, by either stock number or stock category.
    b   Stock status.
    c   Valuation of stock by FIFO, LIFO and average.
    d   Issue report for stock-level work.

In the event the company got most of what it wanted by buying a minicomputer with a full time-sharing operating system, and employing their local friendly salesman and his colleagues to produce the systems.

2.3 Electronic engineering

Traditional methods of designing complex electronic circuitry fall into two categories: either theoretically establishing circuits which will do the job, or 'breadboarding' to find a combination of components which will work. Major designers use, as one would expect, a combination of both methods to gain the benefits of the theory and the practical results of 'breadboarding'.

One such company, a year or two ago, ran into difficulties with a particular circuit, which sent it in search of other methods. The theoretical models were extremely complex, and whilst steady-state analysis was straightforward — if tedious — transient analysis was daunting. Sensitivity analysis to obtain worst-case conditions was virtually impossible because of the complexity of the circuit (it was estimated that a thorough steady-state sensitivity analysis would have taken up to three man-years) and a transient sensitivity analysis just was not on! Normally this was the point at which breadboarding would take over, but due to the configurations of some of the integrated circuits, the leading edge of the transient waveform was very fast — too fast for even the most determined oscilloscopes.

Their search led through to work on which the Xerox Corporation had been engaged. Xerox Corporation had produced software that faithfully mirrored the theoretical models of electric circuits containing resistors, inductors, capacitors, voltage impedance sources, current admittance sources, mutual inductances, transistors (by equivalent circuit) and limited integrated circuit models. by defining circuit modes and the active (or inactive) elements between them, it was possible to quickly model the troublesome circuit.

The programs, using numerical analysis techniques, carry out steady-state (a.c. and d.c.) transient and sensitivity analyses over an automatically scanned frequency range, and produce either tabular output or graphs. Using tabular output linked to a graph-plotter, the 'bugs' were quickly removed from the circuit and, so far as is known, the programs are still being used as a routine design aid.

Run via a bureau, they are undoubtedly expensive, but are both more reliable and less costly than using scientific staff.

2.4 Stock control on multiple sites

A nationally represented retail supplier recently decided to investigate the potential for improving its control of stock at its manufacturing site and at its five depot locations. The company is in a fast-moving business and wanted to:

1   Enable trends in demand to be identified quickly).
2   Improve customer service by maintaining stocks at minimum levels, yet reduce 'out-of-stock' situations.
3   Reduce the cost of stockholding by reporting where maximum levels were being exceeded and by generating data on aged stock.
4   Produce accurate and timely management control information on some of the more sensitive areas, e.g. volume throughput, stock status and out-of-stocks.
5   Save some clerical effort and, as a spin-off from the systems analysis, improve workflow through the warehouse.

Central to their operating requirements was the ability to expand later if business merited, and the facility for entering data from each depot location over a telecommunications link, using either hard-copy printers (teletypes) or VDUs.

These requirements alone reduced the range of computers which would do the job, and a budget of under £20,000 (1979 prices) eliminated others. Even at this price, hardware was available on the market which purported to carry stock control systems and which could provide both hardware and software within the budget. (For a full discussion of the factors to be considered in the purchase of a computer system, see Chapter 9).

The final specification presented to suppliers asked for:

1. Data to be presented at container level, i.e. 5 litres, 2.5 litres and 1 litre, and *not* just at product level.
2. The facility to input re-order points, minimum and maximum stock-levels, economic order quantities and safety stocks manually. There should also be a facility for the computer to calculate/update these automatically.
3. The following transaction types should be available for finished goods:
   - *a* Receipt from production.
   - *b* Rework from production.
   - *c* Return to production.
   - *d* Planned issue.
   - *e* Return to stock.
   - *f* Inter-depot transfer.
   - *g* Miscellaneous receipt.
   - *h* Miscellaneous issue.
   - *i* Inventory adjustment.
   - *j* Stock count — physical.
4. The facility to allocate customer orders to stock, and a means of recording ensuing requests on production. 'Production in the pipeline' information should be held.
5. The system should produce daily:
   - *a* Item shortage lists — detailing date, item code, item description, unit of measure, minimum stock level, balance, quantity allocated by order number. Sequence — item code within depot.
   - *b* Inventory transaction register — an audit trial of those transactions posted to the master files. Contains — date, item code, item description, order number (if applicable) type of transaction and supporting detail, quantity. Sequence — transaction type within item code depot.
6. The system should produce weekly:
   - *a* Sales variance list — for some 150 selected items at product group level a report of actual sales (at head office and depots) in litres against expected issues (either manually input or for the equivalent period the previous year).
   - *b* Item shortage lists — for some 300 items at item level a report of those items below re-order level, those below

safety/danger level, and those out-of-stock.
7 The system should generate at the end of each accounting period:
  a Stock status reports — detailing date, depot, product group, item code/description, unit of measure, accounting period (receipts, issues, adjustments), quantity on hand, quantity on order, quantity allocated, quantity available. Sequence — item within product group within depot.
  b ABC analyses (by movement category), containing date, depot, item code, item category (ABC), item description, unit of measure, item count annual usage.
8 The system should also provide certain *ad hoc* information:
  a Inventory analyses — detailing date, item code, item description, unit of measure, date of last issue, estimated annual usage, EOQ, re-order point, safety stock, ytd issued, ytd receipts.
  b Physical inventory report — contains depot number, depot location, item number and item code, unit of measure. The list provides a turn-round document for warehouse personnel to record actual counts.
  c Variance reports from physical count — reporting on stock check against computer data.
9 The system should provide on-line enquiry on:
  a Item master date, e.g. minimum order level, safety stock and classification.
  b Item balance, e.g. quantity on hand, quantity allocated, quantity on order, date of last issue, period to date and year to date usage.

There is no reason why any company wishing to apply computers to their stock control should not specify a similar system, but it must be remembered that the budget figures mentioned relate to a configuration designed specifically for inventory management. The machine eventually purchased was an SBS (see Chapter 8) with only sufficient storage capacity for the stock-files and essential software. Any attempt to use other elements of the SBS package would have resulted in the need for more computer power, and an increased budget. Remote sites were dealt with initially by maintaining a manual system until the head office machine was fully implemented (Chapter 10), then one-by-one depots were given telephone links to the central computer and VDU terminals.

2.5 Miscellaneous on-line examples

As stated at the beginning of this chapter, it is possible to list literally hundreds of examples of computer applications ranging from the massive to the trivial. This section contains some examples of applications which should have significant cost benefits because they are using the power of the computer to free people from tedious and repetitive calculations.

In every case, the user has had access to a time-sharing service (Chapter 5), either internally or through a commercial bureau.

1   A marketing manager wanted a new holding tank for his petrochemical products, and had to estimate pay-back periods for different sizes and locations of tanks built of different materials. The first three pay-back calculations using traditional discounted cash flow methods took four days to calculate. Then he was introduced to an applications package on the bureau used by his firm. The remaining 20-odd calculations were completed in a morning at a cost of under £100 (or less than the manpower costs of the first three calculations).

2   One of the tasks of design engineers preparing pipework is to calculate frictional losses and to minimise them by adjusting the design. Where necessary, larger pumps or booster pumps may need to be fitted. The arithmetic is fairly simple (just two or three equations) but optimisation can be tedious. On an internal time-sharing service, one such engineer wrote a program in BASIC (Appendix 1) which was only about 30 lines long, but which performed over 10,000 frictional loss calculations (for a 'cost' of under £5) in seconds. Previously he had taken 3-5 days to find a 'best' solution — and then he was not sure if he had the very best!

3   An annual bane in the life of many a finance director of small companies is transferring annual figures to reports, and getting them typed *accurately*. One man got round the difficulty by using a program designed for financial planning. He did not plan with it, he simply formatted his reports, supplied the raw data, and asked the computer to print the results. Total cost was less than his typist's salary for getting it right — and the computer had done all the calculations as well.

4   It takes between three days and three weeks to manually prepare a program for a numerically controlled (NC) machine tool. Even after coordinates have been defined, they have to be translated into the dialect of the NC tool which is to be used and then transferred to a program on either paper-tape or magnetic tape. The program has then to be tested by running it with a product blank to ensure the programming is correct in terms of shaping, drilling and travel. (Users of NC tools will know the result of asking a tool to travel over one of the work-clamps!)

Using a bureau service, a user of NC tools now programs his most difficult pieces (2,000+ locations) in under three days — and the need for testing is reduced because the computer cannot mispunch a hole in paper-tape or put a spurious character on magnetic tape. Work-clamps are automatically avoided, and the same instructions can be programmed for different NC dialects without re-writing the basic specifications.

Chapter Three
COMPUTERS AND PEOPLE

3.1 Introduction

In the 1950s when computers were first beginning to make a significant impact on businesses, a variety of *homo sapiens* developed which the rest of the civilised world viewed as a visitor from outer space. This breed was the 'computer programmer'. Perhaps, because of that unfortunate beginning, there has always been a gulf between the computer specialist and the rest of the world — which has included computer users. The early breed of computer specialist developed an ability to communicate with computers, but somehow lost the ability to talk to his fellow men.

Now, in the early 1980s, new and different skills are required of computer specialists, and of computer users, who will increasingly have to communicate with computers as a routine part of their everyday jobs.

On the shop-floor, processes controlled by microcomputers will need to be monitored by supervisory personnel, who — before they can be expected to meet the challenge with any degree of enthusiasm — will have to overcome the antipathy created by the 1950s model of computers. In the UK, at least, companies contemplating any form of computer application, from payroll to production control, from electronic office to oil refinery control, will also have to consider the effects of the propaganda of the late 1970s which cast microprocessors in the light of a universal replacement for the labour force!

3.2 Social implications

There can be little doubt that in many production applications, microprocessors will replace human operators as the routine controller of a process. In some instances this will lead to a reduction in the workforce at all levels, with consequent implications for unemployment figures. In other instances, more skilled employees will be needed to maintain the equipment, to monitor wear and to deal with emergency situations. The training and re-training implications are considerable not only for the larger company (which will have extensive facilities anyway), but especially for smaller companies that have little or no experience with training.

Users of process-control microprocessors will have to learn a range of new skills, including basic computer programming, and will have to be prepared to give up their 'know-how' to consultants who have been retained to produce the essential systems. If users are reluctant to release all their knowledge and skills, then the resultant systems may be inadequate or even dangerous.

The implications for developing 'correct attitudes' are considerable, and the penalties of not developing these attitudes are even greater.

Some people may argue that efficient methods of task and systems analysis will overcome any antipathy on the part of the workforce but experience has shown — and continues to show — that the adage 'You can take a horse to water, but can't make him drink' is as true today as ever. The potential for inadvertent or deliberate sabotage is vast during the early years of this latest technological revolution, and employers must carry a heavy burden of responsibility for reducing such sabotage to a minimum.

Education, training, a new perspective on leisure, involvement and above all, a realisation that people are now the most valuable asset a company 'owns', will inevitably lead to a reappraisal of the role of all staff, irrespective of status and specialism.

However, it is not the purpose of this book to investigate the philosophical issues of change resulting from the inevitable explosion in computer applications, and such discussion will be restricted to the job implications for computer specialists and users. Nevertheless, people do not respond in the way that one has come to expect machines to do, and introducing computer technology will frequently result in major reappraisals of company policies.

As the roles of specialists and users are developed and inter-related in this chapter, the nature of such reappraisals will (hopefully) become clearer. For the present, let's just say that a company may need to reconsider:

Its organisation.
Functional responsibilities and authority.

Remuneration packages.
Recruitment and training.
Consultation.

The cost of such reviews and the changes resulting from them are likely to be high, both in financial terms and disruption to comfortable work patterns. They are costs which form an integral part of the cost of installing a computer (see Chapter 1) and should never be underestimated.

In particular, they should not be shirked or 'done on the cheap'. The overall effect of trying to cut corners in this emotionally charged area will be much greater than the cost of doing it correctly. For example, one large UK organisation spent nearly £2 million ($4 million) on new mainframe equipment without asking users about alternatives. They now own a £2 million computer which only the data processing staff want. The users are alienated and speak to data processing staff only out of a sense of courtesy — nobody is gaining any benefit from the new machine. Furthermore, many user departments within the company are keeping manual records which duplicate data held within the computer. They claim, with some justification, that reports are not in the format they require, they are late, they are sometimes inaccurate, and there are too many of them. Furthermore, since users have no confidence in the data processing department, raw data is not properly checked before it is sent for processing and users knowing that they are sending 'garbage in' are sufficiently astute to realise they they are receiving 'garbage out'.

Preventing repetition of such a disaster in other companies requires a comprehensive understanding of the needs of people who have to deal with computers, and a thorough analysis of the roles they play.

3.3 Specialists

Big computer installations (naturally) need more specialist people than small ones. They also require a wider range of specialisms, and some of the people, their roles and training discussed here will only be applicable to mainframe computers. Wherever possible, distinctions will be made between the needs of particular computer configurations as they affect specialist staff and their roles.

Systems analysts

This, the first of the specialist positions considered and the one in closest contact with the user, or potential purchaser, will probably exert the greatest influence on users. The systems analyst has evolved from the 1950s 'computer specialist' as a very particular type of person. In the 1960s he was an able analyst who understood computing and computers as well as he understood himself, but who understood people jut about as well as his wife understood him. By the 1970s he began to acquire some skills with people and now, into the 1980s, the systems analyst has a central role to play in any company using, or envisaging, a computer. To add weight to the importance of the analyst's role, it should be said that the growth of computer applications virtually stopped in the early 1960s because of a shortage of analysts. Applications such as sales analysis, payroll and rudimentary stock control were readily implemented, because they were easy to define, generally procedural, and lent themselves to the painstaking attentions of the 'programmer'. Both programmer and user could test the programs under all conditions without talking to each other too often, and without having to understand each other's point of view. But when senior managers became involved as programmers tackled the complexities of production control and forecasting, the lack of compatibility between detailed thinkers and generalists led to an impasse which stunted growth for some years. From this impasse grew the systems analyst who:

1   Investigated existing systems and identified inefficiencies and bottlenecks.
2   Analysed the data flowing in a manual system and restructured it into a form acceptable to a data processing system.
3   Designed a computer system to meet the needs of management.
4   Documented and assisted in the installation of the new system.

Business analysts Nowadays, the analyst has an even more wide-ranging role, and to reflect this he is sometimes called a business analyst. Some organisations even distinguish between business analysts and systems analysts. Where such a distinction is made, the role of the business analyst is:

1   To help management define its aims and objectives, and to assist in the development of a long-term plan.
2   To coordinate the experiences of functional departments in reaching a definition of a business system.
3   To analyse the business system and compare its requirements with the existing structure of the company.
4   To assess the viability of a computer system in meeting the needs of the business system, and to investigate available hardware and software alternatives.
5   To coordinate the installation and commissioning of the computer system.

The role is, therefore, one that requires a deep understanding of business and of people. Large companies and consultancy organisations employ business analysts who have experience in one particular field (accounting, marketing, etc.) and deploy them only in the area of their specialism. Other organisations employ generalists, with general management experience.

From the point of view of a medium/small company contemplating either employing one, or hiring one for a specific project, there are both advantages and disadvantages (as one would expect!).

Functional specialists may locate weaknesses in an organisation which could be overlooked by a generalist, but they might also be unable to 'see the wood for the trees'. Certainly they would have more difficulty encompassing the complexity of a small business and identifying the areas in which 'feel' plays such a significant part. Almost by definition, functional specialists are unlikely to have the entrepreneurial flair of the people with whom they are dealing.

Perhaps the most important quality of the modern analyst, however, is his ability to get on with people. He must be as comfortable in the boardroom as on the shop-floor, and should be able to put his interviewees at ease. After all, he needs to be able to differentiate between fact and opinion, truth and rationalisation; and in order to do this must be able to overcome the defensive barriers that people frequently erect.

Although, as has been mentioned earlier, analysts are frequently drawn from functional specialisms such as accounting, there is an argument for drawing on personnel and/or training staff (where the functions exist in a company) since they will necessarily have an overview of the company and will not be hindered by a bias towards their own functional specialism. In large companies employing several analysts the problem of selection is ameliorated by the fact that people can be drawn from several disciplines.

Choosing and grooming Smaller organisations considering a computer installation for the first time may have more difficulty, and should bear in mind that their first business/systems analyst will probably be their first computer manager (if the installation is successful). Wherever he is found, he should be as well-trained in 'people' skills — group dynamics, inter-personal relationships, etc. — as he is in the computer field. In fact, a list of the qualities of an ideal analyst reads like a testimonial to perfection:

>'Clears high buildings in a single bound,
>Talks to God as an equal.'

- He *must* be relaxed and reasonably extrovert in his dealings with staff at all levels.
  He should be content to spend time 'chatting' — and attending numerous meetings.

He must also be able to apply his rear to a chair for long periods of time whilst preparing specifications.

He should be educated to about degree level (though the discipline is unimportant).

- He should be numerate and have a working unerstanding of business accounts.

He should have a diverse background.

- He must be able to 'step back' and see the aims and organisation of the company as a whole (the 'helicopter quality' identified by recruitment and selection consultants).

He must be able to apply the techniques of systems analysis and should have some programming experience. (By necessity this experience should be limited and secondary to business experience.)

He should be up-to-date with hardware and software developments.

He should have an analytical mind and should be critical (in the critique-al sense) of information he is given.

He has to be able to communicate clearly, both verbally and in writing.

- He *must* understand business and its problems.

It is unlikely that anyone will be able to recruit such an animal, or even hire one from a consultant, nevertheless certain of the attributes (marked ●) should be considered as of greater importance than others.

Costs Companies contemplating employing a systems analyst should give some thought to his career prospects, since the kind of enquiring and free-ranging mind which marks a good analyst may not be compatible with company culture. Would-be employers would be ill advised to choose an analyst for his ability to fit in later rather than for his potential as an analyst, for in that way they will risk poor analysis, weak systems and an expensive mistake. In such circumstances it would be better to hire an analyst from one of the better-known professional agencies. Employees of such agencies are 'highly respectable', extremely discreet and will bring their experiences with other, similar, companies to bear on one's own problems.

Finally, business analysts, systems analysts or just analysts are *essential* to the success of any computer project, whether it is for a multinational organisation spending £5 million ($10 million) on a mainframe, or a three-man outfit spending £2,000 ($4,000) on a microcomputer. (It would seem that, in the UK at least, there will soon be a flourishing second-hand market in discarded microcomputers bought for the wrong reasons. The 'record' to date is 3 weeks.)

Programmers (applications)

Some systems analysts also write their own applications programs and there are certain advantages in operating this way.

The problem of communication between the analyst and his programmer is completely obviated, and delays resulting from uneven work loads can be reduced. However, the list of necessary attributes in the analyst gets even longer and less achievable at a reasonable cost. Those who appear to have the attributes but are left on the market must have some personality defect or they would be directing their own company!

By and large, it is more common for analysts to pass their work to specialist programmers who will translate the proposed system into program code. Large companies will undoubtedly employ their own programmers and smaller firms will hire them from a contracting 'Software House' or, by using a contracted analyst, will delegate responsibility for the selection of the programmer.

The distinction between a systems analyst and an applications programmer is frequently not clear-cut. Inevitably a dedicated analyst will become involved in the coding of programs and an ambitious programmer will always want to move as far into the analysis of a system as possible. In broad terms though, the analyst decides *what* should be done and identifies *why* it is being done. The programmer is involved in *how* the principles are translated into a language that the computer can understand. He can frequently take an analyst's design and without really knowing what is going on, produce a program that does the job.

At the simplest level therefore it can seem as though the programmer 'just codes' the analyst's systems, and whilst this may sometimes be true, the manner in which he writes the code may substantially affect the future success of a company. For example, one company commissioned a suite of programs to control its sales/order processing function. At the time of writing the program suite it seemed that an external computer bureau using a Honeywell computer would be most suitable, and the programmers prepared the coding using all the extensive facilities of the computer and Honeywell's operating software. Viewed as one views a balance sheet (a snap-shot) the suite was ideal. The analyst and programmers documented the system adequately (but did not provide detailed flow charts) and left the company to its own devices. Three years later the firm had grown to the stage where it wanted its own machine, and selected a PDP11. None of the programs written for the Honeywell machine would run on the PDP11, and the firm was committed to spending as much on rewriting its program suite as on its new computer.

One can apportion blame for this type of disaster in various places, but if the programs had been written in a language and dialect that was reasonably transferable between machines, the problem would have been much smaller. Programmers, being no less human than anyone else, will write in a way which pleases them best — unless they are firmly controlled by company management. Elsewhere (Chapter 6) some of the principles involved in selecting an 'application language' will be explored, so it will suffice to say here that every applications language exists in many different forms. FORTRAN, for instance, exists in at least seen versions: II, IV, IVG, IVH, V, SUPER and EXTENDED. Of these, just one (FORTRAN IVG) is internationally standardised, and it follows that programmers should be encouraged to write at this level.

Care also needs to be taken in the selection of programmers to check that they can write in the language required. Many of the languages are very different and people tend to develop specialisms in particular languages. It would appear that the UK is about to experience a shortage of competent programmers as more and more companies develop their own computer applications, which will inevitably increase the cost of programming. At the time of writing, programming costs for major applications packages are approximately equal to the hardware costs, and all the signs are that their proportion of the total cost will increase further.

The role of an applications programmer is normally to:
1   Devise detailed flow sheets (or the equivalent) from the work of the systems analyst.
2   Write programs that will meet the requirements of the analyst.
3   Prepare test data.
4   Test the program and debug it.
5   Document his own work for inclusion in the analyst's systems documentations.

The point to note is that programmers will normally be working for a systems analyst and may not see much of the user. Whilst efficient from the point of view of the programmer's use of time, this approach can lead to some major misunderstandings and discrepancies between what the user wants and what the programmer provides. Broadly speaking it is more cost-effective to insist that analysts and programmers work as a team, both attending meetings with users about any areas of uncertainty. Additional manpower costs are more than compensated for in improved programs (as seen from the user's standpoint).

Training   Present-day programmers, like analysts, should have some skills with people, skills that will need to be acquired through training. Training occupies a significant part of a programmer's year, for new techniques are constantly becoming available which he will want to master. For instance, in the list of roles previously mentioned, item 1 indicates that the programmer prepares flow charts. Recent developments in programming methods, however, seem to indicate that 'better' programs can be produced if the system is viewed less as a 'procedure' and more as a 'structure' (hence structured programming). The change in concept is at once quite simple yet absolutely fundamental. It entails seeing a program not as a process that needs data in order to work, i.e. the user's *data* is a necessary evil, but as a data-manipulation exercise, which also needs processing, i.e. the *calculations* are a necessary evil.

Thus the emphasis is switched from the computer and its requirements to the user and his needs. The resulting programs are much more modular in construction than earlier program suites, and it is (relatively) easy to add new modules without disturbing existing ones. The benefits to users are considerable, but to gain them it is necessary to retrain existing programmers and recruit trained ones. Because the change in emphasis is fundamental it is a difficult change for many to achieve, and training (retraining) time may be considerable.

As users acquire more control over computers, so they demand more meaningful reports, and we are presently seeing a rapid growth of Report Writing languages. Programming staff will also need to be trained to use these languages.

Programming costs Experience is showing that, however certain a company is that it *will not* need to use programmers — it will. Even the best 'packages' from software houses need to be modified from time to time, and whether programming is done in-house or by a consultancy, it will need to be done, and provision for it should be made in the budget.

Selection Choice of a programmer from a software house raises few problems since users will not normally be given a choice (*sic*). Selection for recruitment should also not be too difficult (provided there are applicants at the salary being offered) since most programmers come from recognised training schools, or are able to provide comprehensive references of their track record. Anyone deciding to select and train a programmer from existing staff would, however, be well advised to use an agency to test candidates using one of the several special selection test batteries which have been devised. It seems that programmers should be 'quite good' in a number of areas, but not 'too good', and selection tests are the most effective way of making sure that the people chosen will be suited to the job.

As with systems analysts, thought must be given to career progression within an organisation. In the past, programmers' allegiance has been to their language or computer — not to the company — and would-be employers need to consider whether they should develop a career structure into their organisation. With computers playing an increasing part in everyday life, the argument for integrating programming staff into the career structure of a company gets stronger year by year.

Programmers (systems)

A very different person from an applications programmer, a systems programmer only exists in large installations, or on computer manufacturers' premises. He is the person who writes and maintains the operating system of a computer, usually in the 'assembler language' (see Chapter 6) of the computer. He is responsible for many of the complex functions that a modern computer can perform, for the display screens on minicomputers, for graphics, for comprehensive program-editing facilities, for the file-handling qualities, etc.

It is unlikely that anyone using this book will be employing systems programmers, but it is possible that they may need to retain the services of one from a software consultancy. For example, they may wish to increase the security of their core (see Chapter 4).

The first thing that should be said is that hiring a systems programmer will be expensive — at present-day prices well in excess of £1,000 per week. They will be required for a fairly considerable length of time, and will want access to every part of the computer, its systems and files. Thus, anyone concerned about security will want to select their systems programmer carefully, getting the names of satisfied clients from prospective consultants and checking with those clients that the work done for them was effective, reasonably bug-free (it is virtually impossible to write systems that are totally bug-free) and well documented. It is also important to establish that the consultants can provide an emergency back-up service should things go wrong — preferably sending the same systems programmer who wrote the modifications.

Operations staff

A mainframe installation will normally employ at least:
    1 Operations manager
    1 Shift leader (per shift)
    1/2 Operator(s) (per shift)
    1 Data control clerk
plus, in very large installations

1 Tape librarian
1/2 Engineers

Typical installations requiring this level of staffing could be an IBM 370 series computer, a DEC 10, a Sigma 9, a CDC 6600 or an ICL 2900 series and where a three-shift system is operated, a total staff of 15-20 people might be required. (Such an installation would also have at least one systems programmer.)

Staff for a minicomputer At more modest levels of hardware investment (PDP11 series, two or three minicomputers in a group of companies), the operations requirements will be much smaller — perhaps a manager for the entire installation including systems development and an operator for each machine, who will also control and monitor data movements, maintain tape and disk records and generally look after housekeeping.

For companies installing a minicomputer for specific purposes, e.g. stock control, it will normally be quite sufficient to train the appropriate functional employee, e.g. stock controller, in rudimentary operating routines, which then become a natural part of his job. It must be remembered though, that 'rudimentary' operating routines still require a fair degree of intelligent application, and staff who are satisfactory store-keepers (or who have risen through the ranks to, say, Warehouse Manager), may not be suitable as part-time operators.

In selecting an operator for a small installation, one of the more important considerations will be that the person is able to cope with changing circumstances and will be able to understand the reason for certain of the more esoteric routines, e.g. 'booting'. Whatever the claims of the salesman, there is more to operating a minicomputer than switching on the power supply in the morning, and pulling the plug out in the evening. A busy day might include:

1 Powering-up. Switching on the processor, bringing disk packs up to speed, initiating the transfer of operating systems from disk to core memory.
2 Testing the system to ensure it is operating correctly.
3 At intervals throughout the day, 'dumping' up-dated files from the system disks on to back-up storage (disk or tape).
4 Operating the line printer, separating printout and distributing it to users.
5 Dealing with user queries ('Why won't my terminal work?'), which may require referral to others in the company or to outside agents, e.g. maintenance.
6 Coping with crash shut-down of the computer because of an error (either hardware or software) and trying to identify in gross terms the reason for the shut-down. For instance, although one would not expect an operator to solve the problem of a particular

program trying to write to a protected part of core memory, he should be able to recognise the program that is causing the trouble and prevent users from running it until the problem has been solved. (Otherwise the system will be up and down like a yo-yo.) He should also be able to identify when the 'bug' is in the operating system, not the applications program.

7   Where a minicomputer has a 'batch' stream, he should be able to write the job control that initiates each job.
8   Shutting down the system in the evening, having first 'dumped' all updated files, checked that all terminal users are off the system and run any end-of-day jobs (such as updating the Ledgers).
9   Documenting any unusual occurrences (new disk packs, crash due to parity error, etc.) and all line-printer output movements.

Some companies, in an effort to keep costs to a minimum, are operating minicomputers without any specialist staff at all, and by all accounts do not seem to be unsuccessful. There is undoubtedly a risk in pursuing this course, and there are companies which, because they have not regularly 'dumped' their files, have 'caught a nasty cold' when the disk 'crashed'. In some instances the 'cold' can be valued at over £10,000 ($20,000), in others it is as little as a day's work for functional staff. But, if the functional staff are not aware of the potential need for this form of emergency activity from time to time (say once a year on average) the cost in terms of their increased scepticism about the value of computers might be much greater.

Selection   For the larger installations mentioned earlier, operators can frequently be recruited directly from school or college and trained on-the-job and/or through manufacturers' courses. Most manufacturers run courses on their computers and on the peripherals most frequently associated with them. As with other computer specialists, a significant part of an operator's time will be devoted to self-development — development that employers must be prepared to see go to other computer installations because operators tend to offer their loyalty to the computer manufacturer, and will move to larger installations wherever possible. Career opportunities outside this route are not obvious, though some do train to be application programmers or systems programmers, looking for a career development into systems analysis or software design.

3.4   Users

In the beginning 'users' were a blot on the computer landscape. They made quite unreasonable demands on the computer system, and even expected it to produce an answer *when* they wanted it, and in a form which suited them. Thus the schism developed and computers, when introduced into an organisation, were merely a thorn in the side of a user, to be tolerated but in no way assisted.

Whether the gap between specialist and user has yet narrowed is questionable, and whether it will narrow depends on the approach that management takes to the introduction of new systems. One thing which is certain is that modern computer systems can now communicate directly with users, and if they are to be introduced successfully, users must be aware of, and genuinely accept, the changes that will occur in their authorities, responsibilities and work-patterns.

In order to examine the potential effects on the staff of a company, and the action which can be taken to alleviate difficulties and maximise benefits, let's take an example of a company on a single site which has installed a minicomputer to control its business system. The computer co-ordinates information from sales, purchasing, production and warehousing functions, produces financial data and maintains ledgers. Through a database it allows users to operate a management information system (MIS), producing reports in whatever format is required. Most of its data input and information output is via terminals near the users' place of work.

Senior management

With the system described the first and most significant effect on senior managers will be that they have access to much more information about their own function. They need, however, to be aware of the potential open to them and to the dangers of accepting computer reports as 'gospel'. Somehow, the printed word always carries more authority than the spoken word — and the line-printed word is seen to be accurate to twice as many decimal places as the data from which it has been produced!

It is essential that, through workshops and seminars if necessary, senior managers are made aware of the limitations of the reports they receive. They must be constantly aware that the raw data is being provided by shop-floor and office staff and that their personal motivations may colour (discolour?) the validity of that data. For systems that support flexible database packages, they will also need help to realise that the computer *can* give them *exactly* what they want, in the *exact* format they require. Thus if the marketing director requires a sales analysis for the last 23 days for a single salesman, with sub-totals for different product ranges, he can have it and either he, or his secretary, can write the 'program' that produces that report in a matter of minutes. Already a breed of senior manager is appearing which consumes information produced by the computer as avidly as the computer consumes raw data.

He must also realise that the computer does not just provide a sterile history but can project trends on which far-reaching decisions can be based:
- What is he going to do with them?
- How is he going to translate them into decisions?
- What changes will he make in the structure of his function as a result of consuming this information?
- How will he communicate those changes to his staff? — will he 'blame' the computer by claiming that 'it' says he should act in a certain way (because if he does he will incite sabotage at data input levels)?

Senior managers (and others) will also need to accept that there is a cost attached to these benefits. First and foremost, 'his' data will no longer be 'his' secret. Other senior managers in the organisation will be able to access his data, and compare trends in their departments with his own. Sales managers battling with higher prices against competition in the field will be able to scan factory wastage figures — and production managers *may* be able to see salesmen's expenses. To combat the implications of such revelations, all senior managers will need to accept — sometimes for the first time — that they are working for the same organisation, and that their parochial interests must be secondary to the good of the company.

Parochial interests take a further knock when it comes to feeding the computer with data.
- Who is responsible for monthly sales figures?
    - Marketing?
    - Sales?
    - Accounts?
- And what *are* monthly sales figures?
    - Gross?
    - Gross less VAT?
    - FOB (Free on board)?
    - Net?
- For what period
    - Calendar month?
    - Period (13/year)?

Before the introduction of a computer, each department probably kept its own records, and experience has shown that they frequently (though not invariably) were different. Now there can be only one figure and one person with the authority and responsibility to enter it.

More than one business system has foundered because management could not agree about 'who owned what'. The only answer is negotiation, started well in advance of the introduction of the system — or an autocratic edict from the chief executive, which can be as effective and a lot less time-consuming (and hence less costly).

Either way, the net result could be a redistribution of power, authority and responsibility and perhaps a change in the organisation. Frequently (though for no good reason) control of a computer installation is given to the finance department. Where the chief accountant is a generalist and open-minded this can be an effective move which leads to a reduction in 'in-fighting' between other departments. Where he is of a 'civil service' mentality, however, it can lead to an over-emphasis on procedures and loss of a clear perspective. In such circumstances, the redistribution of power can be a distinct threat to the company and can lead to a proliferation of 'accurate' manual systems running in parallel with the fodder supplied to the computer.

The penalty for starting off in this way without knowing exactly where one is going can run into five or six figures. Since most installations of the type described will need a coordinating manager of one sort or another, it will be worth making him responsible directly to the chief executive. For very small installations where a full-time appointment is not justified and the operator responds to a functional head of department, it might be convenient to consider combining the role of computer manager with that of personnel manager.

Wherever responsibility eventually comes to rest, there will undoubtedly be a redistribution of perceived status (even if it is not backed up by an actual change in status) which needs to be recognised and accepted.

Middle/junior management

It is at this level that the effect on status will be most deeply felt. For many managers and supervisors, their power and status lie in the information which they hold to their chest. For the computer to do its job, all that information must be made freely and willingly available to it.

There is some room for 'face-saving' in that the information can be supplied by the manager via his own terminal, and he can be allowed to write his own report formats. It is a problem that must not be underestimated, and which can only be overcome through consultation and involvement. The subsidiary problem is that nobody will ever admit that they are solely concerned about their own status!

A second potential area of difficulty for middle managers is that gathering information from a computer can have an insidious effect on one's desire to get it from colleagues, with the result that people talk less to each other than to the computer. And linked to this issue is the one mentioned earlier — 'line-printer output is (perceived as) inherently more accurate than any other'. (Those who deny that view normally take up a position at the other end of the spectrum and say that 'line-printer output is inherently less accurate than any other source of information'). Each position is, of course, equally indefensible and time may have to be spent convincing people of that fact. Some will never be convinced, and may have to be moved from their existing job if the system is to work. Too frequently computer systems have been implemented *around* an intractable manager — and have not worked.

Through meetings, discussion, consultation and involvement (preferably in the design of the recording and reporting systems) managers need to recognise that their jobs will change. There will be greater demands made on them for:

Planning.
Security (of information).
Accountability.
Meeting deadlines.
Accepting 'the system' as the major controlling influence on the day-to-day running of their department.

For example, the simplest stock control system will allocate a finished product before it is despatched and free stock, as shown by the computer, will seldom (if ever) match physical stock. Thus there may be 50 widgets on the shelf, but all may have been allocated. Stock controllers, production managers and even directors must *never* try to override the computer allocation by saying 'Just send a couple to Mr . . . .' — as so often happens in manual systems.

Preparing to introduce a computer to provide a control facility for the business is not just a question of dealing with the technical aspects. It requires careful thought about the attitudes of first-line management and the changes in approach which are necessary. Above all, people need to accept that there can be no short-cuts; such as:

1   Orders placed by word of mouth.
2   A change in production or packaging to help a salesman.
3   Stock taken from shelves.
4   Goods ordered from suppliers without an authorisation code.

Through discussion, managers (at all levels) need to be convinced that the reason for the change is not a tightening up of security, but a necessity for the smooth running of the business. It might be hinted that slackness in manual systems might bear some of the responsibility for some of the problems which the computer is helping to solve.

In larger companies using a mainframe computer, and providing functional and service departments with terminal facilities, all the previously mentioned difficulties can arise, and may be tackled in the same way — through on-going consultation. There are additional problem areas associated with larger companies which are more difficult to isolate because of the size of organisation and the number of

responsible managers. Such areas include:
1. Refusal to 'cooperate', resulting in a minimum service to and from the computer.
2. Genuine difficulty in using procedures which may have been designed for/by other departments and which do not transfer easily.
3. Protectionism by maintaining parallel manual records, or a separate data file.
4. Efforts to put passwords on data perceived as 'sensitive' by the supplying manager.
5. Reluctance to discuss new applications with other departments (protectionism again).
6. Ignorance of the range of applications programs available.
7. Reluctance to allocate a budget to terminal operations.

In service functions particularly (technical support for example) much of the benefit of a mainframe can be wasted if the manager is unaware of the potential benefits to be gained from encouraging extensive library programs. In one case nearly two weeks of manual calculations were reduced to thirty minutes on a library program, whilst in another, 3 days of work was reduced to two minutes, after four hours had been spent writing a simple BASIC language program (see Appendix 1). But these savings would not have been made if the technical staff concerned had not been made aware of the facilities, had not been given free access to the system (through the use of their own identification codes) and had not had a terminal close to their normal place of work.

The workers

At the sharp end of business operation come the people who have to input data to the computer and initiate reports and enquiries of a database. For the larger installations just mentioned, the sharp end comprises the technical staff who will use the packages. For these people the extent to which a computer system poses a threat or an opportunity will depend on their existing method of working. To technical people, reducing two weeks' work to half an hour will invariably be attractive, until they realise the potential for staff reductions as a result of improved productivity. Similarly in functional departments (sales/order processing, stock control, etc) the spectre of redundancy often looms large at the mention of a computer installation. In fact, as discussed in Chapter 10, the introduction of a computer seldom reduces staff. It does allow the same number of staff to do more work and thus they usually enjoy it better because many of the more boring duties are taken over by the computer.

Less easy to combat are the spurious arguments based on genuine concerns about power and status — issues which are as important on the shop-floor as in the boardroom. In fact, in some ways they are more important on the shop-floor or office than in the boardroom, for it is here that data is generated. False data (either through negligence or bloody-mindedness) will naturally result in false results and perhaps wrong decisions at higher levels in the organisation's hierarchy.

It is also on the shop-floor that the schedules developed by production-control programs are translated into reality and if the schedules are ignored there is little purpose in producing them.

A story is told of a domestic appliance company which (some years ago) introduced a production scheduling system which, on a particular day, demanded production of machine A. The managing director visiting the shop-floor and discovered that Machine B was being produced. He asked the works manager, the production manager, foreman and chargehand to explain — all without result. As a last resort (*sic*) an *operator* was asked why they were making machine B and he said that the storekeeper had told him. When questioned the storekeeper said that he could not find nameplates for Machine A, so he had changed the schedule!

The story does not say what happened to the storeman, but undoubtedly some of the 'blame' lay with his management who had not dealt with his concerns about loss of power — concerns which he had displayed by proving that he could still 'call the tune'.

Involvement At the risk of being boringly repetitious, it can only be emphasised that involvement at an early stage — though it is expensive in manpower — is the best insurance against such 'sabotage'.

One method of encouraging this involvement is to ask user staff for views and comments on the terminals which are to be used and the form of interface which is to be implemented. (It is being assumed that, in the 1980s, companies will not be installing computers which do not provide direct terminal access for users.) Many users, particularly in offices, have very strong views about the terminal they would prefer to use. Some like visual display units with no hard copy, some prefer hard copy printers as part of their terminal, whilst yet others would like the display unit and the keyboard separated. There are terminals on the market to meet all these foibles, and whilst in a large office it will be impossible to satisfy everyone, there is no reason why the office itself should not decide which type of equipment is to be used. The chances are that the cost of allowing this exercise to take place will be more than offset by the resultant 'Hawthorne Effect', (see Peter Drucker's Management Series) although it must be said that the cost will be high — up to five days/person in the office, plus additional time for selected people to visit manufacturers or suppliers to view equipment.

Interfacing with the computer Direct users can also be involved in designing the type of prompt they get from the terminal, coding schemes, 'HELP' routines, etc. For example, one system required distribution clerks to enter 012 for road transport, 014 for sea, 019 for air and 015 for rail. Needless to say, there were numerous occasions when inland goods were scheduled for sea transportation. How much easier it would have been to enter R, S, A or B (B for British Rail since two R's could not be allowed).

On another system, if a user gets into difficulty he types 'HELP' and is given a list of the commands he is allowed to execute. Typing 'HELP' a second time will keep the data he has already entered in cold storage whilst he is given tutorial help by the computer. Only when he has mastered the steps he is allowed to take does the computer's operating system return him to the original program. Such facilities can be expensive to implement, but can pay for themselves within twelve months in terms of improved commitment from users and fewer errors in execution.

Finally, enough terminals must be provided to allow users ready access. One terminal shared between stock controller and accounts clerk just will not do (unless for some unknown reason these two people share an office) — even if the usage does not objectively justify one each. Making a decision to provide terminals which will lie idle for half of every day can be a difficult one to make, not only because of the cost of the terminals themselves, but also because the computer itself may need to be more sophisticated than originally envisaged (see Chapter 10).

Once again, bitter experience has shown that machines with inadequate terminal or communications capability can lead to enormous losses. In one case, neglecting communications with satellite stations cost a company over £100,000 p.a. until they changed their computers — a further £70,000 per computer. (The recurring costs were revenue items, whilst the £70,000 computer cost came from capital budget. Hence the apparent anomaly in costs.) The machines that failed to meet the company's needs had cost £50,000 and had been chosen because the finance director (who had responsibility for them) hoped to save £20,000 per machine — a total of £60,000. In fact the decision cost the company £320,000 and the director his job (see under 'Senior management' above and Chapter 10). In addition to 'actual' costs, the blunder also cost the company a great deal of goodwill from its employees and the total cost has never been estimated.

Many times throughout this book, I have talked about the human element in computer installations, and at the risk of being boring its importance is going to be emphasised again. People do not respond in totally logical ways as many managers think they should. Nor are they totally naive to the reasons for computer disasters — particularly those which affect their earning power and careers. People are important and costly assets, and must be treated as such.

User training

Such is the sophistication of present day operating systems that user training at the 'nuts and bolts level' can frequently be undertaken 'on the job' with relatively little time required to develop the relevant skills — except perhaps typing. For this reason, would-be purchasers can be forgiven for thinking that user training is a quick and simple process.

Not so. User training can be a lengthy and sensitive business. It is to do with the fears and hopes of staff — their aspirations to greater things in the company and the perceived power and status threats presented by the new toy.

The most successful installations (see Chapters 9 and 10) introduce user training the moment a decision is made to *consider* a computer installation, with departmental managers meeting to discuss potential benefits (see Chapter 1) and to identify potential difficulties — including the psychological ones.

Frequently even senior managers will be totally ignorant of what computers are, how they work, and what sort of impact they might have on the organisation. Visits to (and from) similar companies which have already installed machines, computer appreciation courses and a supply of glossy brochures from manufacturers can be very helpful at this stage. (But, for heaven's sake, don't let a supplier give a presentation. It will *sound* like a high-powered sales talk — even if it isn't — full of meaningless jargon.)

With decisions (involving senior management) made, similar processes are needed for more junior management and the workforce, with heavy emphasis on the quelling of fears, real or imagined.

Each chapter of this book contains some elements which will require user training, and in Chapter 9 we will be looking again at this crucial aspect of computer selection and installation.

Chapter Four
SECURITY

4.1. Introduction

Although 'security' normally means protection from fraud and theft, it means significantly more in the computer context — partly because there are more ways in which information can be lost. For instance, some parts of a computer system are quite capable of changing the input information without anyone being the wiser. 'Security' includes making sure that this does not happen.

As explained elsewhere, computers can be accessed through ordinary telephone networks, and the noises which we often hear during telephone conversations are readily picked up by the computer's circuits and interpreted as data. 'Security' includes making sure that this does not happen — too often.

As with everything else the decision about what is 'too often', and how much it will cost to achieve that level of security is a matter of compromise. For example, some very large computer installations can check every character reaching them to make sure that it is correct. This needs special equipment at the computer and at each of the terminals linked to it. For most installations, that level of security is neither necessary nor desirable.

To impart some order to the subject, this chapter first looks at the threats to a computer installation, then examines some of the ways of combatting these threats. Readers browsing through the book for the first time might find it easier to leave the latter sections to a second reading.

4.2 Threats to data processing installations

Threats to DP Installations can be considered in three stages — threats to the files (and programs), threats to remote terminals and telecommunications systems and threats to the central computer facilities. In many cases, a threat to any one automatically affects the others, e.g. if access to the central facility is restricted it is much more difficult to steal information. This section looks first at threats to files, then threats to telecommunications as part of an installation before finally asking 'Is security adequate?'

Threats to the security of files

It goes without saying that the information stored on files must be accurate, secure and not misused, however it is accessed.

Incorrect information One of the UK's larger suppliers of services discovered that its stock values were about 100 times higher than they should have been. The reason was that a punch-card operator had entered one item as 'price per metre' instead of 'price per drum'. Problems and inaccuracies of this nature are a very real threat, particularly in batch operations, where the person who enters data to the program does not understand it. The threat is significantly smaller where remote terminals are controlled by the users — in this example, the stock controller.

Human error in entering data has also accounted for twins being born to 'Miss' Smith, a 5-year-old being offered a pension (mispunched 65) and I. Jones being refused credit (mispunched J. Jones). Not all incorrect information comes from the users, however. Incorrectly coded programs have produced their share of bills for £0.00, which can only be satisfied by a cheque for the same amount.

But whatever the reason for incorrect data, only meticulous attention to detail in the programming and vigorous validation checks of the input can reduce the threat.

It is also possible for hardware faults to create incorrect data, but the probability of either this happening — or if it does, of it not being trapped immediately by the computer's built-in protection — is very low.

A final source of incorrect data can be the file-handling software of some computers. A few years ago, one commercial bureau advertised a 'file scrambling' facility which was designed to protect files from unauthorised access. The idea of such scramblers is that every character is multiplied by some factor. When the file is read, a further operator converts the character to its original form. In the case of this particularly unfortunate bureau, the reconversion did not work, and many valuable files were converted into garbage.

File scramblers are now fairly generally available, but the chance of the bureau's experience being repeated is small — but not zero.

One of the facts of computer life is that the smaller the computer, the less sophisticated will be its operating system, and the more rudimentary operating systems can impose disciplines on the users which, if not observed, may result in incorrect data being used.

Other, happily infrequent, but not unknown, sources of faulty data on files are:
1   Bugs in the operating system that randomly pick up bits of one file and drop them into another.
2   Stray magnetic fields that corrupt data.
3   Tiny dust particles that settle on disks and prevent the magnetic fields of the disk-drive reaching the disks, or which become magnetised and put spurious data on to the disk.

Unauthorised access   Unauthorised access comes in two forms. Physically, people can walk into a computer centre and remove data. The other form of unauthorised access is through terminals. If the file protection of the computer is inadequate, it is possible, through the normal channels of access to the files, for unauthorised people to read a file and print it at their own terminal. This can also happen if authorised users are careless — and by far the greatest threat comes from carelessness. A typical user will, for example, build-up some data files, taking great care to protect them from everyone else — even perhaps by adding password protection. Then, for any one of a thousand reasons, he agrees to one other person using his data — and the only way of doing that may be by making the files 'public'. Finally he forgets to re-impose the original protection, or leaves it off because he is not certain that the other user has completed his work. At the moment this decision is made, any and all efforts by the computer's designers to improve security is nullified.

Determined espionage can be expensive to protect against. At any time in a computer system, 'scratch' files (files which are needed as one needs scrap paper when making calculations) are available to anyone who knows how to get at them. Protecting them from unauthorised users requires a comprehensive security system within the computer's operating system. Fortunately for the average company, the threat can be reduced to acceptable proportions by much simpler methods — such as keeping the door locked!

The same analysis applies to unauthorised access to old data files, which have a habit of cluttering up disk space to an extent that they sometimes pose a different type of threat. Users may have difficulty identifying which is the most up-to-date file (see previous section).

Loss of information Some of the threats mentioned earlier can, if they occur on a larger scale, result in information being lost totally. A misused set of 'generation' files could destroy all the information stored on a particular file, or a speck of dust on a disk could wipe out the entire contents of one side.

Less of a problem now that nearly all computers work entirely from disks is the possibility of a wrong magnetic tape being loaded and modified. However, in view of the high probability of some form of data loss during the course of a year's operations, it is frequently worth keeping magnetic tapes (or cassettes) as back-up protection.

The very existence of such off-line back-up poses a threat in itself, however, since theft may become a significant possibility. Cases have been documented where complete strangers have walked into a computer installation and walked out with disks, tapes or even printout. Small companies have an advantage over larger ones in preventing theft simply because a strange face is that much more noticeable. But contractor's staff, visiting engineers and even VIPs should be kept away from the computer area and the tape/disk library.

Back inside the computer itself, files can be corrupted, with partial or total loss of information, by bugs in the operating system, or bugs in the programs.

As was said earlier, anything that can cause incorrect data can also destroy data. So the example in that section about a 'scrambling' routine is equally applicable in this section. The cost of closing all the gaps in an operating system, such as one would get with a small computer system, is horrifying, and for most companies it is more attractive to plan to recover data lost due to system bugs than it is to prevent them. Inadvertent program bugs can normally be treated in the same way.

However, cases have been known where program bugs have been deliberate — such as the instance where a programmer wrote a command into a payroll program that wiped out all the company's files if his name did not appear, or the even more publicised case of the bank programmer who rounded-off clients' interest payments and transferred the difference to his own account.

Threats to the security of computer installations

The previous section outlined some of the ways in which files can be directly attacked, or lost. Now let's look at the potential for direct attacks on the hardware of a computer system. Frequently the outcomes will include those already mentioned — lost or corrupt data — but may also be even more far-reaching.

Loss of information Computers, as everyone knows, are sensitive to the conditions in which they are used. If the temperature in the computer room gets too high or too low, if the humidity gets too high or too low (in which case static electricity will develop), if the power supply fluctuates too much, or if the atmosphere is dusty, the machine will hiccough and information may be lost. And in the sense of security, any of the above eventualities can be accidental or deliberate. (It has been known for a disgruntled employee to pour carborundum powder into the air-conditioning.) Accidental loss of information from changes in the environment is relatively less likely with mainframe computer installations (say £100,000-plus at 1980 prices) because environmental controls are usually provided within the premises. With smaller machines and minicomputers the chances are greater because, although the machines are generally more tolerant to change, many companies stretch tolerance beyond permissible limits.

Other natural disasters such as fire and flood can be considered as 'normal' risks for the average company and guarded against in the normal way. The consequences of such calamities can be minimised by back-up:
1   In the form of copies of files in fire-proof safes.
2   In the form of being able to 'borrow' another company's computing facilities.

The likelihood of deliberate assaults on computer facilities will, of course, depend on the attractiveness of the data which might be misappropriated. Few people will not know about the theft of ICI tapes from Holland, or the trouble which their loss caused to the company. And the loss of anyone's customer files would be as disrupting. However unlikely such an eventuality might be, it is always worth guarding against. The same controls on access which prevent theft of tapes or disks, will also guard against the theft of waste. Frequently a computer run will produce as much unwanted paper as useful (to the user) reports. That scrap paper may be invaluable to an industrial spy, or to more a disgruntled operator, data control clerk, programmer or user.

As the trend from massive reports produced by batch runs to interactive computing continues, it is tempting to believe that such threats might be reduced. In fact, they are increased, because terminal users are generally thinking about their problems and not about security. Often terminals are placed conveniently for users (with a waste bin) in a quiet corner. It is easy for unauthorised people to clear the waste and get a great deal of useful information.

All waste, from any terminal, should be treated as top secret and consigned to a shredder. The cost is low and the potential savings are high.

Unauthorised access One large organisation dealing with very sensitive data installed its own line printers to avoid the small possibility of its bureau sending printout to the wrong address, or of having the printout stolen. It then put a notice above its terminals:

    LOG-ON CODE: ....

Admittedly, the premises themselves were fairly secure, but anyone finding their way in (contractors, cleaners, etc.) would have immediate access to many of the organisation's secrets. Some protection can be given if terminals are fitted with 'answer-back' drums, but the inconvenience this causes to the average user has made them unpopular. It is much cheaper in every sense, and just as effective, not to display log-on codes or allow unauthorised access to them by leaving copies in waste baskets.

With malice aforethought, the modern computer installation offers many opportunities. Most contain 'gates' in their hardware and in their operating systems which allow access without going through the computer's security routine. Other 'gates' appear as a result of software bugs. The intentional gates exist for engineers and systems designers who may be undertaking maintenance or updating activities and are generally necessary. The unintentional ones appear at the most inconvenient times and can be very expensive to close.

Once inside the operating system, an unscrupulous user can destroy files, or corrupt them, print out the contents of the main memory, change the operating system programs or even wipe out the entire system.

It is possible, as will be discussed in more detail later, to close the gates, but such a course is usually very expensive. It is much easier to keep people out. As long as unauthorised users cannot get to the computer they cannot browse through output, scan files or modify systems programs. Nor can they plant bugs, monitor electromagnetic radiation or even sabotage the system.

For the most part, active attempts to increase security against the threats just mentioned will not be cost-effective. However, it may be worth taking some action to protect the company against embezzlement. Many knowledgeable users, analysts, programmers and operators have succumbed to the temptation that an unthinking 'money-printing' machine puts in their way. By patching in a small amount of extra program coding (perhaps accessed by an operator through one of the 'gates') it is all too easy to transfer small amounts to ficticious accounts, change the value of a stock item, alter stock records to obscure pilferage, etc., etc. Sometimes an operator may be an innocent party, doing a favour for one of the company's managers.

4.3 Is data processing security adequate?

The whole issue of security must be kept in perspective. Many minicomputer installations work effectively without fires, file corruption, embezzlement or theft, and it would be wrong to suggest that the safeguards built into a modern computer are inadequate when viewed from any standpoint. In fact, experience has shown that any computer installation is normally more secure than the manual system it is replacing. Sometimes staff are tempted by their newly awakened awareness to the potentials for embezzlement, but more frequently, they see opportunities — which may or may not have been exploited — removed. (For example, it is much easier to browse through, or even burn, a Kalamazoo Stock Record Book left open in an unattended office than it is to learn how to access a file protected by a constantly changing password.) Yet it would be foolish to ignore the problems of computer security, because a breach — once achieved — is potentially much more damaging than a week's waste! Thus it is worth asking questions about the security of:

1 The computer installation:
   - *a* Are the rooms housing the computer, any computer staff and the tape/disk libraries sited so as to make unauthorised access difficult?
   - *b* Are all printouts, line printers, terminals, etc., sited so as to make browsing difficult?
   - *c* Are there physical security arrangements, e.g. key cards for access to the computer room.
   - *d* Is there someone who, at any time of the day or night, is responsible for access to the computer installation?
   - *e* Are all the master files kept in a fireproof safe? And is that safe in a secure area away from the computer installation?
   - *f* Is all documentation kept in a secure place?
   - *g* Are all staff aware of the need for security in the computer area?
   - *h* Have the fire-fighting/fire-prevention arrangements been discussed with the local fire authorities?
   - *i* Have all users been trained in the security arrangements? What 'penalties' are imposed for a breach in security?
   - *j* Have all computer specialists been trained in the security arrangements? What 'penalties' are imposed for a breach in security?
   - *k* What systems are used for signing tapes/disks out of/into the library?

2 The computer hardware:
   - *a* What is the extent of the computer's own audit records? How much information does it hold about users?

    b   Are security controls built into the access of hardware restricted areas via 'gates'?
    c   Who can access core memory, e.g. for maintenance purposes, whilst the machine is processing?
    d   Are you aware of any 'gates', either intentional or as a result of bugs?
    e   Are there hardware security controls on terminal access to the system, e.g. answer-back drums?
    f   Are there monitors and audit trails for unusual core dumps or accesses?
    g   Is there protection against residual memory being read by users, either from the operator's console or elsewhere?
    h   What security controls, if any, does the operator's console by-pass?
    i   Do other terminals by-pass security controls?
    j   Is there back-up in the event of hardware failure, e.g. arithmetic software?
    k   Who is responsible for hardware security? Has he been properly trained?
    l   Is there one person responsible for all remote users? What form of control is he able to exert?
    m   Are there monitors to record unusual and unsuccessful attempts to access the system from remote terminals?

3   The software — including files:
    a   Is it clear who has authority to change data? Is it clear who has authority to read data?
    b   Are data files protected against accidental corruption?
    c   Is data validated before it is put on file?
    d   Are data files categorised in some way according to sensitivity, e.g. public, private?
    e   Are passwords used on data files? Who can read password lists?
    f   Are updated files 'dumped' at regular, and frequent, intervals?
    g   Are there periodic checks on data to ensure that it is up-to-date and accurate?
    h   Are there periodic checks of programs (with test data) to ensure that they have not been tampered with?
    i   Are there monitors and audit trails to check for unusual or unauthorised dumping of files?
    j   What are the procedures (if any) for accessing data when the computer is down?

And finally, but most important, because it determines the extent to which security should be considered as an issue in its own right:
    k   To what extent would the corruption, loss or theft of files

affect the viability and operation of the company? Is there data which would be of value to competitors (or customers)? Is there data which, if revealed, could cause the company severe embarrassment, or even cause legal proceedings, e.g. if confidential personal information was made public?

4.4 Additional threats posed by commercial bureaux

By and large, commercial bureaux, either batch or time-sharing, are far more security-conscious than their clients. They provide extensive hardware and software protection and are particularly careful about the security of their premises, which often appear to be impenetrable. Nevertheless, anyone using a bureau service for sensitive information still needs to check the facilities, as the following illustrations show.

In one case, visitors were held in a 'Secure Area' between the foyer and the bureau's offices. Access to the area (in and out) was via doors which could only be operated by key cards held by staff. Unfortunately, there were no washrooms in the secure area and one visitor was told: 'Go down the corridor, turn left through the computer room. . .'.

In another case, the computer facility had been designed to make access between reception areas and the computer almost impossible. So successful was the design that computer room staff invariably keep the fire doors to the car park propped open to ease transference of printout to their 'secure' data delivery service.

It should be said, however, that these examples only serve to illustrate the high quality of security against unauthorised access practised by most bureaux.

Perhaps the weakest link in a bureau's security system against information loss through theft comes in its data control. Even with the best will and the most dedicated data controllers there is always a small but finite possibility that printout will be sent to the wrong addressee whenever an envelope is used. The solution as at least one bureau has discovered is to use heat-sealed plastic bags with the name and address on the printout itself showing through.

Protection against unauthorised users is unfortunately not so universally comprehensive. Some bureaux (particularly those engaged in the time-sharing business) insist on up to four levels of identification for each user, each of which must be accurate in every way. Others give users a single log-on code which may consist of only six characters. Such 'security' systems were designed for in-house installations (though many would consider them inadequate even then) and have not been extended for commercial service.

File protection, or lack of it, normally mirrors access security, and the protection procedures of some bureaux are so comprehensive, it is difficult to access one's own files. With others, any, and every, file is considered to be public unless defined otherwise; a hole which should be far too large for any user to accept.

To sum up, any company considering the use of a bureau should be assured that all the threats mentioned in Section 4.2 are covered, that all the questions in Section 4.3 can be satisfactorily answered, and that the small additional problems raised in this section do not occur.

4.5 Providing protection

Whilst this section aims to introduce the more common ways in which computer installations and files can be protected, it does not pretend to give any technique detailed treatment. Some of the ploys have had books written about them in their own right, whilst other important criteria, particularly in the personnel area, form part of a larger system.

People

Many of the threats mentioned earlier in this chapter will only arise if two or more employees collude to defraud the company. Some of the protection techniques described later are only necessary if equipment and files are being protected against their users. Thus anything which can be done to reduce the range of threats posed by employees (and visitors) will reduce the cost of alternative protection and the risks.

One of humanity's fundamental traits (if you believe McGregor) is that they respond to reason and react to bullying. If follows, therefore, that comprehensive training for both users and computer staff should reduce the risks (both deliberate and accidental) to computer installations. Where people are *told* that a computer is to be installed and that their jobs are to change, the natural reaction is one of non-cooperation. On the other hand, where they are involved in the development of new systems, the structure of and responsibility for databases, the design of interfaces and the selection of terminals, experience has shown that only a few fail to respond (see also Chapter 9). And they seldom get any support from their colleagues.

Training Such training will not be cheap, amounting to about 0.5 per cent of emoluments for a small company employing external consultants. Internally prepared courses and seminars will probably cost about half that amount, but care will have to be taken that the training sessions do not become briefing sessions in which the delegates feel they are not being involved in the significant decisions. Too frequently one sees objectives of the form:

'To inform delegates of the benfits of the XYZ computer system.'

A feature of any training for employees should be an understanding of the need for security, and a developed awareness of the necessity for controls and restrictions. Such an understanding and awareness can *only* be created by the delegates themselves. It cannot be externally imposed. Thus it might be superficially attractive (and much cheaper) to impose regulations which:
1 Minimise personnel knowledge of the computer's internal security.
2 Minimise personnel interactions within the computer department, and between departmental staff and users.
3 Split knowledge.
4 Minimise what people see.
5 Avoid single control, where one person has authority and responsibility for important processing.

However, in practice, such regulations will inevitably be counter-productive in all but the most regimented of large installations.

Job descriptions and security There is an argument for making security a substantive feature in everybody's job description, if necessary by rewriting them when a computer is installed. The cost of this re-emphasis of the importance of security is not high. Such an activity will also clarify the roles of selected 'security staff' who will be responsible for checking the security controls. Above all, proper standards will have to be set [see the publications of the National Computing Centre (NCC)], implemented, monitored and reviewed.

Protecting the computing facility

Physical considerations It hardly needs saying that computers, their associated equipment and (especially) their files should be protected against fire. The fire service will normally help with fire-fighting equipment, alarms and the like, but it is worth noting some of the issues peculiar to computer installations.

Firstly, fire extinguishing systems (automatic or manually operated) should be gas systems (carbon dioxide or BCF) in preference to foam or sprinkler systems, because of the damage which the latter systems cause to equipment. The only value of water extinguishers is for small waste-basket fires, and one of the strictly enforced security procedures should be that the only combustibles in computer rooms should be *on* the line printer (plus an operator's log). There is, then, no need for any waste baskets in the room and all printout should immediately be taken outside to another secure area.

Obviously, anywhere near the computer is a NO SMOKING area. The use of smoke detectors (as opposed to heat detectors) will also discourage staff who smoke, particularly if they are told one of the many true stories about hotels being evacuated because of a pipe-smoker sitting under a detector.

One further, useful, protection against fire is to maintain a reasonable level of humidity in the room. Not enough to rust a print-bar, but sufficient to avoid the static discharge that one frequently experiences in modern office blocks with air-conditioning and nylon carpets. Static can build up very quickly on line printers, card readers and any moving parts, and can cause fires. Effective air-conditioning can help greatly, and will also maintain the reasonable temperature needed by all computers — whatever their salesmen might say!

Finally, in case fire should break out, make sure that the company's data does not go up in smoke by having back-up tapes/disks in a fireproof safe. For preference, the safe should be in another room, or even in another building — in which case, both buildings should be physically secure.

Access to even the simplest of computer systems should be restricted, the easiest way of doing this being by using key cards — with a door that closes automatically. Low-security sites probably need no more complex a system than that used in car parks, where a single code is punched (or coded) onto everyone's card. As security increases, cards of the 'cash card' variety become necessary, where the user identifies himself by manually dialling a code whilst his card is inserted in a reader. High-security installations may require changing codes at irregular intervals.

It should be remembered that access is only as secure as its weakest point, and comprehensive controls at the 'front-door' are useless if the 'back-door' is left open — either literally (as in the case mentioned earlier of the bureau whose data controllers propped the fire-doors open to make access to the car park easier) or figuratively — as in the case of insecure (or open) windows, skylights or false floors.

Incidentally, picture windows, attractive as they may be, are a disaster for computers. They bake the equipment and can cause fires on sunny days, attract the attention of would-be theives and vandals at night, and are generally a security liability. Showing-off a computer with internal plate glass windows is also not to be recommended, and more than one tape-trolley has been inadvertently pushed through a closed glass door with subsequent injury to body and pride.

Physical protection can also be provided against the less likely risks of 'bugs' (listening devices), wire tapping and reception of stray electromagnetic radiation.

Having protected the installation from attack by Acts of God and the ungodly, the memory and its data must be similarly protected. This will be rather more technical in places, and first-time readers might prefer to just scan the headings, then go to another chapter.

Memory protection   As explained in Chapter 5, programs and data are constantly moving in and out of the main memory of a computer, and the area of core used varies according to the size of program used. A standard feature of any large machine should, therefore, be a means of preventing a user printing out any part of core which he is not occupying for his own programs and data. This type of protection should also be extended to minicomputers where multiprogramming facilities exist.

If a user does try to access a protected part of core, control should be transferred immediately to the executive and a diagnostic message printed to both user and operator. Such 'read' protection is fairly normal either as standard or as an optional extra, in which case the cost is small. However, if the computer does not contain this facility, the cost of implementing protection will be high. The same is true of memory 'write' protection, which is essential if multiple users are to be protected from (at least) each other's errors.

It is also necessary to protect the memory and its contents from physical breakdown of core. For example, one byte might get 'stuck' at a particular character (say, '3'). Without protection, the damage might only be spotted when a program tries to read an alphabetic character from that location. The usual method of dealing with this potential problem is to incorporate 'parity' checks.

(Chapter 7 explains in some detail how the computer core is built and shows how each character is normally sorted in a 'byte' of eight 'bits', where a 'bit' is a circuit representing one of the two binary numbers '0' or '1'. For example the number 5 would be represented by the byte '11110101.' A parity bit is an additional bit added to every byte, and set so that there is always an even number (2, 4, 6 . . .) of ones. The parity bit added to the representation of 5 is therefore '0' — since the byte already contains six ones. The binary equivalent of 7 (11110111) would have a parity bit of '1'.)

In the days when core was expensive (up to the mid-1970s), parity was expensive to incorporate. Nowadays it is automatically incorporated, and need seldom concern purchasers (except in so far as they might want to understand why the machine has stopped.

Various other hardware devices are also incorporated in a modern computer to protect it, its executive and its programs from itself. These include: 'lock-out bits' — which provide additional protection to certain areas of core; 'read-only executive' — which prevent the executive from being accidentally overwritten; 'resident executive' —

which means that the executive is permanently stored within the computer, and like read-only memory, cannot be overwritten.

Many of today's minicomputer installations are completely 'open' to their operators and are only protected by a locked door from intruders. Particularly in small companies, such precautions are completely adequate, since strange faces are quickly spotted and challenged, and sabotage or fraud on the part of the operator is highly unlikely because of the relationships which exist within the firm.

Provided staff are co-operating in the use of the computer, and are committed to the success of their employer, the only hardware protection which needs careful and detailed consideration is that related to accidental damage.

The same is true of software protection. Before moving on, however, it is important to mention one other feature of hardware security.

Back-up Computers are no different from other pieces of equipment which always break down at the most inconvenient times. Just as the TV set collapses just before the World Cup Final, so a mini will crash immediately before the year-end accounting run.

Each company using a computer will have to decide what action it is going to take to alleviate its inconvenience when the inevitable occurs by providing some form of back-up, or standby facility.

At the simplest (*sic!*) level it may be possible to arrange for a local company with the same equipment to run important jobs whilst the engineers are at work. Because language implementations are sometimes different from one computer to the next (as a result of over-enthusiastic programmers) it *may* be necessary to keep two versions of the programs. Akin to using a neighbour's facilities is using demonstration machinery at the manufacturer's premises.

Every computer purchaser will have seen his equipment demonstrated before he bought, and will probably have used demonstration equipment for some program development. That same machine should be available in case of breakdown of one's own computer. It is worth writing a clause to that effect into the contract when a new machine is purchased — a precaution which becomes doubly necessary if a manufacturer cannot show companies already using their computers for one's applications.

Peripherals — terminal, card readers, magnetic tape driver, disks, etc. — are also prone to breakdown; to a much greater extent than the main Central Processing Unit (CPU), in fact, since they contain so many mechanical parts. The same options to use other people's computers whilst repairs are effected are, of course, open to a company. However, it might be worth avoiding the inevitable disruptions by purchasing standby equipment. The economics of the situation will hinge on an equation balancing average 'downtime' against the cost — in every sense — of delay.

Large companies and groups may find it advantageous to think of their computing requirements in terms of a 'distributed network', in which several 'small' computers take the place of one central machine. Properly planned and implemented, it is possible for one computer to be taken out of use entirely without affecting any user, though a more usual arrangement would be for the subsidiary owning the damaged equipment to be severely affected, and others less so.

In the final analysis, however, most medium-sized companies which have installed data processing computers find that they can cope with the occasional delay without too much disruption, and that the more esoteric and expensive back-up options are just not justified.

Software protection Many techniques are available for improving the security of programs and the computing facility in general. Unfortunately, as software costs rise, none of them are cheap, though by careful planning at the design stage some can be implemented with relative ease. As elsewhere, two forms of protection are necessary, one against accidental damage, the other against deliberate attack. In this latter category comes all the forms of log-on and password protection which are available within present-day executives. Such protection may be expensive to implement, and can be tedious to use but may be necessary for high security against deliberate attempts to violate programs and data. Where terminals are confined to secure premises, and for many companies that will mean their own offices, it will probably be sufficient to maintain a simple log-on sequence.

Systems using a telecommunications network, or with multiple users, e.g. a group, will almost certainly want one of the more extensive protection options. They may also need 'Residue Protection'.

Protection of software from accidental corruption of the executive, programs and data is best provided by arranging for 'graceful degradation' when the computer shuts down, and by constantly striving to remove bugs from the executive. 'Graceful degradation' means that when the computer shuts down as a result of an error of some kind, it should not do so 'instantaneously', but should dump its core onto a disk, and should protect the executive from being written to. There will always be occasions when degradation will not be graceful, however carefully written the protection might be, but it is a useful addition to most operating systems. The cost will not be high if provision has been made by the designers of the operating system, but could become prohibitive if a user decides to make his own modifications as a result of an unfortunate experience. In such cases it would probably be more cost-effective to arrange for regular 'dumps' on to magnetic tape.

The process of regular 'dumping' is one which is routinely

undertaken by large installations and bureaux. It means that at regular intervals (say, every 3-4 hours for maximum security, daily as an absolute minimum) every file which has been edited since the preceding dump is transferred to tape and stored. Thus, no matter how serious the 'crash', files can always be reconstituted from the previous dump.

Finally, in this section let us deal with the software routines for general security, which should be available to a greater or lesser degree on all mainframes and on the larger minis. First of all, the operating system should maintain a continuous audit of all activities performed on the computer:

    Entering jobs
    Logging in/out
    Creating, opening, closing, editing, deleting files
    System start up/shut down

For each of these should be recorded:

    What the event is
    The date and time
    Identities of the user, the files, the jobs, etc.

The process should not be expensive to run, though it may be expensive to incorporate into an operating system which does not contain an audit capability. The overhead of writing a few words to store will be small, and although it may be necessary to provide some back-up storage to avoid filling up the disks, it may sometimes be thought of as a 'Blackbox Flight Recorder' — only retaining information over a given period, and overwriting itself.

In high-security areas, it will certainly be necessary to keep a complete audit trail, and because of the sensitivity of the information on the audit tape, it may be necessary to restrict access to it to privileged terminals. It may even be necessary to 'scramble' the code it contains.

A useful line of defence against unauthorised access which can be considered a routine measure is a system of reprisals against attempts to violate the security of the computer. At its most rudimentary level, this might mean dealing with hiccoughs on a telephone line. Since all user activities are routed through the operating system, which must anyway check them for validity, it is tempting for systems programmers and security-conscious data processing managers to devise draconian reprisals. It is, after all, as easy — sometimes easier — to implement a severe reprisal as a mild one. For example, anyone failing to log on correctly after three attempts could be suspended or even deleted from the list of authorised users. Easier, any illegal attempt to log on over a GPO line could result in the line being disconnected.

Some reprisals should be built into an operating system, but they should work progressively. The programming costs may be slightly higher, but the majority of users will benefit from not being penalised because they hit the wrong typewriter key. Reprisals that are too harsh have been known to turn users against a computer system, with much more expensive consequences than a few more days of programming time.

Protecting programs and data

Much of what has gone before has been concerned with safeguarding the integrity of a computer system against either deliberate attempts to steal or modify data, or errors made by users. The same techniques may also be used to protect data files from the same security threats.

This section deals mainly with protection against faults in the computer system itself, from hardware malfunction to spurious noise on telephone lines.

By hardware The most secure and certain method of providing security against faults is to maintain back-up files. Their use has already been mentioned under software protection. In that context it was the executive software that required modification to control dumps. It is mentioned now under hardware protection of files because back-up files require additional hardware for their maintenance. The theory is that three copies are always available — a working copy, the previous version and the one before that ('grandfather, father, son'). When files are changed the grandfather file is destroyed, to be replaced by the father file, the son file becomes the father file and the new file is the new son. The technique was developed in the early days of computing, based on magnetic tapes, and although modern disk-oriented systems wil probably work perfectly safely with only father and son files, the grandfather file provides a second level of back-up at relatively low cost. However, the cost may rise considerably in database applications where a single file may easily require 3 Mbytes of storage, and the cost-effectiveness equation may have to be looked at in some detail.

There is one situation in which it is essential to maintain effective back-up, and that is where the operating system allows files to be edited directly, i.e. editor commands work directly on the disk version of the file, and not on a copy of it held in the main memory. Thus any changes are irrevocable, and positive action to establish father and son files (at least) is mandatory.

The manner in which such back-up is provided can vary considerably, ranging in concept from the operating system providing all the protection which is necessary, e.g. by creating a new file every time a change is made and identifying it with a suffix, i.e. CUSTFIL(1),

CUSTFIL(2) , . . . , to the responsibility being laid squarely on the shoulders of the user (even to the extent of 'losing' his working file if he simply forgets to save it). For most purposes some form of system lying between these two extremes is probably most acceptable.

The same sort of compromise is reasonable when it comes to parity checking, already mentioned in the context of installation protection.

Finally, in this section, hardware protection against overwriting files must be mentioned. The cost is either negligible or very high, depending on whether the equipment has been designed to carry such protection. For magnetic tapes it is normally necessary to fit 'write permit rings' to allow writing — without them it is only possible to read the tape. Note that the ring protects, or allows access to, the *whole* of the tape. Thus for effective security, only one file should be kept on a given tape, which could not only be wasteful but also tedious if many tapes have to be mounted. In general it is probably more satisfactory to rely on software protection.

Disks are more difficult to protect by hardware since they are almost certainly shared by many users. The only way is to arrange switches (operated either manually or by relays) which 'protect' a given track. With moving-head disks, the potential for error introduced by mechanical switches and the reduction in access speed will usually outweigh any benefit derived from hardware protection. The equation is rather more finely balanced for fixed-head disks, where each track may be separately protected.

However, software protection is again a more flexible option. This should not be expensive to implement, since nearly all operating systems provide it as part of the package.

By software In the last section we finished by looking at ways of protecting whole files, and this section will use that as a starting point before moving on to examine ways of protecting items on file.

Nowadays one can reasonably expect an operating system to be capable of protecting files from being either read or written to, as a matter of routine. Data files should be protected from all other users of the system by the log-on sequence, and should be capable of having additional passwords added to them. Where operating systems do not provide this level of protection, or cannot be persuaded to provide it at negligible cost, any security-conscious user would be well advised to consider another system.

It may also be possible to 'scramble' data on files so that, even if an unauthorised person manages to copy it, the data is still meaningless. (The normal method is to use a 'key' which operates on every element of the file being scrambled.) Security against accidental revelation is virtually 100 per cent.

Since software file protection is usually implemented by adding special instructions to the leader of each file and/or to its 'End of file' marker, the only limit to software protection is the ingenuity of systems programmers. Since many systems programmers are very ingenious people, there is a greater danger of authorised users being unable to access their files than there is of unauthorised users walking off with the goodies!

Protection within data files of individual values is very much a matter of common sense, and a recognition that the computer relies on its programmers for its 'thinking ability'. Thus checksums (where all the 'words' of a block of data are summed), hash totals (say the total of all account numbers, even if they are not numeric [*sic*]), check digits, counts and sequence numbers are widely used to ensure that each file contains 'the file, the whole file, and nothing but the file'.

Further protection against both fraudulent and accidental data errors can be provided by adequate validation, built into the applications program:

1 Do all the variables contain the right type of character? For example, has a price been entered as £26.H4. Such checks are particularly important when users are non-specialists in the computer field, when they might confuse the letter O (capital oh) with 0 (the number zero), or a blank with a null (difficult to illustrate, since they both appear as " " on a printout!). Sometimes, for instance in statistical work, a blank, a null or a zero may all be shown as "—" on coding sheets, which requires even more careful validation checks, perhaps by comparing two or more values.
2 Do the variables fall within the correct range of values? Such checks may be absolute, e.g. there are only 12 months in a year, or relative, e.g. Widgets Mk I are sold at prices from £2 to £3 whilst Mk II Widgets range from £3.50 to £3.75).
3 Is the data consistent? Certain values may be incompatible with other items in the record. For example, fuel oil deliveries to Birmingham are unlikely to be made in 2,000-tonne loads, but deliveries to Rotterdam may be.
4 Is all the data there? This check is not so necessary where on-line disk is the normal storage medium, with updates via on-line terminals. Whenever cards are used, however, it is useful to check that the card-reader has not swallowed one.

Other protection procedures are available, and anyone wanting to delve more deeply into the subject should consult one of the many specialised books on the subject.

Chapter Five

OPERATING CONFIGURATIONS

Computer processors used for data processing can be used in several different configurations or modes. Some modes have particular benefits or disadvantages for specific applications. Unfortunately, but predictably, the configurations best suited for a majority of user-oriented applications require the most sophisticated computer systems — both hardware and software. Conversely, configurations that are machine-efficient can be, and often are, frustrating for the user.

Throughout this chapter, examples of the type of application to which each configuration is best suited are given, together with examples of applications that are totally inappropriate. In this way potential users should be better able to assess the mode of operation best suited to their overall needs.

5.1 Batch

The original form of computer configuration, batch machines process one job at a time. The user's view of the machine is often through a hole in the wall into which he puts his data, and from which he collects reports.

Batch operation is inherently machine-efficient and in the days when computers were 'slow' and core was expensive, there were powerful arguments for maximising the efficiency of the computer. Users and computer department staff (for pure batch processing requires a computer department) become slaves to the machine. In this mode of operation, jobs are usually entered via punched-cards prepared by dat preparation staff. The jobs require 'Job Control' which specifies who the job is for, how much time is to be allowed (in case something goes wrong), the priority of the job, etc. Writing job control statements is a skill in its own right (on some IBM installations it is a full-time job within the computer department) and mistakes here will cause the job to abort. It can, therefore, take a day or more to enter user data and initiate a program.

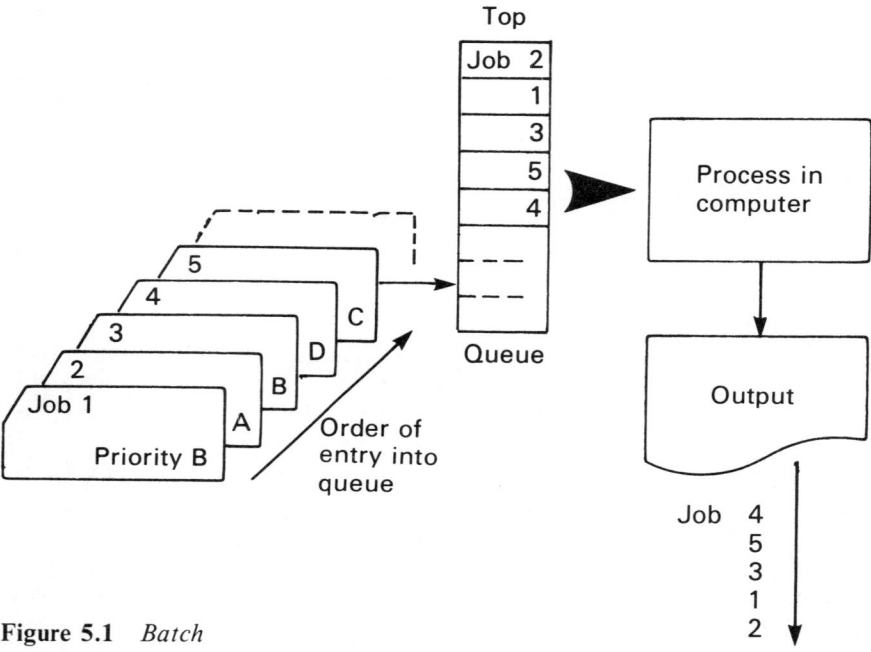

Figure 5.1 *Batch*

Once inside the computer, a job takes its place in a queue (see Figure 5.1), and — one at a time — jobs are processed in order of priority. A second job cannot be started until the first has competely cleared the system. Priority systems are also quite rudimentary. There may, for example, be four levels:

```
IMMEDIATE  — A
RUSH       — B
STANDARD   — C
OVERNIGHT  — D
```

This would mean that a job entered as priority A will be put in the queue *before* all the B, C and D priority jobs — but *after* any existing priority A jobs. To provide a time perspective a priority A job on a large mainframe installation (say an IBM 370/155) will probably be run within the hour if it is entered during the busiest time of day. At slack times, it may even be run immediately (as the name implies). Of course, if the machine is idle (say at 0300 hours) a priority D job will be run immediately.

It is normal for batch installations to charge users a premium for A and B priority jobs, and to give a discount for D priority jobs. Thus users can be seen playing games with data controllers in an effort to get their jobs run quickly and cheaply. This is fine for the computer, but appallingly wasteful of manpower.

The advantage of batch processing is that the operating system of the computer only needs to control one job at a time, needs no communications capability and is, therefore, small and simple. In turn it requires less space within core and allows more room for user programs. This means that big programs can sometimes be run on medium-sized machines.

Suitable applications

One can say that any application not requiring the close involvement of the user is well-suited to batch operations. Those that stand out are:
1   Commercial:
    — Payroll
    — Ledger consolidation (but see Section 5.4)
    — Invoicing (but see Section 5.4)
2   Technical:
    — Stress calculations
    — Waveform analysis (but see Section 5.5)
    — Production scheduling
    — Program compilation

Inappropriate applications

Because batch processing screens the computer from the user and introduces a lengthy time delay, any application that finds these requirements frustrating is unsuited to a batch environment. In the late 1960s, however, many such applications were mounted on batch machines and were 'made to work'. The reader may, therefore, find areas listed below which he knows to be working on batch machines. However, he would be ill-advised to try to implement them now.

Examples of inappropriate applications include:
1. Commercial:
   — Sales/order processing
   — Stock control
   — Management information systems
2. Technical — any 'short' calculation needing a quick answer, for example:
   — Friction losses
   — Bending moments
   — Network analyses

5.2 Remote job entry

Remote job entry (RJE) is best thought of as long-range batch processing. The processor works in exactly the same way, but instead of having just one input job stream from the resident data controller, it has several. The terminals serving each job stream may be in the same building as the computer, or may be many thousands of miles away, connected to the centre by special telephone lines.

The user is even further away from his job — even if he is in the same building as the computer — since the jobs coming from the other side of the world may arrive at any time and demand a higher priority.

Where international connections are used, machine loading is more uniform through local night-time, and local users could well find themselves worse-off under RJE than standard batch processing. Typically, UK-based computers have RJE terminals around the country and on the Continent to deal with data from sales offices and subsidiary sites.

Suitable applications

Anywhere that large volumes of data have to be collated at a remote site and transmitted to a central computer for processing. Examples are:
1. Commercial:
   — Payroll
   — Invoicing (but see Section 5.4)
   — Ledger consolidation
2. Technical:
   — Stress calculations
   — Waveform analysis (but see Section 5.5)
   — Production scheduling

Inappropriate applications

Since RJE is essentially similar to 'pure' batch processing, any application which is unsuited to batch is equally unsuited to RJE. Commercial examples include:
— Sales/order processing
— Stock control
— Management information systems

5.3 Multiprogramming

This is a variation on batch processing (Section 5.1) which divides the central computer core into 'partitions', each one dealing with a single program (see Figure 5.2). It is rather like putting several batch machines of different sizes together and controlling them via a single

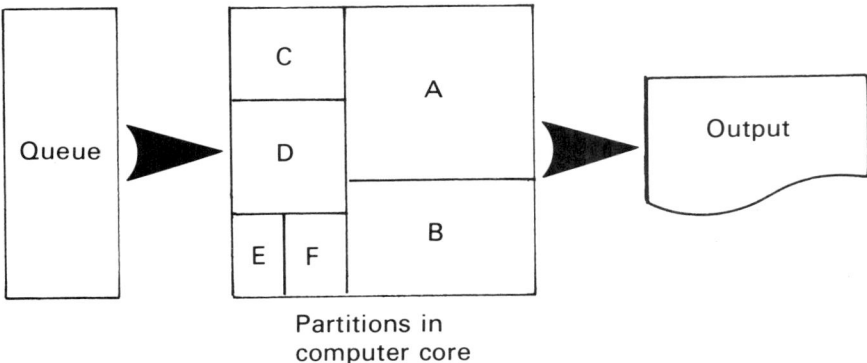

Partitions in computer core

Figure 5.2 *Multiprogramming*

operating system. Depending on the size of the core, the effect may be a general speeding up — or a general slowing down! If the core is large enough to partition into smaller units, each of which is big enough to hold the programs requested by users, then the queue will be reduced more quickly and users will get a faster turn-round. On the other hand, if the partitions are too small, then there will be no difference between a multiprogramming machine and a batch machine — except that the operating system will be much larger, and user core will be reduced still further. The net result will be slower processing.

To illustrate the principle, imagine a queue of jobs, each requiring a specific amount of core. (Core is measured in 'K', where a 'K' is roughly 1,000 characters. A full explanation is given in Chapter 7.)

Queue   *(ignoring priorities)*

		Partitions(1)	Partitions(2)
1	64K		
2	24K	A — 64K	A — 64K
3	10K	B — 32K	B — 8K
4	32K	C — 16K	C — 8K
5	4K	D — 8K	D — 8K
6	8K	E — 4K	E — 8K
		F — 4K	F — 8K
			G — 8K
			H — 8K
			J — 8K

Assume that there are two choices of computer, one with partitions(1) (Figure 5.2) and the other with partitions(2). For (1) the entire queue can be cleared in only two operations (assuming equal time in core and equal priorities):

Operation 1 —   1 into A
                      2 into B
                      3 into C   Partition F is idle
                      5 into E
                      6 into D

Note that, although high in the queue, job 4 has to wait until there is more space.

Operation 2 —   4 into A or B, whichever becomes available first

System (2) is much slower:

Operation 1 —   1 into A
                      5 into B   Partitions D-J are all idle!
                      6 into C

Operation 2 —   2 into A   All other partitions idle

Operation 3 —   3 into A   All other partitions idle

Operation 4 —   4 into A   All other partitions idle

Large numbers of partitions do not necessarily mean quick processing — whatever the computer salesman says. Some modern machines, mainly mainframes but occasionally minis, run with multiprogramming configurations that, like those in the example, are fixed — either for all time (unusual) or by a command issued by the computer operator. Other machines have even more sophisticated operating systems which alter partition size depending on the size of the jobs in the queue. Thus in the example, four partitions would have been set up: 64K, 24K, 32K and 8K. These process jobs 1, 2, 4 and 6, i.e. the entire core would be used, even though it meant that some jobs were by-passed. Slightly less sophisticated machines would set up partitions for jobs 1, 2, 3, 5 and 6, omitting 4 because of insufficient space, but otherwise respecting the authority of the queue.

Clearly, multiprogramming requires a careful study of the available configurations which should be matched to the estimated needs of the organisation, remembering always that more sophisticated operating systems require more space (except for machines operating under 'virtual memory', as is explained in Chapter 6) and hence leave less space for users.

Since multiprogramming is a variation of batch processing, it is possible to incorporate both RJE systems and multiprogramming. Most modern mainframes carry sufficient operating system to deal with both variations.

Suitable applications

Application areas are precisely as for batch and RJE, *viz*:
1   Commercial:
    — Payroll
    — Ledger consolidation (but see Section 5.4)
    — Invoicing (but see Section 5.4.)
2   Technical:
    — Stress calculations
    — Waveform analysis (but see Section 5.5)
    — Production scheduling

Inappropriate applications

Again, applications not conducive to batch processing are obviously not going to be suitable for multiprogramming:
1   Commercial:
    — Sales/order processing
    — Stock control
    — Management information systems
2   Technical:
    — Any short calculation needing a quick answer, e.g. friction losses, bending moments and network analysis.

5.4 Teleprocessing

We are now moving into an area in which the user is in direct contact with the computer. No longer is there a 'buffer' between him and the machine, no longer can he imagine that he is working a manual system. Users now use terminals of one sort or another (see Chapter 7 — Peripherals) to input data and commands directly to the machine (see Figure 5.3). Time delays between initiating a job and getting the results comes down from hours to *fractions* of a second. To the user it appears that the computer is dealing only with his demands — if the teleprocessing is good. If it is poor, 'response time' can be several seconds or even a minute or more. If even that sounds fast, note that the slowest response time acceptable to the world's largest manufacturers of computers is 4 seconds — and to a regular user, 2 seconds 'feels' slow!

Teleprocessing systems with a response time of 10 seconds or more can be considered to be useless, and need replacing if working efficiency of users and morale is not to deteriorate.

Within the core of the computer, a typical teleprocessing system is very similar to the multiprogramming system shown as partitions B-J in Section 5.3. Often there is one additional large partition which contains programs and other necessary software, but the many small partitions are individually dedicated to single remote terminals as shown in Figure 5.3. If the user is not operating that terminal, then his partition is idle. In other words, each user has, in effect, his own batch machine. Typically, user partitions will be quite small (4K-8K) and will

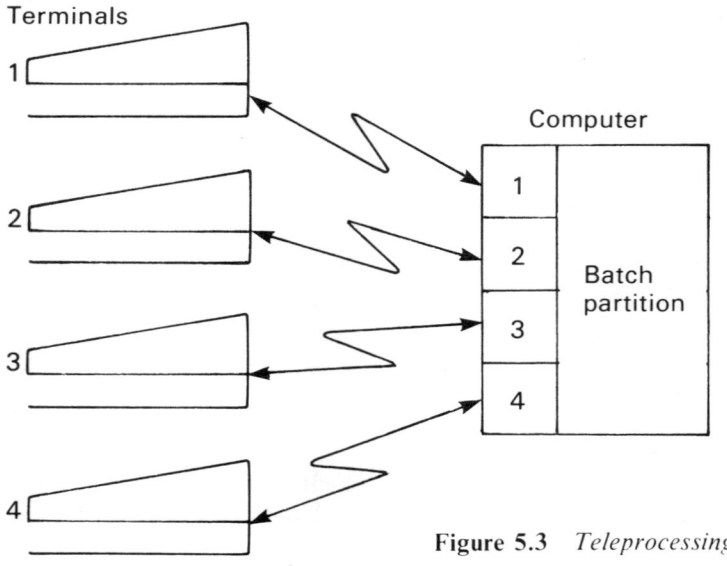

Figure 5.3 *Teleprocessing*

contain some of the program as well as data. On a modern large mainframe machine of 4,000K capacity an awful lot of users can be 'on-line' at the same time. Such systems, however, require very sophisticated operating systems and the total cost of the system is probably in excess of £1 million ($2 million).

For most users teleprocessing means up to 8 (sometimes 16) users linked to a small mainframe or a minicomputer. The normal method of teleprocessing at this level is to divide core equally between users. Thus a mini with 32K of user core and two users will give each 16K. Four users would only get 8K each and eight users would get a miserly 4K, which is hardly big enough to write your name in!

At this level, response time for eight users, based on experiences to date, is diabolical! Would-be purchasers of teleprocessing minicomputers would be wise to insist on demonstrations in which the computer is handling its maximum number of users in order to decide for themselves if it meets expectations.

At the present time, most minicomputers work on a teleprocessing principal. Some have terminals permanently connected to core, others allow remote (teletype) terminals. Either way, operating system demands are considerable, and may occupy more than half the computer's core and processing power. For instance, one minicomputer now on the market needs 32K of its 48K for the operating system. However, one can buy extra core in 32K 'lumps'. But in order to cope with the additional demands of the first extra lump, a bigger operating system is needed — this occupies 64K. Nett gain to the user — nothing! Happily, further units of core can be added without additional operating system, to a maximum of 128K — giving eight useful terminal partitions.

Suitable applications

It is difficult to conceive any situation in the management of a business where direct user control of the computer is not preferable to computer control of the user [provided the political problems have been sorted out (see Chapter 3)]. But teleprocessing may not be the best method of establishing that control, as will be explained in Section 5.5.

The most fruitful areas for introducing teleprocessing are where routine processing is being carried out, but there is a high demand, on a continuing basis, for immediate response to enquiries. Thus we find applications in the areas of:
    Sales/order processing
    Point-of-sale stations, e.g. supermarkets
    Stock enquiries
    Customer (credit, etc.) enquiries

    Work-in-progress
    Direct ledger postings
    Direct invoicing
    Management information systems
    — preparing report formats
    — accessing data
    — printing reports

Provided the teleprocessing system incorporated in a user's computer will allow different users to run different programs (some require that there is just one program in a large area of core, as mentioned earlier) and users are prepared to wait while a batch job runs (seldom more than a few minutes), teleprocessing systems can 'double' as batch machines. This considerable versatility has made them exceptionally popular and 'standard' for minicomputers, where the inclusion of a host of recent developments allows considerable flexibility in a small space.

5.5 Time sharing

To users, a computer running in time-sharing mode may look no different from a teleprocessing configuration. They share the advantage of direct user access to the computer and its files, but their methods of achieving it are very different. Whilst teleprocessing (TP) is, in reality, a rather special kind of batch operation, time sharing literally gives each user in turn a slice of time on the whole of the available core (see Figure 5.4). Thus a 64K (user) core machine with eight terminals can only give each user 8K in TP, but all 64K in time-sharing mode (TS). In TP mode that 8K is always available. In TS mode the 64K is only available for about 1/10th second, then the entire core content is 'dumped' on to a disk and the next user is allowed in. When everyone using the system has had a turn, the first user's 'core image' is replaced in the computer and processing recommences. The cyle is repeated for as many times as is needed for the job to be completed.

At the time of writing, few minicomputers have a truly effective time-sharing system, but it is possible to give figures for the best of the mainframe time-sharing systems, running on Digital, Honeywell or Sigma machines for example, and those available on Prime and Digital minis. Here, it is almost inconceivable that response time will be more than about 5 seconds. Other computers, adapted to, but not designed for, time-sharing work, can keep the user waiting for a very long time.

Some minicomputers have a 'roll-in roll-out' capability which approximates to time-sharing, for enquiries to files (in a management information system) whilst normally operating in TP mode. This

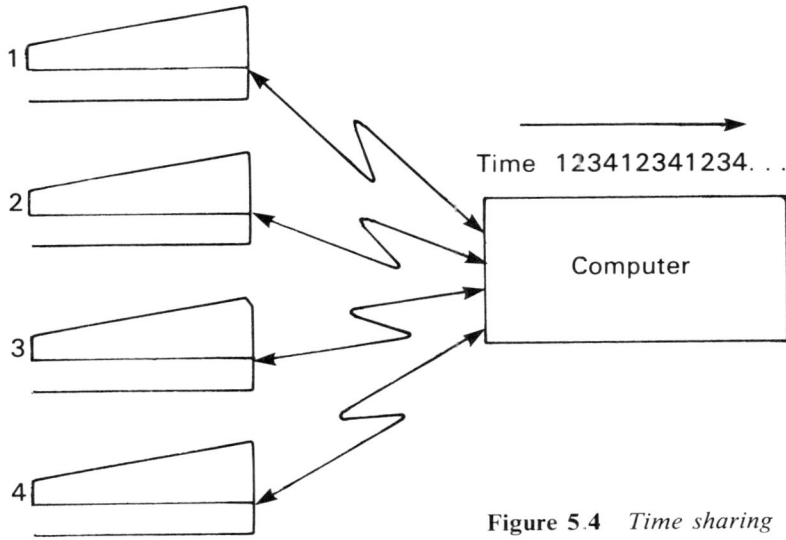

Figure 5.4 *Time sharing*

provides a powerful enquiry facility without inconvenience to on-line users.

Suitable applications

The area in which time sharing really scores is where instant access is needed to large amounts of computing power. Thus, although it is equally acceptable in all the applications listed in Section 5.4, it is the best means of supplying instant help in:
- Modelling (market, financial)
- Program development, e.g. FORTRAN
- Work-in-progress
- Technical support
- Engineering calculations
- Laboratory work

Inappropriate applications

Since TS depends on using core for only short periods of time, it follows that operations which require a lot of time are not suited to TS systems:
- Ledger consolidations
- Stress calculations
- Stock updating
- Payroll
- Program compilation

5.6 A comprehensive system

A modern mainframe computer will have a hardware design and operating systems that permit any of the configurations discussed in Sections 5.1-5.5 to be used — though not necessarily at the same time. Thus one can imagine a machine with multiprogramming batch partitions in which stock records are revised overnight as a result of data input in teleprocessing mode throughout the day. At the same time, in another partition, a systems programmer may be compiling a program that has been developed by using a time-sharing partition in the same machine. And throughout the day, senior managers have been able to access data, design reports and study trends through a time-shared database system. Such systems are now running successfully, but are restricted mainly to multinational companies and bureaux.

For the small to medium-sized company, such a system — even if there was a need for each type of application — would be an expensive folly. Smaller companies need to select the mode from which they will get the best return. For most this will mean using a teleprocessing system with a small business machine (see Chapter 7), and linking to a commercial bureau for other requirements.

5.7 Real time

Real-time processing has been separated from the other configurations because it cuts across all of them. Literally it means any mode of operation in which the computer is working at the same rate as its user. This normally interprets into a system in which a computer is dedicated to a single program. On-line airline seat bookings is a good example of real-time computing controlled by users.

Other real-time applications link the computer to equipment controlling strip-mills, chemical plant, aircraft landing sequences, space shots, etc.

Within the strict meaning of the term, teleprocessing (Section 5.4) is a form of real-time computing — since that part of the core dedicated to any given terminal is idle if that terminal is not actively being used. However, for the sake of clarity we shall treat them as separate modes.

Suitable applications

As we have defined real-time computing, the most suitable applications lie in the control of industrial processes:
   — Chemical plant   — Steel mills
   — Numerically controlled machine tools   — Sugar refineries, etc.
This brings us face to face with microprocessor technology.

	Batch (5.1)	Remote job entry (5.2)	Multiprogramming (5.3)	Teleprocessing (5.4)	Time sharing (5.5)	Real time (5.7)
● Suitable						
O Unsuitable						
Payroll	●	●			O	O
Updating ledgers	●	●	●	●		O
Updating stocks (etc.) files	●	●	●	●		O
Preparing invoices	●	●	●	●	O	O
Preparing mailing lists	●		●	●	O	O
Technical 'number crunching'	●	●			O	O
Production scheduling	●	●			O	O
Critical path analysis	●	●	●			
Sales/order processing	O	O	O	●	●	●
Stock control	O	O	O	●	●	●
Purchasing	O	O	O	●	●	
Scientific calculations					●	●
Information systems	O	O	O	●	●	
Database systems	O	O	O	●	●	
Warehousing	●(1)			●(1)		
Modelling, scientific					●	
Modelling, financial	●(2)			●	●(2)	
Direct postings	O	O	O	●		●
Direct invoicing	O	O	O	●		●
Program development					●	
Program compilation	●					

1 Input data via teleprocessing, run programs in batch.
2 Depending on the complexity of the model. Extremely complex models may need to be run in batch mode.

Figure 5.5

5.8 Summary

Figure 5.5 summarises the applications particularly suited to a given mode and inappropriate applications. No mark at all means that the application and mode are not incompatible — no more, no less.

Chapter Six
SOFTWARE

6.1 Introduction

However a computer is configured, whether it is operating in batch, time sharing or real time, it needs programs to make it work. The general term to describe such programs is *software*, and strictly speaking anything that contains instructions and is input to a computer can be thought of as software. Within the trade, though, there are clear distinctions between different types of software, and in this chapter, each type will be looked at in turn. In simple language, the split distinguishes between:
1. Software that controls the computer — known as *Operating software*.
2. Software that performs calculations — known as *applications software*.
3. Software that manipulates data — known as *database software*.

Before looking at each of these forms of software, however, it is worth clarifying what is meant by the 'language' a computer uses — for all three forms of software have to be written in some language or other. The choice is between languages that are 'easy' for the computer and those which are 'easy' for humans.

6.2 Languages

The simplest language with which we can communicate with a computer is the code which it uses internally, or some other code which very closely resembles it. At this level, every move the computer is to make has to be written by a programmer. Each core address (see Chapter 7) has to be individually ascribed to its variable. Every time a calculation is performed, instructions must be written which extract the contents of a given core location, transfer them to a register in the arithmetic processing unit (APU), extract the contents of a second specified location and transfer it to another register in the APU. Then a further instruction adds (say) the registers and yet another instruction transfers the result back to a core location which must again be specified by a programmer. Thus adding two numbers together requires several lines of programming.

Not many people write in machine code.

Clearly many of the steps in any program are repeated, and by giving the common functions (ADD, MULTIPLY, PRINT, READ, etc.) specific 'names' (+, *, WRITE, READ, etc.) it is possible to set up an index within core that recognises the names used by programmers and translates them into machine code. By setting up a further index which keeps a record of the core locations which have been allocated to variables, this part of machine code programming can also be dispensed with — though if a programmer wants to, he can still access individual addresses.

A 'language' is therefore developed which, whilst leaving the programmer in direct control of core locations, frees him of some of the more tedious detail. This language is called ASSEMBLER and every computer has its own individual assembler language.

It was in assembler that the programmers of the 1950s wrote their programs — which was largely responsible for the rapid growth of computer mystique, and slow growth of business applications. Assembler programmers needed to expend so much energy and time communicating with the machine that they had difficulty communicating with people. (And those who could were rapidly promoted to data processing managers.)

Although there was clearly a need for languages that were easier to use, the need for assembler was not diminished because it allowed programmers to use core efficiently. It kept the indexes (or directories) to a minimum and it allowed programmers to access individual bytes and bits (see Chapter 7 — Hardware).

To this day, most operating software is written in assembler language, though with reduced costs of core and the vast storage potential of modern disk packs, more and more suppliers are turning to 'high-level' languages for their operating systems. They are finding that, by extending existing languages to allow byte handling within them, they can get the best of both worlds — the flexibility and efficiency of assembler, and the ease of use of a high-level language (see Figure 6.1).

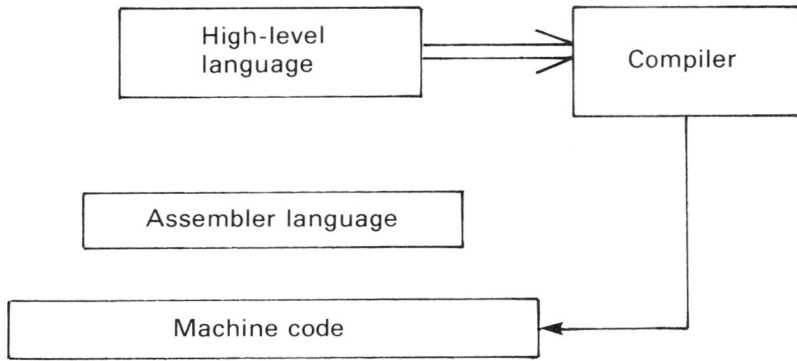

Figure 6.1 *Computer languages*

So what is a high-level language? It is a language that has combined many of the commonly used assembler routines into a directory and given the group a name — just as assembler is a directory of machine code statements. For example, "INPUT A,B" is a statement in one high-level language which will perform all of the following functions:

1 Recognise that INPUT is a particular command; that 'A' is a 'name'; that ',' means another 'name' is to follow; and that 'B' is that other name.
2 Set up core locations which will henceforth be referred to by the names A and B.
3 Add the names (A and B) and location addresses to the operating system index of locations.
4 Print a '?' at the particular terminal in use — which means opening up a channel to that terminal, retrieving the code for '?' from the operating system and sending it over a communications network.
5 Set up and monitor the communications network mentioned in (4).
6 Wait for a response from the terminal, and suspend processing of the program until a response has been received. This entails transferring command for the program to an interrupt handler within the operating system, which will itself be a very complex prgram.
7 Recognise the response from the terminal and identify a space or a comma as the means of separating two inputs, e.g. 12A, FRED.
8 Put the first value (12A) into the location for A and the second value into the location for B.
9 Recognise that the process is complete and transfer control to the next program statement.

Each of those processes will entail many machine code statements, and the single command "INPUT A,B" could require several pages of machine code. Thus we have high-level languages which are relatively inefficient in their use of core, but efficient (to a greater or lesser degree) in the use of human resources.

Almost all applications software is written in a high-level language, the choice of language depending on the application.
- COBOL and RPG for commercial work
- FORTRAN for scientific work
- APL and PL/1 for general work
- BASIC   Originally intended as a simple interactive language for students. Now extended beyond all recognition

Many more languages have been devised by manufacturers or software houses to meet special requirements.

One might reasonably expect programs written in a given language to perform equally well on all machines with the appropriate dictionary. Unfortunately this is far from the case.

Compilers

In order to translate 'source code' into machine code, programs are loaded into the computer with a compiler — the jargon term for the language dictionary. Since many compilers are written by manufacturers, they have slight differences which can completely prevent translation. For example, one compiler might accept either a space or comma between input names (INPUT A B or INPUT A,B). Another might only accept commas, and would interpret the first command as a single input name 'A B'. [Remember that a space is simply a different EBCDIC code (see Chapter 7) to the computer.]

The American National Standards Institute (ANSI) have prepared very detailed standards for some of the languages — notably COBOL and FORTRAN — but others (like BASIC) have no such standard. Even where standards are laid down, there is no requirement for suppliers to meet them.

The language jungle is just that!

Compiling programs can be a lengthy and expensive business, since the entire program has to be written, then submitted to a compiler. A program cannot be executed until it has been compiled, so even the tiniest mistake may not be spotted until the program is compiled. For example, a report may have a heading which turns out to be a couple of spaces too far to the right (putting say £ over the p column). In order to correct the error, the source program must be changed (naturally), then the *whole program* must be recompiled. If programs have been written in 'subroutines' some compilers only require the corrected subroutine to be recompiled, which is a clear saving in time and money.

To ease this burden on users, some languages — especially BASIC and frequently APL and PASCAL (a language particularly suited to microprocessors) — are 'interpretive'.

Interpreters

With an interpreter, each statement in the high-level language program is translated immediately. This means that instructions can be added or deleted and their effect tested immediately. Interpreters are especially useful to novice programmers as a form of self-learning facility.

6.3 Operating software

Later, in Chapter 7, the coding systems used by computer hardware — the physical computer — are explained in some detail. For the present, take it as read that the computer uses codes which are very simple, and that every activity undertaken by a computer has to be controlled by software stored in the computer in this simple code (machine code). To be only marginally useful, a computer (in addition to performing calculations) must:
1. Accept input from a user.
2. Take data and programs from storage devices, e.g. disks.
3. Route data and instructions (from a program) around the processor.
4. Send finished data and programs to either a storage device or printer.
5. Maintain records of:
   — authorised users
   — charges
   — files (both data and program)
   — storage devices
   — available space in the computer
   — queries
6. Establish security for core and files (see Chapter 4).

In order to be really useful it must also cope with the range of configurations discussed in Chapter 5, control screen formats, i.e. visual display terminals, provide HELP facilities, deal with input errors sympathetically, allow several different ways of handling files and many other housekeeping functions.

These are the roles of the operating system (OS).

In many ways, the operating software of a computer system is the most important element of the system, and its integrity and quality determine the effectiveness and efficiency of the installation. If a programmer makes a mistake when writing an OS, he can cause havoc, and all manufacturers spend a considerable amount of time and effort testing operating systems to ensure they do not contain 'bugs'.

Inevitably, one sneaks through the net occasionally, and we hear stories of a new OS that ignores the first number on a line of data (perhaps turning £1,000,000 into £000,000) or which 'scrambles' files (just like a telephone scrambler) but which refuses to unscramble them! Operating software, written by systems programmers, is undoubtedly the most complex and difficult part of any computer system, and many machines have been purchased solely on the quality of their operating software. Manufacturers tend to be justifiably proud of it and create new names to describe it:

Monitor
Executive
Supervisor

and then give different types of OS names of their own:

CICS, DOS, GEORGE, COMMANDER,
COSMOS, BTMX, etc., etc.

Computer specialists will then tend to nod sagely when they hear that a computer is 'having trouble time sharing 36 terminals *under* George', thus implying quite accurately that control and performance is determined by the OS.

One of the perennial problems of a manufacturer is to create an OS which is powerful and flexible, yet which does not occupy all the available space within the machine. After all, users will need some space to run their own programs. For example, in order to implement real time access to some very large data files, followed by on-line optimisation of programs, one manufacturer found that his OS was occupying 75 per cent of the total space available. With other 'overhead' activities, the poor user was left with not much more than 20 per cent of the computer! In batch mode, the same machine was able to use a much simpler OS, and the customer got 70 per cent or more of the available space.

Thus many computers have a range of operating systems which are called in from storage by the operators, depending on what type of configuration is being used.

Would-be purchasers of computer systems are well advised to check the OS they are being offered against their requirements, and to ask for a demonstration. Recent (the last five years) developments have seen the arrival of operating systems which are enormous, but which require very little computer 'core'. The effect is achieved by using *virtual memory*.

Virtual memory

If one imagines that a normal OS, i.e. one that is permanently in core (Figure 6.2a), is written on a large sheet of paper, then a virtual memory system is like a book, with only the contents page and a few other pages in core (Figure 6.2b). The rest of the OS sits on one of the storage devices waiting to be called in. (Some virtual systems are actually called 'paging' systems.)

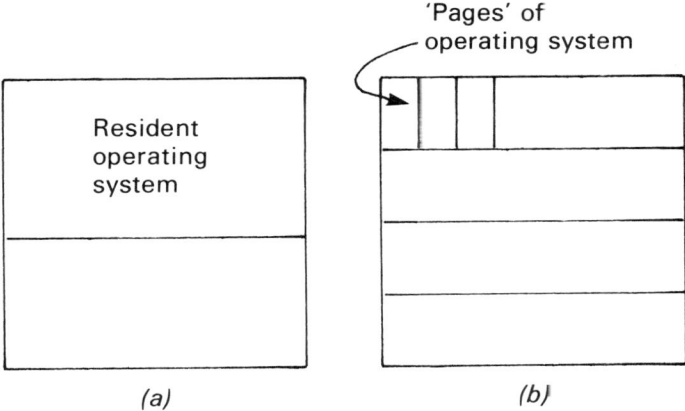

Figure 6.2 *Holding the operating system in core*

Once virtual memory has been implemented, the potentials are enormous because one can have an OS 10 times larger than the core of the machine which it is controlling, yet which requires only 10 per cent of core to perform all its functions. In order to do this, however, the machine must itself be powerful in order to 'page' quickly enough to prevent a degradation in service to the user; its files of cross-reference tables must also be very rapidly accessible on fast-access storage devices.

The system by which locations, either on disk or in core, are accessed by the OS has a very significant effect on the speed of the computer. It also determines how much space is needed for file (or location) directories, and even what type of applications can be effectively undertaken.

File management

Although we are talking here about managing files, many of the core management principles are equally applicable. There are basically two ways of accessing information held in core or on files: sequentially or randomly.

A sequential file consists of a string of records organised in the order written. New records are added to the end of the file, and may be of any length. A record of a day's activity on an order entry terminal would provide a good example of a sequential file.

In order to distinguish between records on a sequential file an 'End of Record' mark is put on the disk, but records are not marked in any other way. Thus there are no keys, no index. The result is that the file is easy to create, occupies the minimum space — and is fast to read in its entirety. But finding any single given record is an exceedingly slow process, because every one has to be read and checked in turn.

Random files are generated in a way that allows a user to access any single record directly. They may be of either fixed or variable length and invariably the first item on a record provides a key by which the record can be identified. One of the OS pages (in virtual memory) will contain an index relating keys to locations (either in core or on file) and the record can be accessed directly. Frequently, several keys are used to locate a record, and when this is done one has the makings of a database system.

Since this section is essentially about operating software, it should now be said that whether or not a computer will accept random-access files depends entirely on its OS.

So far as disk storage of random files is concerned, since every record is separately indexed, there is no need to store sequentially, and one can find the elements of a file scattered haphazardly over a disk pack. From the disk's point of view, however, it is more efficient to keep all the records of a single file together on one or more consecutive 'tracks' (see Chapter 7), and in this form files tend to be called *index sequential*, since the file *is* sequential but is accessed via an index — thus making it *random*. Quite!!

There are many variations on indexed and index-sequential files to suit the operating software and the application. Clearly using customer names as keys will be a great help in dealing with a customer data file, but for developing applications programs it is going to be easier to refer to records by line number.

Some operating systems identify locations by a starting number and an increment, e.g. 2C00F + 5A — in hexadecimal of course! This saves space in core (if virtual memory is not implemented), but will probably necessitate fixed-length records, with subsequent wasted space on disk.

By and large it does not matter what system is used provided it does its job properly. The foregoing is really intended as ammunition to be used against salesmen who make extravagent claims for their own OS facilities — or who offer a 'database system' using sequential files!

Utilities

Operating software also includes a number of utilities — small programs which link applications programs into the OS (for file and screen handling, for example). Once again they are 'transparent' to the user and only become significant if the OS is so badly written that their inclusion in an applications program increases its size to an unacceptable extent, i.e. it is too big for the available core. This in itself can only happen if virtual memory is not available.

The time when file-handling utilities can be useful is when users are writing their own programs where the ability to SORT and MERGE files, COPY files, ANALYSE files and LINK files to other computer systems can be very helpful.

Editors

Users who start writing their own programs soon discover that mistakes can be easier to make than correct unless the OS contains a powerful Editor (a facility which frequently goes hand in hand with random-access files). More than rapid access to a record is needed because one will probably want to change a single character within a record, or will want to change every occurrence of a particular string of characters to a different string. [When this book was first drafted, Chapter 5 was Chapter 8, but in order to explain some of the jargon, it was later transposed, with consequent changes to other chapters. It would have been very nice to have been able to say "Change all 'Chapter 8' to 'Chapter 5'! with similar simple editing commands to other chapter headings — but it was not typed on a word processor (see Chapter 2) and the changes had to be made manually.]

Illustrating good editing facilities could occupy a further 20 pages, so just one example will be given. A mistake (as shown) in the line:

THE QUICK BROWN FOX JUM*ED OVER THE LAZY MOON

would, with a poor editor, require the line to be completely retyped. With a good editor, the * is changed to P by the command:

/*/S/P/

Screen displays

Many of todays minicomputers and microcomputers are using much more sophisticated displays to prompt users than would have been considered possible a few years ago, and which are still not generally available on mainframes. Sometimes the displays are generated and controlled by the operating software of the computer. Operating software is, on occasions 'plumbed in' to the hardware using microprocessor technology (Chapter 11).

Operating system costs

One can reasonably expect the best available OS on mini- and microcomputers to come 'free' as part of the hardware package (that's right — the *hardware* package) because without it, the machine is useless. With mainframes, manufacturers' policies vary and one may be faced with a choice of OS ranging from £2,000 to £50,000 for either purchase or lease.

As with everything else to do with computers, one can only make a decision when one knows exactly what the OS is going to be asked to do.

Operating systems are *not* like ordinary programs, and you should never buy one thinking it can be changed to meet your requirements. Any attempt to modify an OS (except by experienced — and expensive — systems programmers) will not only surely fail, but may create total chaos — remember the file scrambler example on page 46. So make sure that the manufacturer's OS will meet your requirements
    — Time sharing   — Screen displays
    — Random file access — Security
and add its cost (if any) to the cost of hardware for the purposes of comparing costs.

6.4 Applications software

When we talk about 'programs' we are almost invariably referring to applications software. These are the programs which send old ladies gas bills of £9,999,999.99!

Any program that does a job for someone falls into the category of applications software, and Chapter 2 lists just a few of those jobs. The intention of this section is to outline some of the issues that should be considered when reaching a decision about the software to be implemented.

Packages

Many business tasks are common to all firms — even though a lot of firms would refute any suggestion that they are other than unique. Ledger transfers, credit control, payroll, stock holding and sales analyses are all examples of routine activities common to most companies and which can be prepackaged by suppliers. Small business systems (Chapter 8) base their hopes of success on a general acceptance that their packaged software will meet the needs of a wide range of businesses.

Uniqueness in firms usually appears in the detail of input and output formats, or in the volumes: details which are catered for in most good packages. Sometimes it comes as something of a shock to a managing director to discover that what he considers to be large ('We carry 2,000 stock items!') is considered by the supplier to be small ('In that case we can supply a smaller disk!') Sometimes companies do present unique problems ('We have 2,000,000 stock items') which might stretch the credibility of a package, but by and large packaged software will cope with most situations.

The advantage of a package is that it will have been thoroughly tested by the supplier and (unless you are foolish enough to be a pioneer) by other users. (Always ask for the names of other users.) Packages will also be updated from time to time, and these upgrades can often be a cheap and efficient means of improving operations. In particular, tax legislation changes can be dealt with much more cheaply through a package than through DIY or custom-built software.

However, not all packages available today are suitable for the 1980s and to explain that fact we need to look at the philosophy underlying the structure of a package. Some started life as a set of disparate programs solving disparate problems:
— Stock control
— Sales/order processing
— Ledgers, etc.
calling in whatever data was needed for their individual needs and printing 'comprehensive' reports.

Packaging consists of tying these elements into an untidy bundle, using a terrifying range of sort/merge utilities to create some semblance of compatibility between sets of data. Such packages are not suitable for companies looking for flexibility. They can be identified by asking for a change in report-formats and watching horror cross the face of the supplier. A lot of packages available through bureaux services fall into this category and are to be avoided like the plague! They *will* cause trouble, they *will* delay your activities ('Since we went onto the computer, it takes us three weeks to get our sales analyses — and then they're in the wrong format'). But they can be superficially very attractive to a financial director because they are cheap.

Other packages have a fundamentally different philosophy. They

start with the premise that a business runs on information and that, in order to achieve that information, 'something' has to be done to the data which the business generates (orders, stock, cash flow, etc.). That 'something' is:
— Stock control
— Sales/order processing
— Ledgers

which *follow from* the needs of the business. Such packages lead to database applications (see Section 6.5) and flexible operations. They are also easier to change when circumstances alter.

Finally, using packages may mean that you need not employ programming staff.

Anyone considering a small business system will, of course, be offered an applications package with the hardware, and, for many such firms, the most significant 'software' cost is the cost of converting their own systems and procedures to the computer's. It may be necessary to add or delete customer/product, etc., codes, change the size and structure, e.g. alphanumeric (AB01) to numeric (2001), redefine territories, change the basis on which stock is valued (FIFO to average value, say) and so on. If such costs are just too high, either in financial, staff or organisational terms (particularly if the firm is a subsidiary of a larger parent company with defined and inviolate regimes), then the applications software will have to be either custom-built or home-grown.

Custom-built software

If pre-packaged software does not, for one reason or another, meet the needs of a company, then custom-built software may be the answer. There are many good consultants and scanning the last set of UK Yellow Pages produced over 700 names, ranging from one-man outfits, to major software houses employing several hundred people. Unfortunately, there is no way of knowing whether a consultant is competent to undertake a specific job unless he has already prepared an almost identical one, and his client is prepared to talk about it. With small firms the people (or person) concerned may be very good, yet may not have been given the opportunity to prove himself. (Many small consultancy firms have been set up by entrepreneurs who feel confined by the regulations of a large company.) However, some consultants are in business by themselves because a larger firm discontinued their services. References from existing customers help, particularly if the consultant can produce someone who has given him repeat business. Large companies give an aura of respectability and competence — and most are both. But the reputation of a company may not reflect the competence of all its consultants. Watch out for references which quote the same individuals — particularly if the list does not contain the person who is being offerred to you.

In reality, most firms choose their consultant on the impression he makes on them as a person. If he is to be helpful to a company, he has to be closely involved in its life and work, and in order to do that effectively he must be able to get on with its people. It is a very crude measure, but if you feel happy with him you will probably be satisfied with his work. The danger is that you may be satisfied even if the work is poor.

Conversely a less likeable person may produce very good work, which is 'unsatisfactory' because he does not present it well.

Whilst we are going through a period of indecisive 'on-the-other hand . . .' arguments, it is important to mention the cost of consultants. National software houses will charge over £200 per day for a senior consultant (some want £30/hour for a seven hour day) whilst one-man outfits may charge as little as £50. Which alternative will prove cheaper is a matter for conjecture, for a major software house may be able to link together a series of fairly standard program suites compiled by one of the country's leading authorities on the subject (whatever it might be).

A 'new' consultant without experience would have to design systems from scratch, gleaning all his knowledge of the subject from the client's (highly paid) staff. On the other hand, the one-man outfit may *be* the leading authority, and the software house may be breaking in a trainee. Only close attention to what a supplier is offering, supported by comments from business colleagues, can help one to decide who to use. And do not forget travelling and subsistence costs for consultants who have to stay in hotels.

If a decision has been made to use a consultant, the next decision is to assess where he should start. It is tempting to try to cut costs by specifying the system oneself and ask only for programming expertise (which will be significantly cheaper than a senior consultant). The danger is that some crucially important point may be overlooked, which could result in significant losses when the programs are installed.

The fresh approach provided by buying a few days of senior consultant's time usually pays for itself very quickly, and provides a useful check on all the work which has gone before. The presence of a senior consultant also provides an important liaison for ensuring adequate testing and documentation of the applications suites.

The software itself should fulfil all the requirements of the purchaser and meet the criteria suggested above for packages.

Once again, a user may expect to be able to survive without systems analysts and programmers.

User-prepared software

A prerequisite for user-produced applications packages is that analysts and programmers are already on the payroll. This will usually mean that the company has a mainframe machine. By and large, home-produced commercial suites will not be economically viable unless this condition is met. In fact, some large organisations still find it sensible to use software houses (see above) for major suites of programs, even though they have staff available. Such staff are employed on 'special jobs' and program maintenance (see below).

Where user-prepared software can be of particular value is in the non-standard areas of the business (which usually means non-commercial areas). Scientific and engineering applications programs are frequently produced internally, sometimes by the technical staff, using a language such as BASIC (see Appendix 1) or FORTRAN. (In such cases it is useful to have interactive operating software.)

A company planning to move into the ranks of computer owners and also considering in-house software would be best advised to appoint a data processing — or computer — manager and allow him to assess the need for internal staff. He will also be best placed to advise user departments in the preparation of their own software.

Program maintenance

The 'normal' route towards internal programming staff arises when applications packages or custom-built suites need to be changed. The life of any suite of programs can be likened to the life of a motor car. In the first year, there are teething troubles. In the second year, operation is trouble-free (well, almost!). In the third year, maintenance (repairs) are needed, in the fourth year, maintenance becomes a nuisance and by year five it's nearly ready for the scrap heap.

For custom-built programs, maintenance can be carried out by the original suppliers, or by local consultants if the suppliers are based some distance away. The approach has advantages in that no increase in establishment is required, but suffers the disadvantage that expertise is never built up with the firm.

There may also be 'unacceptable' delays when software houses are making the changes. For example, a change in tax regulations will affect all users, resulting in overwhelming work for the software houses tying up their staff for some considerable period. Alternatively a 'bug' appearing during a monthly consolidation (always on Friday afternoon!) may have to wait until the following week before it can be tackled. Captive staff can be 'persuaded' to work 24 hours a day over the weekend!

Users should always be looking ahead to the next three to five years of computer operation, and there is a better than evens chance that usage will increase, putting greater demands on coordination and control of systems, thus forcing companies to employ some computer staff. Program maintenance is not a bad starting point, and a good young programmer might aspire to being the firm's first computer manager.

Users of packaged software will probably have signed a maintenance contract with their suppliers and any legislative changes will be made 'automatically'. Likewise, 'bugs' will be of considerable interest to the manufacturer whose very reputation relies on keeping them to a minimum, quickly eliminating any that do appear (and there will inevitably be some).

6.5 Database software

To say that database software manipulates data is true, but rather underestimates the complexities involved. Properly designed, a database management system (DBMS) will enable users to pick the data they need from a vast file quickly and efficiently. They will be able to order the data in a number of different ways without the need for a 'SORT' utility (the old way of changing a customer list from code order to alphabetical order) and will be able to change their data requirements, often without recompiling the program which is processing it. The DBMS thus provides a means by which an organisation can monitor and control its resources.

The cost of a good DBMS is high, and it requires significant computer hardware backup, but the potential returns are high.

Fundamental to a DBMS are a number of concepts which differentiate between 'data files' (which we have always had) and a 'database'.

Data is independent

The separation of data from procedures provides a basis on which a DBMS can be built (see Figure 6.3). Traditionally data files have been defined within programs; if at a later date it is necessary to change a program this may involve changes to the data structure, which in turn frequently leads to changes in other programs using the same data. If the data can be defined independently of the program, then changes to either the program or the data structure should be possible without the necessity for change to the other. In practice, program and data must be related at some stage, and data independence becomes a matter of

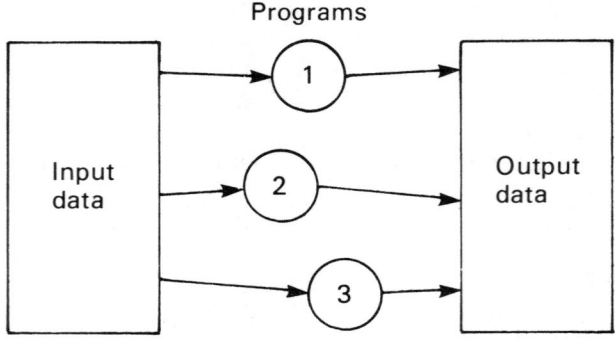

Figure 6.3 *The database concept*

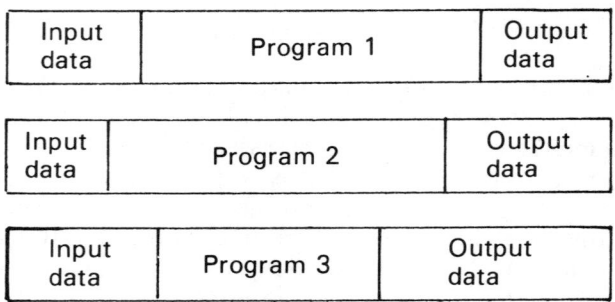

Figure 6.4 *Traditional programming*

delaying this 'binding' as long as possible. In traditional programming binding occurs when the program is written (see Figure 6.4); it is fairly easy to delay binding until compile time, but much more difficult to delay it until run time — which is what a good DBMS achieves.

Data is integrated

When data is defined within programs, it frequently happens that the same data is defined in two or more programs, perhaps slightly differently, and it becomes necessary to hold a separate copy of the data for each program. This poses two problems: wasted storage space and possible discrepancies between two versions of the same data. For example, the term 'Monthly Sales' can take on many different meanings:
1   *Monthly* could mean:
    — 30 days

  — Calendar month
  — 4 x 1 period (13-month year)
2 *Sales* could mean:
  — Out of factory gate
  — Invoiced
  — Paid for
  — Ordered, etc.

Even this simple example gives 12 alternative meanings for, and hence values of, 'Monthly Sales'.

 Databases aim to store an item of data once and once only. This aim is not always achieved because duplication of some data items may be necessary for security purposes. However, within a database system such duplication (or *redundancy*) is kept to a minimum. A secondary benefit is that as little disk space as possible is occupied by data.

Data has integrity

This should result from data integration. If there is only one copy of a data item, it should be easier to control it, to ensure that it is up to date and that it is never corrupted. This implies a central control on access and security measures, which in turn frequently means a database administrator — an ultimate authority to whom all disputes and brainwaves about database design must be referred.

Data is retrievable

If data is organised to provide independence, integration and integrity, then it should be possible to use the data in more ways than was originally intended. This may be done formally by designing further programs to use the data, but perhaps more important, it should be possible to retrieve data directly from the database using a high-level DBMS language, and to re-organise it in any way. ('List the one-eyed, left-handed, blond-haired employees in the North West of England'.) In order to achieve such flexible data access, the software must be sophisticated, and the data must be carefully organised.

Data organisation

The organisation of data can most easily be explained by comparison with a manual system. Imagine a registry system in which all a company's files are kept in one place under the control of a registry supervisor. The *physical* data (pieces of paper) are kept in folders under headings, e.g. company codes. The folders are then stored in an order under other headings, e.g. regions. We can think of the two sets of headings as access 'keys'.

Managers wanting to use the data (say for handling customer queries) will ask the registry supervisor for certain information, which will entail a clerk getting several sheets of paper (physical data) from disparate parts of the filing system, doing some calculations on the data (perhaps producing a summary) and then presenting a copy of the relevant information to the manager. This represents *logical data*.

In a DBMS physical data is stored on disk in a database file, and with many users accessing a database there may be many logical data structures needed to meet different needs. The trick is to find a way of defining the access keys which will allow logical stuctures to be flexible.

By creating 'physical' and 'logical' data as separate concepts, it is possible to modify either one without damaging the other; users need never know how the physical data is organised (as with the registry) and more complex searches can be developed by improving the database software (retraining the filing clerk).

At this time, no industry standards exist for DBMS designs, though two very different philosophies are emerging for getting at data elements, called *pointer systems* and *inverted file systems*, respectively.

Pointers (see Figure 6.5)

In this system, each data element has, stored with it, pointers which direct any searcher to the logical elements that either precede or follow that element. Thus access to any given bit of data allows the rest of the logical structure(s) to be explored. This approach is rather expensive on storage space (since each data element carries a number of pointers) and it is relatively difficult to change logical structures. However, searches make fairly efficient use of computer time, since — once started — retrieval follows naturally.

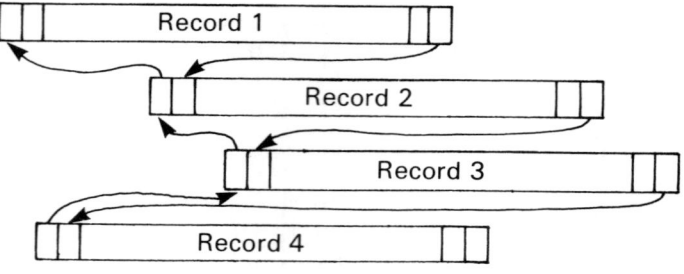

Figure 6.5 *Schematic of 'pointer' file*

A second level of search is provided by creating a hierarchy of elements which may be searched using the pointers, or sequentially. In some DBMS, lower hierarchical levels are only amenable to sequential searches.

Database management systems which rely on pointers (in one form or another) include IMS (from IBM) and TOTAL.

Inverted files (see Figure 6.6)

This is a somewhat misleading term since the file is perfectly normal. However, every file created under this system carries with it a second file which provides an index to the location of data on disk. The index files are normally stored with the operating system, each entry containing simply a logical name and an address. Disk space is used efficiently, and access can be very rapid indeed (random access systems normally depend on some form of indexing anyway).

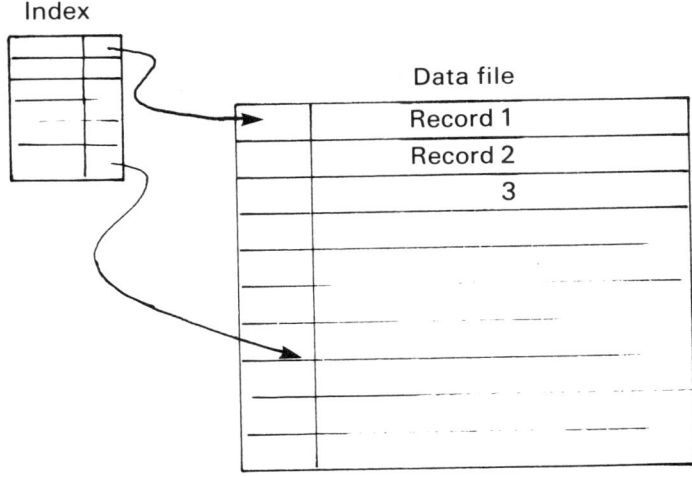

Figure 6.6 *Schematic of 'inverted' file*

Databases formed in this way can be compared directly to a book with a comprehensive index and DBMS utilising this philosophy are generally well liked by users. Problems can arise if new names are to be added or deleted, and since records are not stored sequentially on disk, the term 'sequential' search loses its meaning. Thus routine 'sequential listings' are as easy (or difficult) as a random search. Database management systems using inverted file access include ADABAS and SYSTEM 2000.

Choosing a DBMS

Both vendors and users claim significant benefits from database systems over conventional programming techniques, but in order to gain the greatest benefit users need large hardware configurations. Of the systems mentioned, only TOTAL can run effectively in less than about 200K bytes of core with at least 1Mbyte of disk storage. Neither figure provides any difficulty to a mainframe installation, but is rather outside the range of most minicomputers and small business systems. At the beginning of 1979, fewer than 15 per cent of the eighty or so SBS manufacturers provided a full DBMS — though many have adjusted their operating system to give a pseudo-data management facility.

The distinction is unimportant until such time as a user wants to move his data onto another machine.

As with hardware, the choice of a DBMS involves weighing a number of conflicting criteria and one must start with the question: 'Which systems will fit on the hardware I intend to use?' This question is itself preceded/succeeded by the question: 'What hardware do I need to support the DBMS I hope to instal?' By going in ever-decreasing (or increasing) circles one finishes with some sort of fit, and can then choose between the available systems. Since most companies embarking on a DBMS will already have a computer manager, we will not deal with the criteria to be considered in any detail, but will simply list some of those most frequently mentioned by users:

1. Data integrity must be assured — if there are several copies of the same piece of data floating around, a large part of the benefit of a DBMS is lost.
2. The DBMS must be reliable and fairly free of 'bugs' — it's no use having 50 time-sharing users held up whilst programmers frantically plug holes in the software.
3. Programs and data should be independent of each other.
4. It should perform well — in a test a few years ago on some 400,000 records, one DBMS took 9 hours, another 50 minutes!
5. It should be easy to use — some DBMS require a lot of on-going maintenance and a brain like a computer to penetrate the barbed-wire entanglements with which they surround themselves. (Of course, to some computer-professionals, those entanglements may appear as additional degrees of freedom!)
6. Security.
7. The DBMS should not require additional staff to support it [see (5) also], nor should naive users have to lean heavily on computer staff support.
8. The supplier should be credible, and should be able to provide quick, effective support in the event of trouble.

9   The system should be well documented, and contain training aids.
10   Cost.

Within the selection criteria themselves, one can also see the benefits which might accrue from the effective installation of a database system.

Looking to the future, it is quite likely that the pressure on users to select carefully will diminish as new applications languages are developed which include within their basic structure the elements of a good DBMS.

Chapter Seven
HARDWARE

7.1 A brief history

One tends to think of computers as a very recent development of the 1950s and 1960s, but computers of one sort or another have been with us since the days of Stonehenge. Five hundred years or more BC, pebbles in grooved boards were used for counting, though it took until AD100 before the abacus was in common use in the East. In the early 17th Century great advances in computational capabilities resulted from Napier's work (the introduction of logarithms for instance), but it was not until two centuries later that Babbage developed his 'analytical engine'.

By the beginning of the 20th Century, increasing interest in computational aids was being shown by commercial organisations, and the concept of data processing began to develop. Hollerith invented a machine which sorted cards with holes punched in them — and the first card-reader was born. Today's card-readers owe a great deal to Hollerith's early work.

Between the First and Second World War, developments in electronic valves progressed rapidly, and in the 1940s the first 'computer hardware' appeared. This first machine would hold only a few bits of binary information, had nothing in the way of software or coding systems, but was able to *store information* for extended periods.

By the 1950s fairly complex computers were being used which employed valves both as an internal storage medium and within the arithmetic registers — that part of the computer which gives it its computational facility. However, computing power was strictly limited because of the problems of dissipating heat from hundreds — later thousands — of valves. The problem was that valves could only be used to represent 'switched on' or 'switched off' states. They could therefore only count as far as ONE. (OFF = 0; ON = 1) and the number of valves needed to represent any sizeable number was somewhat large! Dissipating heat was a major problem, and the most important feature of these early machines was the air-conditioning, which frequently occupied more space than the computer and all its peripherals.

Information was fed into the machine via a card-reader and output was typically via a card-punch. Storage was by means of magnetic-tape machines using 1,200-ft (later 2,400-ft) lengths of tape similar in nature to the tape used by hi-fi enthusiasts on spool-to-spool tape decks. Access was fairly slow and accuracy somewhat haphazard.

During the 1950s came the first of two major technological advances which have revolutionised computer hardware design. Transistors replaced valves. They were cheaper by a factor of between 10 and 100, they were more reliable, they were more robust, their characteristics were more stable — but above all they used electrical power much more efficiently. Air conditioning to dissipate 99 per cent of the total power consumption which had been converted to heat by valves could now be replaced by equipment that only had to dissipate 30 per cent of less) of one tenth of the power consumption for the same size of computer.

By this time, the memory of a computer had changed from valves (or even transistors) to small 'cores' of a metal based on iron-ferrite. These 'cores' were sewn (literally) together on frames and their magnetic properties were such that they could be used to act as simple counting devices — they were magnetised positively (equal to the number 1) or negatively (equal to the number 0). Because 'core storage' had to be sewn together, the process of building core was very labour-intensive, and hence expensive. 'Core' became not only the universal measure of computer size, but also a measure of the purchasing organisation's pocket-book!

By the end of the 1960s, computers capable of storing many thousand characters in core (at great expense) had been developed and, in parallel, software designers and programmers were using that power to make the hardware perform in more and more sophisticated ways.

Throughout the 1960s, space exploration provided the spur for lighter, smaller and even more reliable devices than the transistor, and 'microelectronics' appeared. The first 'chip' hit the market in 1969. This was a tiny piece of silicon which was capable of storing the same number of characters as a bank of cores. Later (about 1974), the 'chip' was extended so that the same sized piece could contain the same number of characters as a few thousand cores (say 4,000).

Now, in 1980, 'chips' which are equivalent to 32,000 cores are commonplace — and prices have plummetted (see also Chapter 11). Consider, for instance the calculator market. When 'chips' were first introduced into calculators, one containing the equivalent of 30,000 transistors — and hence several chips — would cost over £200 in the UK. Nowadays, for just £10, one can buy calculators containing the equivalent of over 200,000 transistor and 'core' circuits. Computer hardware costs have come down to the same extent and the main memory is now the *cheapest* part of a computer system.

Within five years (and probably a lot less) it is likely that 'bubble' memory will be storing 500,000 to 1,000,000 characters in less space than it takes to write the number. (This compares with the 1950s computer which needed space equal to the volume of this book to store a single character.)

The remaining sections in this chapter deal with how computers use the power at their disposal, but because the technology is easier to understand, they are written in terms of 1960s technology, using ferrite cores as the main storage medium. The principles have not changed, only the mechanisms.

7.2 Elements of a computer system

Television programmes that show computers with whirling tapes and a myriad of blinking lights are showing not so much the computer but its peripherals — those parts of a computer system which get data into the machine, store it, and take it out. The computer itself, the Central Processing Unit (CPU), is the small box in the middle of the room which displays no histrionics. It is the CPU that forms the heart of any computer system but which cannot function to any purpose without its peripherals.

The elements which make up a complete system are therefore (see Figure 7.1):
1 *Input devices* — which convert data intelligible to humans into a form intelligible to the computer. They also increase the rate of data transfer from the snail's pace at which we can handle it, to something approaching the speed at which the computer works.
2 *Storage devices* — which hold data until the computer is ready to process it and hold the results of the computer's labour. Storage elements will hold information indefinitely and can be removed from the computer room for safe-keeping elsewhere. They can frequently be transferred between machines.

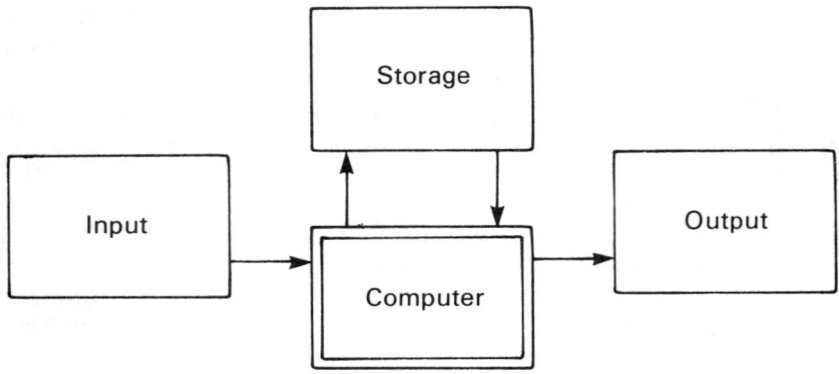

Figure 7.1 *Basic configuration*

3   *Output devices* — which translate the results of processing into a form that humans can interpret. Usually that means a printed copy or a television screen.
4   The Central Processing Unit — *the computer.*

Modern hardware architecture

Central processing units have much in common with large office blocks. Their architectural design can significantly effect the type of task to which they are best suited. Open-plan offices with many entrances and exits to any 'department' contained within the office are ideal for rapid and random access to anyone in the building.

Office blocks with long corridors and enclosed individual offices give some degree of freedom of access, but the process can be slow. Some offices designed in this way will have comprehensive indexing systems posted in the lobby to help visitors find the way round — but it can be slow.

Nobody designs offices so that, in order to reach an office at the far end of the building from the entrance, one has to walk *through* every other office — but if they did, progress would be very slow — unless the visitor needed to visit every one in the building, in the order in which they were allocated offices.

Computer design has tended to follow the examples just cited, but in the reverse order. The first machines were dedicated to doing certain things in certain ways and both programs and data 'visited each office in turn' on their way through. For batch processing of routine data, such architecture made very efficient use of the facilities, and did not cause any problems for the user. Files were accessed and written sequentially (they had to be, since magnetic tapes treated them in that way, and magnetic tape was the only available storage medium) and processing proceeded in like manner.

As more flexible storage devices, i.e. disks, appeared and more flexible operating systems emerged, architecture gradually changed to mirror 'open-plan' offices. Where manufacturers were not able or not prepared (perhaps because of the extent of their investment in existing architecture, or maybe because their designers had become locked into a particular way of thinking) to change their architecture radically, they tried to write operating systems that provided the part of the indexing system described in the 'corridor office block' illustration. In some cases the operating system was so complicated it took up nearly 90 per cent of the computer's available power, which resulted in stories in the papers about '*** computer only delivers 25 per cent of the service which we were promised'.

The most modern architecture now has a mix of 'open-plan' and 'indexing' which allows operating systems to run *efficiently* in multiprogramming, teleprocessing, real-time and time-sharing modes (see Chapter 5) — all at the same time.

It is difficult to see how less sophisticated CPU architecture can expect to survive through the 1980s, even though some of the major suppliers to the UK market are persisting in the development of 'corridor office blocks'. Irrespective of architectural design, however, all CPUs have much the same type of circuitry and have similar functions to fulfil.

7.3 Central processing unit

The CPU has a number of separate functions to fulfil. Firstly it has to receive data from the storage devices and take that data into a store of its own. It then has to hold the data until its arithmetic processing unit (APU) is ready to perform the calculations. Data in its new form is returned to storage from the APU and is then translated through an 'output' unit to either external storage or directly to an output device such as a printer. Finally the CPU has to perform a control function that coordinates all those activities and the usage of the external devices.

The CPU of a computer, therefore, has five functions to fulfil (see Figure 7.2):
1   Control.
2   Input.
3   Storage.
4   Arithmetic.
5   Output.

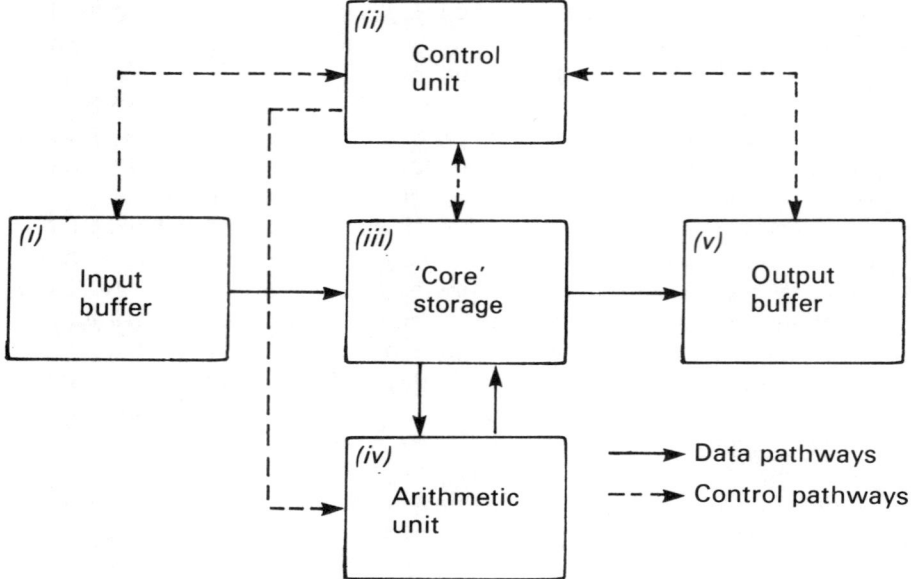

Figure 7.2 *Central processing unit*

Of these five functions, that of control is by far the most crucial. In present-day computers the design of the control unit (and of the program which it uses) determines the range of applications for which the computer is efficient. It also determines the number of processing jobs which can be undertaken at any one time and to a large extent it determines the size of each computing job. In addition the control function determines accounting, security and priority of each job entering the machine.

Despite its complexity of function, the control unit like the others in the CPU — apart from some parts of the arithmetic unit — was originally made from very simple electrical circuits. Now, in 1980, field-effect transistors (FETs), 'chips' and other electronic magic have revolutionised the circuits. They are now infinitely more complex, yet strangely much more reliable. (The mean time between failures is measured in 100,000+ hours of continuous operation.) However, the fundamental concepts on which their operations are based have not changed.

Binary codes

Basically, the circuits within the CPU are arranged to act as switches which can only be in one of two states — on or off. Every element of a

CPU (except the arithmetic registers) is based on this premise. Before seeing how the circuits are connected, however, it might be helpful to digress to look at the codes that are used.

Binary arithmetic is not as horrifying as some people make out. Whereas our decimal system is based on the assumption that there are ten numbers to deal with, binary only allows two. In that respect it is much simpler than the decimal (or denary) system:

Denary   0 1 2 3 4 5 6 7 8 9
Binary   0 1

The method of counting on in binary is exactly the same as is used in denary, i.e. a second column is used in which the first available character is placed. The full range of numbers is then repeated.

Denary   10 11 12 13 14 15 16 17 18 19
           20 21 22 23 24 25 26 . . . . . .
           and so on to 97 98 99
           at which point, it is necessary to start a third column.
           100 101 102 103 104 . . . . . etc.

The difference with binary is that limits are reached much more quickly:

Binary   10 11 — and that is all before the third column is required
           100 101 110 111 at which point a fourth column is needed
           1000 1001 1010 1011 1100   etc.

It is possible, clearly, to represent any denary number by a binary equivalent, and by using 'switches' inside the CPU any number can be represented. Zero (0) being equivalent to the switch being 'off', and one (1) being equivalent to the switch set 'on'.

Denary:	0	1	2	3	4	5
Binary:	0	1	10	11	100	101

Denary:	6	7	8	9	10	11
Binary:	110	111	1000	1001	1010	1011

Denary:	12	13	14	15	16
Binary:	1100	1101	1110	1111	10000 . . . .

So far as counting within a computer is concerned, there are two significant points to note about the table above. Firstly, all denary *characters* can be represented by a binary number consisting of no more than four figures, i.e. 9 = 1001. Thus, it would be possible to create a code using 4 binary dig*its* (henceforth called *bits*) to represent each binary character. Secondly, if such a code were devised, there

	0000	0001	0010	0011	0100	0101	0110	0111	1000	1001	1010	1011	1100	1101	1110	1111
0000	NULL				HT								STOP			
0001	DS	SST	FDS	TM	LF						DC1	DC2	FF	CR	SO	SI
0010							BS				DC3	VT	FS	GS	RS	US
0011											EM	ESC				
0100	SP															
0101	&										¢	.	<	(	+	⌐
0110	-	/									!	$	*	)	;	⌠
0111											≮	-	%	-ο-	>	?
1000		a	b	c	d	e	f	g	h	i		#	@	-	=	"
1001		j	k	l	m	n	o	p	q	r						
1010			s	t	u	v	w	x	y	z	SOH	DLE	CAN	NAK	SYN	ETB
1011									STX		ETX		EOT	ENQ	ACK	BELL
1100		A	B	C	D	E	F	G	H	I						CAK
1101		J	K	L	M	N	O	P	Q	R						DAK
1110			S	T	U	V	W	X	Y	Z						DOS
1111	0	1	2	3	4	5	6	7	8	9						◇

Figure 7.3 *Extended binary-coded decimal interchange code (EBCDIC)*

would be spare figures in the range 1010-1111 (10-15), which could be used for other purposes.

EBCDIC (Extended Binary Coded Decimal Interchange Code) The code devised to interchange binary and denary is called EBCDIC and is almost universally used in the world's largest computers. It recognises that 4 bits can be used to represent any denary number, and it also recognises that we need to represent letters and special characters (*, !, ", /, @, £, etc.) as well. In order to do this the code (see Figure 7.3) puts two sets of 4 bits together, uses one set to represent a value and the other to form a code (or zone) which defines whether the character is a letter, number or special character.

The concept is probably most easily explained by taking some examples from the illustration:

```
1010  1000 is equivalent to y
1110  1000 is equivalent to Y
1111  1000 is equivalent to 8
£          is equivalent to 01001010
u          is equivalent to 10100100
```

There are also numerous special codes that control special switches within the computer or which activate parts of terminals. For example 10111111 makes a bell ring on a 'teletype' terminal and 00010101 (LF) makes a line printer go onto a new line. (It can be helpful to explain the code to typists who are used to typing lower case L for the figure 1, or the letter O (oh) for the figure 0 (zero) to help them see why it is important that they do not do it on their computer terminal — even though they look the same on paper

```
l = 10010011
1 = 11110001
O = 11010110
0 = 11110000
```

One further point worth noting (and which will be used later) is that *all* numbers start with the zone 1111.

Lately, other internal codes have been introduced, the most widely used being ASCII. The principle is exactly the same, only the cyphers are different.

Core configuration

We can now return to the computer hardware and see how EBCDIC or ASCII code is incorporated. As of today's date (early 1980) most 'mainframe' computers — the very big ones (IBM 370, DEC10, Sigma 9, etc.) — still use some of the core circuitry developed in the 1960s.

Minicomputers and microcomputers use a combination of transistorised circuits and 'chip' (TTL or MOS) memory.

We will talk exclusively about 1960s core because it is so much easier to understand. The entire CPU with the exception of the APU comprises ferrite rings sewn together with three wires (see Figure 7.4). Two wires pass through at right angles to each other and are used to set up a magnetic field within the core which can change the sense of the magnetisation of the core. The third wire picks up a pulse of released

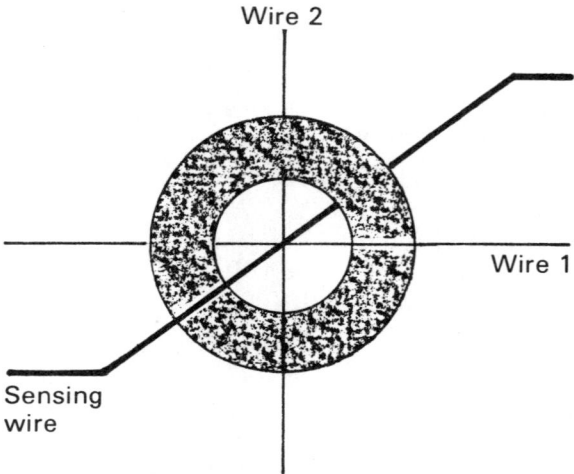

Figure 7.4 *Ferrite core*

magnetic energy if the core's field changes direction. Thus, if the core is magnetised 'clockwise' and electrical pulses which are complementary to a clockwise magnetisation are sent down the two 'change' wires there will be no field for the third wire to pick up. If the pulse down the change wires forces the core to flip to an 'anticlockwise' magnetisation, then a pulse is picked up in the third, sensing, wire.

By defining 'clockwise' = 1 and 'anticlockwise' = 0, a single ferrite core can be used to count in binary. Stringing eight cores together enables any EBCDIC character to be stored. And by trying to flip all the cores into (say) the '1' state, it is possible to read what the core held. For instance, if we use 'F' to mean that a core has flipped, and 'N' to mean that it has not, then FNNFNNFF contained 01101100, which is the EBCDIC representation of the percentage sign (%).

For the core to retain its original value all the flipped cores have now to be flipped back again! The process is tedious, but not inherently difficult. Complexities and enhancements have occurred as scientists have tried to find better and faster ways of reading core.

Within a mainframe computer, there may be many thousands of cores sewn together to allow many combinations of EBCDIC code, and each group of cores (or *bits*) representing a single EBCDIC character, i.e. 8 bits, is frequently known as a *byte*.

Computer size is normally measured by the number of bytes of core storage. A byte is usually the smallest accessible unit of core.

Some computers combine two, four or even more bytes together and use this new grouping as the smallest independent unit of core storage — in which case the generic term used to describe the unit is a *word*. (And just to really confuse us, some people talk of 8-bit *words*.)

When investigating core size, it is usually worth checking to see whether the manufacturer is measuring size in bytes or words. This is becoming particularly important with microcomputers where 16-bit words are being introduced as a standard. (But more of that later in the chapter on microprocessors).

A final word on core configuration. Core size is normally expressed as 'K', which approximates to 1,000, but which is strictly 2^{10}, or 1,024.

Using core memory

It has already been mentioned that core memory is used for all but some parts of the arithmetic unit of the CPU. Thus the input and output (I/O) buffers, the control unit and the user's storage area have to be contained within the available core.

Manufacturers should *always* be asked how much core is available for user programs. For example, a minicomputer (which had better remain nameless) offers a core of 48K bytes — which on the face of it is amply large enough for most commercial programs designed for minis (say 16K-32K bytes). However, investigation showed that of the 48K bytes, 32K were needed for the control unit (usually known as the operating system). The user, therefore, has only 16K bytes. 'But . . .', says the salesman, 'you can buy a further 32K of core for only £1,700' (or $1,800 in the USA, since it's cheaper there). This will ostensibly give 48K of user core. However, it transpires that additional operating system is needed to control the extra core, and instead of OS Mark I, one has to instal OS Mark II. This requires a total of 64K bytes. User core is still 16K. To gain any benefit, one has to buy a further 32K bytes of core, which with the additional costs of the Mark II software, puts the price of the computer up by over £5,000 ($5,000). So how does a computer allocate its core, and how is it used?

Firstly, the crucial operating system (Chapter 6) has to be placed within core. Many computers require all the OS to be resident in core, others use virtual storage in which most of the OS is held on one of the peripherals — either a disk or a drum (see Section 7.4.) — and is brought into core a bit at a time as required. Where the OS is entirely resident in core, it can use anything from 4K to 128K bytes or more.

Secondly, I/O buffers have to be allocated to deal with data being transmitted to and from the peripherals. In comparison with the OS they take very little space, often requiring no more than 1K on minicomputers. For a mainframe, one could expect 4K in each buffer; for a microcomputer, as little as 80 bytes.

Having allocated space to its own needs, the computer allows the user access to remaining core — provided it at no time needs more itself. Typically a mainframe using a time-sharing OS (see Chapter 5) will expect to process a certain number of users each second, and a routine within the OS will be constantly checking to see that there is no degradation in service to users. With some machines, any degradation beyond a certain point causes the operating system to grab more core in order to run a program of its own which is supposed to establish why the response time to users has deteriorated. The problem is that this is just the moment when users want more core — not less. Extra core used by the OS inevitably reduces service even further — and it grabs more core in a further effort to find out why! The fairly obvious result is that the computer eventually grinds to a complete stop.

These problems apart, users will have a certain amount of core in which to run their programs, and store their data. For 'user core' has to contain everything that the user needs. If the program has been written in one of the high-level languages such as COBOL or FORTRAN, it may need to be 'compiled' (see Chapter 6) and the compiler will also have to fit into user core. (It is for this reason that many DP managers who have limited core capacity do not like changing programs, because source program, compiler and the results of the compilation take up a much greater amount of space than compiled program and data. The concepts of compilation are explained in more detail in Chapter 6.

Let's take a typical scientific application where an engineer wishes to plot the frequency response of a circuit for a range of resistor and capacitor sizes.

At some time the applications program will have been written either by a programmer or by the engineer himself. This will be in a language such as FORTRAN, which needs compilation. We can assume that the source program has been stored on disk and is now ready for processing. When it is called by the OS from the disk, the entire program will probably be put into core and, in order to compile the program, so also will the compiler. Together a compiled version of the program is produced, which must also be stored in the user's core When compilation is completed, the compiler version is stored on disk, leaving the CPU through the output buffer (a bit at a time) and the source and compiler copies in core are discarded. Note that there is no need to save them since the original copies still exist on disk.

As compilation is taking place and EBCDIC codes for each step and variable in the program are being stored in bytes within user core, a directory is also being set up in the OS core which links variable names to the place in user core where its value is stored. In this way computers can operate without ever knowing what they are operating on.

The equation $C = A \times B$, for instance, is solved by reserving spaces in user core for the values of A, B and C, whatever value they might take. Only later when the program is run are numbers put into the reserved spaces — or *addresses*. So $C = A \times B$ requires three addresses and three entries in the OS directory (or index) which allow the correct numeric values to be put in the correct places. The direct result of such 'addressing' is that OS core must have sufficient space in it to contain not only the OS software, but also the user core index. Similar indexes are needed to locate files on disks, which must also be held in OS core.

Unless some form of 'paging' is used (by which only parts of OS software and indexes are held in core), the OS core requirement will often account for up to 75 per cent of the total core of a machine.

In the days of expensive core, this set a very serious limitation on the complexity of operating system software and on user core. Nowadays, with core being the cheapest part of a computer system, the restrictions need no longer exist. Mainframe machines are now being built with more than 10M bytes (10,000,000 bytes) of core storage, and they cost no more than a 64K-byte machine of 10 years ago. Minicomputers are now being built with 1M byte of core, and even microcomputers can be purchased with 64K bytes of core, for a basic price of less than £2,000 (in the UK).

With so much core, it is possible to create really sophisticated operating software to run machines in both multiprogramming and time-sharing modes. (The first microcomputer with a time-sharing facility was announced in February 1979.)

7.4 Peripherals

Input and output

In the 1980s, emphasis and interest will switch from CPU to the peripherals which provide fodder and regurgitate the cud. Increasingly, the emphasis is away from input devices (which require computer departments to interpret the user's notes into punched cards) and towards direct control by the user. Much of this movement would not have been possible without the dramatically reduced costs of core.

A similar move is underway with output devices, with results of computer processing being delivered directly to users via screens or the printed word.

Thus we are moving into a period of considerable development in terminal design, providing not only the written word but also high-level graphics capability — which means that terminals must contain microcomputers to facilitate their control. With increasing core capability has also come specialised forms of input device — such as optical readers (for cheques) which recognise characters by the position of light and dark areas. Recent developments have also produced input devices that recognise handwritten characters. Users write on a sensitised pad and combinations of pen-strokes are compared with stylised characters stored in the terminal's memory. Yet other devices are able to recognise voice patterns and translate them into instructions for the computer. Such sophistication is unlikely to be available on any widespread basis for a few years yet, however, and much terminal design effort is being directed towards producing interesting and flexible displays which are driven by either the computer or the user (via a keyboard). Particularly in the area of minicomputers, one can find displays that highlight the information users have to input next, that complete words for them and that automatically 'turn pages'. All this is directed towards the novice computer-user in order to make life easier. Hence, sales office clerks, warehousemen, accounts clerks, engineers, managers, etc., etc., can have displays designed for their own particular purpose.

The day of equally high quality displays on mainframes are, however, not yet with us. The reason is that the very structure of the core of a computer determines the ease with which it can communicate with 'intelligent' terminals, and whereas minicomputer designers have always had the smaller commercial customer in mind, mainframe designers have tended to design for the computer professional — who will often think of such 'pretty' terminals as 'unnecessary frippery'. One can see the different underlying philosophies of designers by comparing the displays produced by IBM on their System 34 Small Business System (see Chapter 9) and Sperry Univac on their BC/7 Small Business System. Strangely, therefore, bigger machines seem to have less 'friendly' interfaces with the user!

The trend to user control and visual display terminals (VDUs) rather than separate input and output (I/O) devices is also revolutionising the role and design of printers. The line printer is still, and probably always will be, a crucial element in any computer system, but increasingly it is needed to print occasional user-generated reports, at times when something more than a screen-full of information is required. The demand for line printer reports is, therefore, reducing, but the layout is becoming more complex and easier to read: a move which puts increased demands on the flexibility of the printer. For instance, a typical chain printer will only have a couple of '*' characters on the chain, but may contain ten or more 'E's. Users who want their reports to look nice may use * liberally and slow the printer considerably.

Modern printer design uses ink-jets which create characters from a matrix of dots ▦ and any character, including Russian or Chinese, is equally easy to generate. Microprocessors, within the printer, direct the ink-jets. Such printers as well as being much more flexible than traditional designs are also a lot faster (over 4,000 lines/minute). Unfortunately, they are also much more expensive, and may even cost more than the CPU!

Whilst such facilities form an important element in modern computer installations, users are increasingly demanding their reports 'NOW' — not some hours later after they have been printed, put in envelopes and distributed in the internal mail. (More than one DP manager has been known to view such demands as 'unreasonable'!) Thus printers are being developed which run relatively slowly (200 characters/minute at up to 80 characters/line) but which can be sited close to users' terminals. Thus a sales office with (say) six VDU terminals may have one printer in the corner, and the accounts department along the corridor has another.

Such configurations are by no means limited to mainframe installations. Many medium-sized companies installing minicomputers have seen the advantages of flexible printer output linked to high quality terminal displays, which staff use, either to print large reports, e.g. sales analysis and production schedules, or to copy the contents of their display screen to paper for discussion with other members of staff, e.g. slack has disappeared from a critical path in a start-up operation, or a customer has exceeded his credit limit.

As was said earlier, CPU costs are now so low that the concepts of the relative costs of different parts of an installation current in the 1960s and 1970s have to be reviewed. Thus printers of the type just described are considerably more expensive than *micro*computers and one additional printer could add 10 per cent to the cost of a *mini*computer installation.

Finally, it should be mentioned that although, like the core, remote I/O devices use binary codes for all their characters, unlike core, they do not normally use EBCDIC. A seven-bit code has been developed which has generally been found to be more satisfactory for transmission over long distances and nearly all mainframe computers expect their remote terminals to use that code — ASCII.

Minicomputers driving high-grade display screens, however, still tend to treat the terminal as an extension of the CPU, and drive it in EBCDIC. Thus, would-be purchasers of equipment could find that they need to buy expensive additional hardware to drive terminals designed to operate in ASCII and which are more suitable — and frequently a lot cheaper — than the terminals offered by the CPU manufacturer. Some minicomputers are designed to operate with both EBCDIC and ASCII codes (the Digital Equipment PDP11 family, for example), in which case purchasers have a much greater flexibility in their choice of terminals. To illustrate the point one can look to ASCII terminals which cost under £500 and compare them with one manufacturer's cheapest EBCDIC terminal at £2,500.

Storage

In line with advances in processors and I/O devices, there has been an increasing demand for instant access to data held on files. This has resulted in an almost universal acceptance of 'on-line' storage where data and programs are stored on disks, permanently accessible to the CPU.

Disks The disk itself is not unlike a gramophone record that has been coated with a material which can be magnetised to represent binary codes. As the disk spins, 'heads' similar to those used in tape-decks on home hi-fi equipment transfer codes to the disks to represent program names, programs, data file names, data, etc. Unlike records the information is not on a single 'groove' which gradually winds into the centre, but is on a series of concentric rings or *tracks* (see Figure 7.5). Frequently, the smallest track (near the centre of the disk) is used to define 'track length', and longer tracks at the periphery of the disc are subdivided into units of this length and — just to confuse — are also

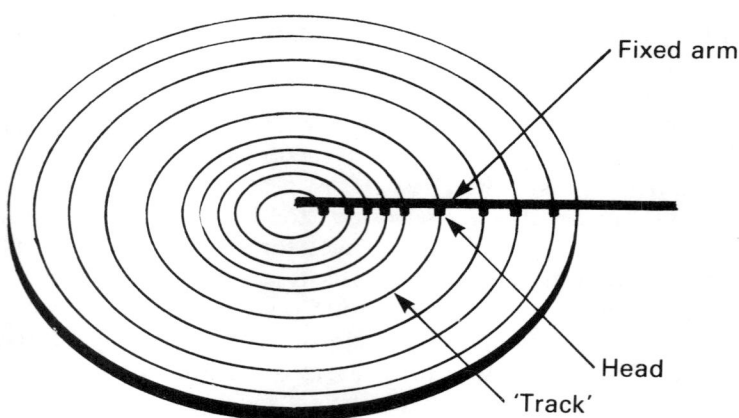

Figure 7.5 *Single disk*

sometimes called tracks. Thus a disk with 100 tracks could be called a 1,000-track disk — if you see what I mean! The information transferred is accessible to the *read head* each time the disk rotates past it, which may be once every thousandth of a second. Access time to any part of a disk, and therefore to any item of information, is of the order of 1 millisecond ('slow' disks may have an access time of 200 milliseconds).

For all practical purposes, disks are the only form of on-line storage used at the present time, and for most people are the best form of storage for any purpose. With microcomputer developments, we are now seeing 'floppy disks' (about $8\frac{1}{2}$ inches in diameter) and 'diskettes' (generally reserved for $5\frac{1}{2}$-inch diameter disks, but check because the equipment is so new that a common language has not yet been established). For storage purposes, we can think of these more recent developments as the same as disks. Their capacity is, of course, smaller and there are some doubts about their durability, but they store information on tracks and allow rapid access, just like the bigger disks. In terms of storage capacity, a modern floppy disk will hold up to 2M bytes, i.e. 2 million characters, and a small diskette about 90K bytes. A big 'cartridge disk' (a term used to discriminate between the large disks and the new breed of small ones) can hold up to 2,000M bytes (or 2,000,000,000 characters).

Two types of cartridge disk are in common use, each with its own advantages and disadvantages. The most common type used with minicomputers is a 'floating-head' or 'moving-head' variety in which there is a single head, traversing tracks looking for information as it goes. The second type of disk has 'fixed-heads' (see Figure 7.5) with one head situated over each track. This second type of disk tends to be more expensive but has the advantage of faster access time, since the head does not have to first position itself over the correct track. (A directory showing file names and the track number on which they are held is stored on the first track accessed.) A further advantage of fixed-head disks is that they are not subjected to the wear that the mechincal parts of a moving-head inevitably suffer.

Wear in itself is not serious. Trouble occurs when heads sag towards the disk, pick up dust and then 'touch' the disk through a dust film. The effect is to create a 'magnetic scratch' on the disk. This effectively destroys all the data under the head. Such an occurrence is onamatopoeically called a 'head crash'. Head crashes are fortunately rare, and with improved air conditioning within the disk drive units, a fairly dust-free atmosphere can be obtained. However, the risk is undoubtedly reduced if fixed-head disks are used. But, quite recently, IBM have introduced moving-head disk packs, in which the head is sealed into the disk pack itself and is not part of the drive unit. Thus as there is no possibility of dust getting into the pack, crashes should not occur, especially since a head only moves when its associated disk is mounted on a drive. Which brings us to another variation on the disk theme.

Cartridge disks come as 'fixed' or 'removable', which has nothing to do with the heads! It simply means that a disk or a pack of disks (say five in a pack) are either permanently fixed within the drive unit, or can be removed from it.

With some confidence, one can say that would-be purchasers should never purchase a disk system which does not contain some removable elements. Most installations (from minis to mainframes) will contain at least a disk drive holding two disk packs. The lower pack will be fixed and will store the operating system, compilers, directories, etc., and the upper pack will be removable and contain applications programs, data files, etc. Both packs can allow the full range of file accessing methods discussed in Chapter 6.

Magnetic tape   In addition to on-line storage, there is a need for 'back-up' storage, i.e. storage that holds the same information as on-line storage but which, for security reasons (see Chapter 4), is held away from the computer installation.

For minicomputer installations, it is normal to use either floppy disks or removable cartridge disks as the back-up medium. On larger installations, magnetic tape is frequently used.

It was not long ago that magnetic tape met the bulk of all storage requirements. With machines operating in batch mode, there was no need for access within a few milliseconds and in the distant past of 1970 disks were both limited in capacity and expensive.

Today, magnetic tape is seldom (except on obsolete equipment) used as anything other than back-up. The principle of a magnetic tape system is very similar to hi-fi reel-to-reel sound entertainment systems. Codes (in binary, of course) are put on to the tape which is then held off-line. The great advantage of tapes is that they are easy to handle, and can be transferred from one installation to another. The only features worth further mention are that files must necessarily be accessed sequentially and different tape drives 'pack' characters more or less tightly.

To explain what is meant by that, it is necessary to look at the codes used on magnetic tapes. Because the tape is 1 inch wide, it is possible to write a character 'across' the tape — either in a seven-track ASCII code or a nine-track [EBCDIC-based plus parity (see Chapter 4)] code. Thus each character written onto a tape uses a length of tape equivalent to only one 'bit'. The density of a tape refers to the number of 'bits' (and hence the number of characters) per running inch of tape. Typical packing densities are 800 bpi (bits/inch) and 1600 bpi. Thus a 2,400 foot tape will contain a maximum of 2400 × 12 × 1,600 bpi = 46,080,000 characters, and since a character is represented by a byte in core storage, one can say that a 1,600 bpi, 2,400-ft tape can hold a maximum of 46M bytes.

In practice things are not that simple as it would be virtually impossible to identify any particular string of characters from a continuous stream of bytes. Tapes are, therefore, subdivided into *blocks*, each of which will usually contain a single file record of normally 255 bytes maximum. There is then a space in the tape before the next block. A tape specification might, therefore, read: 2,400 ft; nine track; 1,600 bpi; 255-byte block. Switches on tape drives can then be set to the appropriate parameters and the tape may be read into core.

Miscellaneous storage Other storage devices do exist. Many microcomputers use cassettes identical to hi-fi cassettes. Some installations still use punched cards as a storage medium, and many process control applications store the parameters of a process on paper tape for later transfer to a data processing machine. However, even in this area, floppy disks are taking over as a more convenient and equally secure holding medium and it is doubtful if the media just mentioned will be around for very much longer.

Chapter Eight
SMALL BUSINESS SYSTEMS

8.1 Introduction

In Chapter 7, the terms minicomputer and microcomputer were used with some degree of abandon, without any serious attempt to define the difference between them — mainly because the difference is difficult to define. Mainframe computers are easy to recognise by their size and the number of staff needed to feed them. Microcomputers are relatively easy to recognise because their newness has put the names of the best of them on to people's lips — PET, APPLE, NASCOM, etc. (see Chapter 11). Minicomputers lie somewhere in between these two extremes, having some of the attributes of mainframes, sometimes requiring support staff, and frequently including the technology of microcomputers.

Small business systems (SBS) are specially developed minicomputers with well developed interactive facilities (see Figure 8.1). What distinguishes an SBS from a raw minicomputer is its design as a complete system. Hardware and software are normally bundled together in the one package (though they may be charged separately) and it is quite impossible to take the programs contained within one SBS to another manufacturer's computer. In fact, in many SBSs, part of the operating system is actually wired into the hardware, or is provided in ROM (Read Only Memory: see Chapter 11 on microprocessors to see exactly what that means; for the present, ROM is a piece of hardware into which a program can be 'photographed'; it cannot be changed, but it can be 'read' and used).

Since neither hardware nor ROM can be transferred, anyone buying an SBS is totally committed to it and its manufacturer. Any

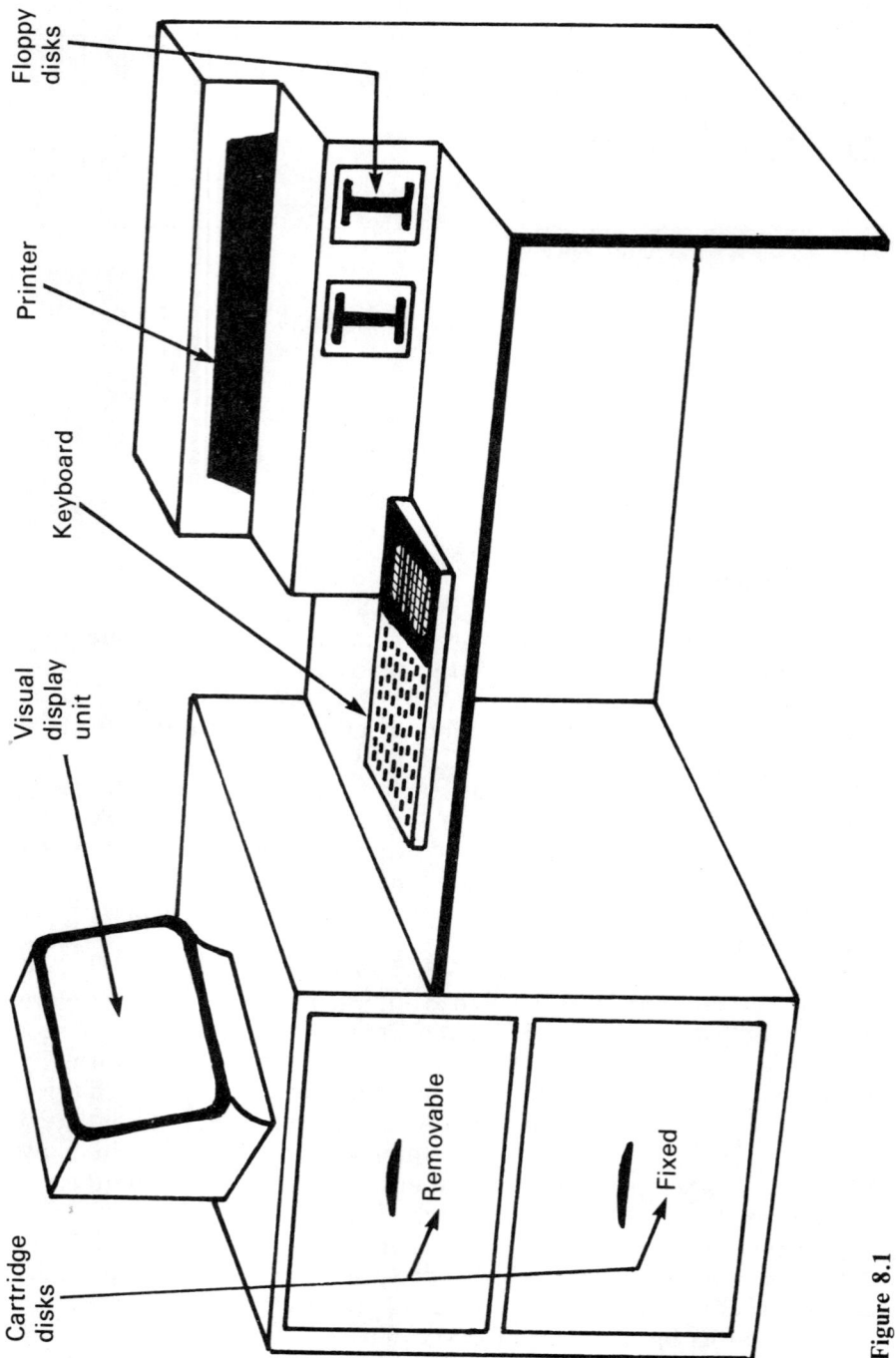

Figure 8.1

enhancement to the system that the user requires must be done through the SBS hardware/software system.

Frequently special languages which users will be required to use have been written for a particular SBS, whilst in many cases only a very limited range of 'ordinary' languages can be used. For example, at the time of writing, the Datasystem 300 series (by Digital) will only accept DIBOL (their own variety of COBOL) and the NCR 8200 series accepts only COBOL and BASIC.

Thus there are very significant limitations on SBSs which might encourage some potential purchasers to buy a minicomputer and have software prepared by a software house. (Beware, even some so-called small business systems require one to buy software separately which rather diminishes their claim to be a true SBS.) On the other hand, there are very considerable benefits for the first-time user to be gained from using an SBS. The most significant is the fact that they are buying a complete business package, which requires the minimum of modification before it can be used, often by up to eight interactive users concurrently.

8.2 SBS hardware

Many of the details of hardware design are common between mainframes and minicomputers, and hence SBSs. CPU codes, I/O buffers, APU and control units (see Chapter 7) are all common. The CPU may be either core or integrated circuit (I/C) with as much as 128K bytes in a typical system. Many of the core-size limitations of the mid-1970s (when minicomputers could not get above 8K bytes) have been totally overcome and a CPU of 2M bytes is already available to anyone who feels the need.

But anyone contemplating an SBS still needs to be careful to distinguish between CPU size and the amount of core available to the user. Several 64K byte machines need 32K for the operating system and buffers, so unless it has a virtual memory OS (see Chapter 6) there may be space limitation problems. Remember also, that more core requires more OS in order to control it and provide addressing (again, see Chapter 6 and Appendix 1). Salesman's claims that 'you can buy add-on memory in 16K blocks which you just plug in', have to be countered by the question 'Does that need a bigger operating system?'

As explained in Chapter 5, CPUs can handle programs in a number of different ways, depending on the architecture of the machine and its OS — and to the uninitiated user different configurations can look very much the same. In Chapter 5 the similarity between time sharing and teleprocessing was highlighted as was the difference in operating efficiency between these two modes where multiple users are involved.

Most SBSs available in the UK have been designed to work in teleprocessing mode, with each user being given a specific area of core. Thus the 96K-byte core of one particular computer, which gives 32K bytes of core to the user, can support:

    2 users — 16K bytes each
    4 users — 8K bytes each
    8 users — 4K bytes each

Another well-known machine operating in time-shared mode gives:

    2 users — 32K bytes each
    4 users — 32K bytes each
    ⋮
    64 users — 32K bytes each (but with some degradation in response time: about 1 second)

This point is being laboured because, in the UK at least, a number of SBS salesmen do not appear to know the difference between teleprocessing and time sharing and will claim that any form of instant response mode is 'time sharing'.

Potential buyers would be well advised to be suspicious of any SBS that claims to operate in time-sharing mode because very few do — and most of those are *minicomputers* that have had software packages bundled with them.

Before reviewing the software of an SBS it is perhaps worth identifying the hardware features that distinguish an SBS from a minicomputer. Firstly, an SBS will almost invariably come with two or more work stations linked directly to the CPU, i.e. two clearly defined teleprocessing partitions. The work stations are sometimes built into the cabinets housing the core, but will always need to be close enough to the computer to be refreshed directly from core memory. With a rudimentary SBS one cannot have terminals on a remote site.

Having said that, however, more and more SBS manufacturers are developing communications capabilities which will allow remote users to access the core, through either time-sharing or teleprocessing monitors (or operating systems). Work stations and remote terminals are nearly always VDUs with a keyboard (but seldom with a print facility).

Secondly, SBSs have cartridge disk drives, and sometimes floppy disk units, built into the cabinet containing the CPU. The rationale is that since one is buying a system, it is sensible to have a neat package. By and large the rationale is sensible, and cabinets contain two cartridge disks (typically of 5M bytes capacity each). One disk will be fixed, and will contain the operating system and all the standard programs; the second will be removable and can be used for back-up storage. SBSs do exist with one fixed disk only, but nobody with any sense would buy one!

Thirdly, a printer will either form an integral part of the cabinet, or will be designed to look aesthetically pleasing with the rest of the equipment. Again we see the emphasis on a single package for all the hardware necessary for a complete system.

Just about every SBS has the hardware attributes just mentioned, whereas mini's come as a set of totally separate boxes which are plugged together. The end result is functionally the same, but with an SBS the user does not have to think as deeply about alternative equipment.

If the SBS hardware is both 'necessary and sufficient' for the firm's needs, there is no problem. However, if the user wants additional peripherals, he could be in trouble. Several SBSs will not accept paper-tape readers or punches — and some will not even accept a magnetic tape drive (which can be so useful for maintaining daily ledgers).

Anyone thinking about an SBS should be asking the following questions:

1. Am I prepared to commit myself to one manufacturer for all time?
2. How much of the core is available to the user?
3. How is that core used — teleprocessing (multiprogramming is the term now normally synonymously employed — albeit misleadingly) or time sharing?
4. Is virtual memory available if core partitions are small?
5. How much does core upgrade cost?
6. Does an upgrade mean a new operating system?
7. How many work stations will it support?
8. How many remote terminals?
9. What form of mass storage is offered? Disks or floppies?
10. Is there a removable disk element for back up?
11. Is the printer fast enough for the volumes envisaged?
12. Can additional printers and disks be added?
13. Can other peripherals, e.g. magnetic tape, be added?

8.3 SBS software

Much of the flexibility, security and 'idiot proofing' of an SBS comes from its operating software. One of the axioms of an SBS is that it can be used by non-specialists who may never have seen a computer before. Thus starting it up in the morning, loading the operating system and programs, dealing with back-up and switching off must all be completely 'idiot proof'. Similarly, the programs themselves must be easy to use and 'self-correcting', with the OS taking over if a 'bug' is encountered. Of course, all these requirements are equally attractive on mainframe machines; they are just difficult to achieve! Where they have been achieved on SBSs it is largely due to the fact that the OS and programs are frequently interconnected and have had vast development resources poured into them. The underlying concept has been to create a software package that will be acceptable to thousands of small firms and to recover development costs through volume sales.

The advantages are clear:
- The software is thoroughly tested.
- Costs are kept down.
- Maintenance is kept to a minimum.
- Flexibility is built-in from the start.

The disadvantages are equally clear:
- A user is tied to the supplier.
- Some details of the package may not be quite right, requiring modifications to the firm's method of operation.
- Applications *may* be limited to those supplied in the package.
- Other, useful, languages may not be supported.

Picking up this last point, it is disturbing to find that many SBSs will support only one or two languages. What is more disturbing is that, in some circumstances, the restriction is not a technical one, but one which has been imposed for marketing purposes. For example, in 1979 the Data General 'CS' series only supported the COBOL language, even though technically it could have carried compilers in one or more of the other widely used commercial languages.

Anyone contemplating the purchase of an SBS needs to check very carefully that they will not find themselves facing unnecessary restrictions.

Operating restrictions

A feature of SBSs is that about 30 per cent of those available on the UK market have part of their operating system implemented in the hardware. This means that some of the operations normally carried out by programmed instructions are performed by switches within the computer. The effect is that those functions are performed more quickly without any possibility of error (for example, through file corruption). Core memory which would otherwise be needed to store those operating instructions is also freed for the user.

By further linking the display screens of work stations through hardware to the OS, it is possible to create some very flexible screen 'formats', which are cheaper to manufacture and program than simply writing one line at a time, one beneath the other. For example, if a list of alternative activities is listed on the screen some SBSs allow users to select the one they wish to undertake by positioning a cursor over its code number. Or, with a list of customer names, more details of a particular customer can be obtained by repositioning the cursor. Such 'firmware' (as hardware-implemented OS is sometimes called) is also used to link screens directly with disks, without even using the CPU. Thus customer details can be pulled off disk and displayed at the terminal without the user occupying core. Where a lot of enquiries are being made, such a facility is obviously very useful. In fact, if the core is being used in teleprocessing rather than time-sharing mode, it may be absolutely essential for the successful use of the computer system.

With high-quality links between screen, disk and CPU, the user is freed by the OS from many of the problems normally associated with applications programs (Chapter 6), once again reducing the potential for 'bugs'. Of course, not all SBSs achieve these links through 'firmware'; many retain the traditional form of programmed operating system, developed to a high level of flexibility. Because SBS manufacturers *expect* users to use their applications packages, and make no pretence that programs are transferable to other machines, operating systems also generally take care of most of the 'idiot proofing' normally necessary within applications programs. For instance, data-entry errors are trapped in the OS whereas on a mainframe they would have to be caught within the program. Special instructions (like 'HELP') are picked up by the OS at any time and systems utilities are implemented as appropriate.

It is not exaggerating to say that the relative strength of an SBS depends entirely on the quality of its OS and the ease with which it can be used by the company's non-specialist staff.

Screen formats

It has been rather taken for granted that any SBS is used interactively and, to keep users satisfied, that requires extensive, fast and flexible screen format facilities. Since many companies will want their own particular layout to match existing styles of invoice, stock report, etc., the screen formats should also be easy to change. (Note that this does *not* mean that the programs are changed — people will frequently have to adapt their methods or coding systems to suit the applications package.)

Many screen management systems (within the OS) will allow users to construct a large variety of displays including 'menus' (of which more later), data entry formats, graphs, bar charts, etc., using simple language. There are others, one should be warned, which allow users to do these things only after enduring a gruelling battle with the OS. The best way to find out how easy it is to create a new format is to ask the salesman to do it. If he says that 'most people find our displays adequate', there is a better than evens chance that his OS falls into the latter category.

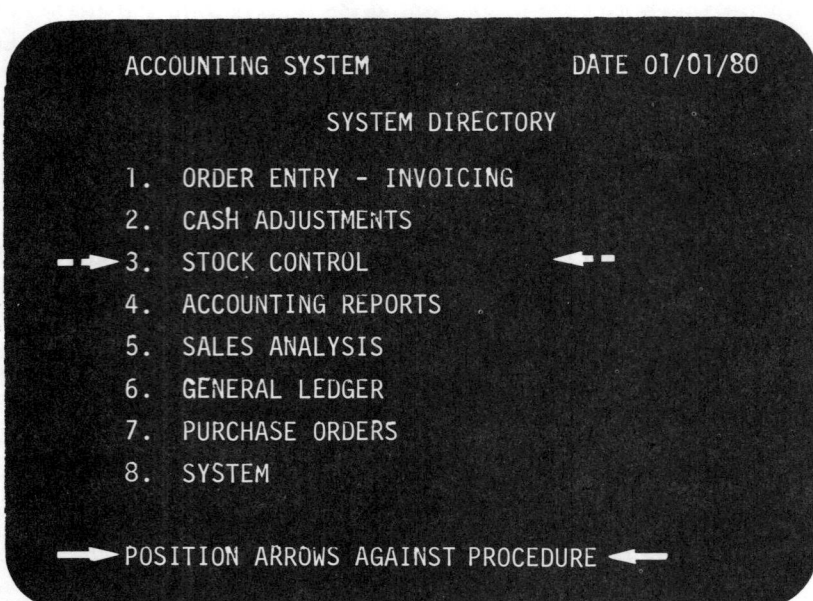

Figure 8.2

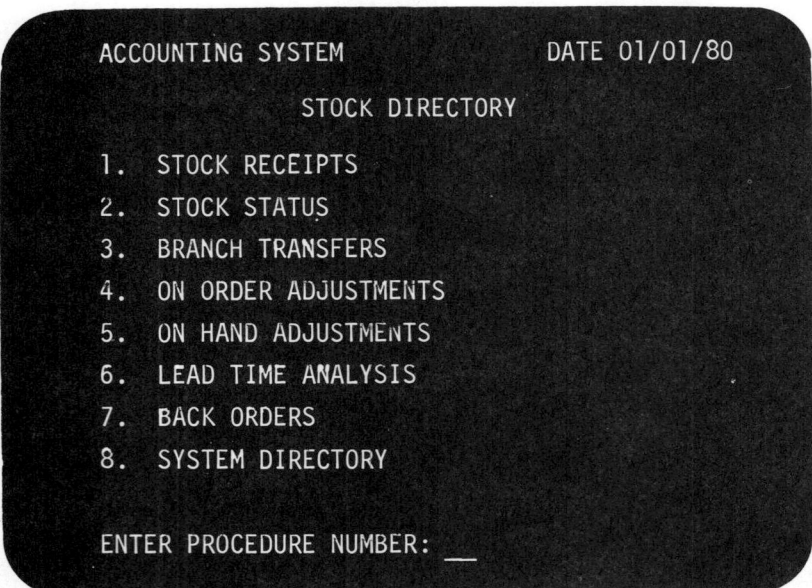

Figure 8.3

Menus Almost every SBS uses menus from which users choose their next activity. They are the single most important technique for making a system easy to operate. For example, a user signing on to an accounting system might be presented with the display illustrated in Figure 8.2. By hitting the (↑) key, the user positions the arrows against the part of the system in which he is interested (in the diagram on the previous page, marked — ➤ ◄ —). Alternatively, the command might be 'ENTER PROCEDURE NUMBER', in which case typing '3' would achieve the same effect — the screen illustrated in Figure 8.3. The kinds and complexities of menu are virtually limitless — provided the operating system is well written. When the procedure number is entered in Figure 8.3, the display automatically enters either data entry or enquiry mode. Note that although the applications program will control the files and calculation, the interfaces will probably be controlled by the OS.

Data entry formats A good operating system will allow firms to create a complete screen of data with blanks to be filled in by the user. These blanks are positioned by the needs of the company rather than the estimates of the applications programmer. For example, procedure 3 (above) might produce the display shown in Figure 8.4. The cursor would automatically position itself alongside DEPARTMENT and would wait there until the user had entered a code. It would then move to STOCK NO. and on receipt of a code, the corresponding description

```
ACCOUNTING SYSTEM              DATE 01/01/80

STOCK
                BRANCH TRANSFER   BRANCH LOCATION
                                  CODE
DEPARTMENT         [    ]
STOCK NO.          [    ]           1    ALTON
                                    2    BIRMINGHAM
                                    3    STIRLING
                                    4    WARRINGTON
                                    5    YORK

DESCRIPTION QTY FROM TO CHARGE TO
            [  ][  ][  ]  [    ]
                        RETURN TO STOCK DIRECTORY? [  ]
```

Figure 8.4

would be printed to allow visual checking, before the cursor moved to the next box. The data being entered will, as mentioned earlier, be dealt with by the program, but the screen format will be OS-controlled.

At the end of the stock entry the cursor would move to the bottom right-hand corner where the user has the choice of returning to the earlier menu ready for the next procedure, or of entering another stock transfer. If the latter choice is selected, the cursor would return to STOCK NO., and a new description would be printed underneath the existing one. Thus both stock transfers can be viewed.

Depending on the needs of the firm, there might be space for up to 10 descriptions to be displayed at the one time. More than this and the first description would 'scroll' off the top, all others would move up one, leaving space for the new stock item at the bottom of the screen. No data would be lost, because as soon as it is entered, the applications program takes care of it, but it would no longer be possible to print a complete list of the transfers by asking the operating system to 'PRINT SCRN'. With a good screen control, it should be easy to set up a display in which the stock items scroll, but the 'form' does not, i.e. 'ACCOUNTING SYSTEM. . . .' does not disappear off the top of the screen.

Inquiry By using the links between screen and disk described earlier in this section, it is usually possible to call up formats that produce displays for pre-planned enquiries, e.g. aged debtors or transfers to a given branch. Once again, the results seen by the user are a joint effort between the applications program and the OS.

Analysis The data the system collects as a routine consequence of daily operations is invaluable to decision-making at all levels of management. It is data which is particularly accessible because of the packaged nature of an SBS — often much more so on an equivalent mainframe — and its potential should not be neglected.

Unfortunately, relatively few SBSs have an OS that allows the novice user to quickly write an analysis program and link it into the data files — *without using the applications programs* in any way. This last point is really quite important because any applications program can have analysis routines written into it given the time and dedication. What is needed is a form of Database Management System (Chapter 6), a facility that is available on only about 20 per cent of the SBSs available at the time of writing.

Watch out for sales brochures that say 'An applications system could readily have an MIS (Management Information System) section for analysing this data and presenting it in ways particularly suited to management needs'. Most management has considerable difficulty defining its information needs in advance, particularly when it is in the throes of selecting a computer, and wants the freedom to set up its own analyses at a moment's notice. ('How many companies in the NW Area with more than 500 employees have recruited instrument technicians from a Government training centre?' is not the sort of analysis which is likely to be thought out in advance!)

Utilities Finally, under the heading of operating systems software, the availability of, and access to, utilities is worth a brief mention. Most, one is tempted to say all, SBSs have utilities that perform routine calculations or file-handling procedures (see Chapter 6) which will allow (or not) random access to particular data items, thus easing (or not) the analysis programs' tasks. Choosing an SBS with good file-handling utilities can mean the difference between waiting half a second for a screen-full of analysed data or 50 seconds.

A relatively recent development in utilities is one that allows equations which would normally be held within a compiled applications program to be held in a separate file, with indexes from within the applications program. Thus frequently changing equations need not be buried but can be constantly available for modification. As the supplier of one such 'Formulae Interpreter' puts it: 'PIXIE will be used to greatest advantage in applying —
- Variable invoice calculation formulae.
- Changes to PAYE and National Insurance calculations.
- Complex product-related commission or freight-charge calculations.'

8.4 Applications software

Throughout this chapter, the systems orientation of SBSs has been emphasised to contrast with the modular approach of the raw minicomputer. The hardware comes as a system, the OS comes as a system and, finally, the applications software comes as a system. Sometimes it is a system that has elements in common with the OS — as, for example, in the use of formulae interpreters. In such instances the would-be purchaser can be certain that there is no way in which he can change manufacturers in mid-stream. He can also be certain that any additional programs he writes — in whatever language — will only run on the machine he has purchased. The reason is very simple. He, or his programmer, will inevitably use the facilities offered by the OS for file handling, error checking, inquiring, requesting help, etc., and these utilities will be unique to the system. In many instances manufacturers offer 'upwards compatibility', which infers that a program written on one of their small machines will run on one of their larger systems without any modifications.

Upward capability, in reality, is very difficult to achieve and whilst it works sometimes, any SBS purchaser should be prepared to spend some time and effort modifying programs for larger machines from the same manufacturer.

Clearly, the better a purchaser understands his long-term needs before he purchases, the better his chance of making his acquisition last out its useful life of (say) five years (see Chapter 9). Otherwise, increasing volumes, more applications programs and greater traffic will either overload the operating system or overflow core within a very short time.

Some SBS suppliers avoid the problems of increased numbers and types of applications programs by limiting the number of languages that can be implemented. Few engineering departments, for example, will be happy writing in COBOL (see also Chapter 2). In fact, few SBSs allow more than two applications languages, the first being COBOL, in which the package is probably written, and the second being either RPG or BASIC. Almost inevitably the COBOL compiler will 'contain improved screen-handling facilities' or will be 'an ANSI implementation *with other features*'. Once again the purchaser is tied to his manufacturer. (For anyone who is now feeling that buying a computer is like walking into a cage, remember that these comments refer to SBSs. Mainframes and raw minicomputers need not impose the same restrictions.) For SBS users, the restrictions seldom cause difficulty because they will be developing a working relationship with their supplier which only rarely turns sour. They will be using the supplier's package, and further applications will almost certainly be in the same fields of operation as those of the package.

Other applications will probably be best undertaken on a second small computer (possibly a microcomputer) which can transfer data to the SBS via a floppy disk. Any disadvantages will be outweighed by the integration of applications that the SBS offers.

The following list has been culled from a typical SBS Applications Package. It is not a comprehensive statement of the package's facilities, but is intended to illustrate what a 'standard' SBS might be expected to offer (see also Chapters 2 and 9):

- Order entry:
  - Acknowledgement of order
  - On-line checking of credit status
  - Discount analysis
  - Non-account customers
  - Non-standard products
- Order processing:
  - Warehouse selection
  - Forward orders
  - Alternative stock items and warehouses offered

- — Picking lists
- — Aged order reports
- — Stock availability
- Sales invoicing:
  - — Variable formats
  - — Discount calculations
  - — Export including foreign languages and currency conversions
  - — VAT
- Stock management:
  - — Alternative ways of evaluating stock
  - — Price and cost adjustments
  - — Bulk stock options
  - — Reorder levels and EOQ
  - — Tabulations and reports
  - — Random stock level inquiry
- Bill of materials processing:
  - — Parts file
  - — Alternative stock items
  - — Stock withdrawals
  - — Parts explosion
  - — Enquiries
- Production scheduling:
  - — Works order creation
  - — Factory documentation
  - — Master scheduling
  - — Cash flows within schedule
  - — Open orders
  - — Purchase orders including chasers
- Material requirements planning:
  - — Purchase order requirements and schedule
  - — Maintaining MRP reports
  - — Exception reporting on purchase orders and work-in-progress
  - — Maintaining cash flow analyses
- Ledgers:
  - — Purchase ledger
  - — Cash flow optimisation
  - — Aged creditors and debtors reports
  - — Remittance advice
  - — Sales ledger
  - — Updating of customer files
  - — Export accounting
  - — General ledger
  - — Financial reports and cost-centre reporting
- Information retrieval:
  - — DIY preparation of reports using interactive inquiry language

8.5 Physical requirements

Most of the glossy brochures illustrating SBSs show great areas of carpet and pretty girls, giving no indication of the amount of space needed. There is, however, one very nice illustration in Data General's brochure which shows their CS/20 system in a room not much larger than a store cupboard — and which actually appears to be doubling as a store cupboard.

Admittedly the CS/20 is a very small system, but it does illustrate the reality of environment in which an SBS will operate. Because the hardware is neatly packaged into a volume little greater than an office desk, any small office will do. Accessibility (if several people are to use the one work station) is important, but that apart, an SBS will work almost anywhere that can provide a clean power supply; (but see Chapter 10 for a more detailed discussion of the physical requirements for any form of computer).

8.6 Suppliers

Any effort to produce a comprehensive list of SBS suppliers is doomed to failure because it will be out of date before it is even printed. With the emergence of commercial systems on microcomputers the task of keeping up to date becomes even more impossible. However, listed below are some of the more well established suppliers, who can provide SBSs for under £50,000 (1979 prices). (Note that in the USA, small business systems seem to sell for half the price of systems in the UK. The list below will, therefore, represent US costs of less than $50,000.)

Burroughs
Computer Automation
Control Data Corp.
Data General
DEC
General Automation
Hewlett Packard
Honeywell
IBM
ICL
Interdata
Jacquard
Litton
Microdata
NCR
Philips

Singer (ICL)
Sperry Univac
Sycor
Texas Instruments
Wang

Chapters 9 and 10 deal with the choice and installation of computer systems in general, and although some of the considerations discussed there may be short-circuited for SBSs, much is relevant.

Chapter Nine

SELECTION OF A COMPUTER SYSTEM

In this chapter it is going to be assumed that the reader is looking for a minicomputer on which to mount the systems needed to control a business — accounts, raw materials, production (analyses), finished product stocks, sales and marketing. Alternatively, readers may be looking for a small business system (Chapter 8) prepackaged into a form to which they can adjust their internal systems.

That is not to say that mainframe and microcomputer systems will not be subjected to similar analyses, but the general thrust of the investigations and their thoroughness will be different. Thus a realistic feasibility study directed towards the purchase of a £1,000,000 mainframe would undoubtedly cost more than the cost of a full-blown minicomputer installation. And therein lies the rub. Because without a feasibility study, how is one to know what type of machine is needed?

The first and most important question to ask is whether a computer, of any sort, is justified. The question should be asked with some commitment to the answer — NO. If one is not, in all honesty, prepared to continue in business without a computer, then try to find someone who is and ask him to identify your need. Too many systems have been hurriedly conceived, expensively installed and continue to be a drain on the company's resources. This is as true of a small computer in a laboratory (dedicated to the solution of such intractable problems as three-dimensional noughts and crosses, Startrek and Carnoustie golf course) as it is of a business-oriented machine which will only produce inadequate data two days late.

The most frequently heard reason for contemplating the purchase of a computer (see Chapter 1) is that it will save staff. The realities of the situation are that it is only infrequently that staff can be cut; more frequently numbers increase initially.

The most frequently heard reason for *not* buying a computer is that it will take over, dehumanise jobs and act as Big Brother. Reality (for businesses at least) is that many staff need to develop new skills often at a higher level, and since computers will only do what they are told to do, any Big Brother tendencies can be laid directly at the door of the managing director.

It is, therefore, essential to view the potential for a computer in an objective way, weighing costs against benefits. The first stage in this analysis is to find out exactly what is needed.

9.1 Identifying the need

Overcoming difficulties

At an early stage, and without outside help, any businessman can ask questions about his firm that will indicate whether a computer installation might be worth considering.
- Do we know how much people owe us?
- What is the average period of debt? — Do we know how much we owe to others? What is the average period of our credit? How do our debtors and creditors compare? How much do they cost us in interest payments?
- What are our profit margins by product and market?
  — How do we stand in relation to our budget (expenditure) figure? How do our sales figures compare with planned figures?
  — What is our service level to customers? Is it what we expect it to be?
  — Are there delays in deliveries due to material shortages or finished stock shortages? Do we know why these shortages have occurred? Can we forecast shortages and plan to overcome them?
  — Do we have control over overtime working? Or does excessive overtime sneak up unexpectedly?
  — Are there delays in the production of invoices and/or statements?
  — What is the labour turnover rate? How does it compare with the average for the area? Is there a higher than average (for us or for the area) rate in clerical functions?

If most of the answers to those questions are 'happy answers', then the potential benefits of a computer system will have to be very considerable to make one worthwhile. On the other hand, if your company's problems have just been listed for you, then the potential the computer can provide for climbing off the slope to bankruptcy turns the more positive benefits into icing on the cake.

Positve benefits

Staff It has been said before, and by many other people, that introducing a computer system will *not* reduce staff numbers. No apology is made for saying it again. Ever since one of the Banks claimed it would cut its staff by 20 per cent, then increased it by 30 per cent, users have known that any attempt to reduce numbers is futile.

Inevitably, numbers will increase, even if only slightly. The *positive benefit* appears as a company expands its markets and products. Additional people are no longer needed to work out sales statistics. More invoices can be processed in a day, and it is no more difficult to post 1,000 items to the ledgers than it was to post 100. Thus staff costs can be stabilised.

Decision-making 'Knowledge is business' as every successful businessman knows, and one of the more persuasive benefits (but also one of the more addictive) is the ability of a good computer system to provide comprehensive accurate and up-to-date information at no additional cost, on which decisions can be based. Let's illustrate that point by considering a company that employs two clerks to produce monthly sales analyses by product/salesman/customer category against budget figures. Suddenly there is a 'need' for an analysis in mid-month by district manager/customer size/salesman In all probability, a manual system would not be able to provide the information, and if it could, it would be at the expense of something else. A computer can (and does, for many organisations) provide the analysis without a single perturbation in the smooth running of the sales department.

And managers have more information on which to base their policy decisions. The information processing aspect of a computer installation is particularly valuable when the board needs answers to 'what if . . . ?' questions.

>What if. . .inflation goes up by 15 per cent?
>. . .raw materials go short?
>. . .we have a strike?
>. . .new firms in the area spoil our labour market?
>
>Etc., etc.

The computer does not make any decisions but, properly programmed (see Chapters 2 and 6), it can provide the trends and information that render the decisions easy — or less difficult.

Inventory Some companies who have introduced a computer to monitor inventory levels have been shocked to discover that their inventory level has actually increased. The reason is quite simply that they had so many lines 'out of stock' that computer-based control, by providing a properly balanced inventory, increased their stock holding. For most companies, however, a detailed knowledge of turnover rates, critical levels, economic order quantities (for bought-in parts and materials) and the application of mathematical equations to what were previously rule-of-thumb estimates will result in significant cost savings over the year.

For example, a company carrying only £100,000 worth of stocks could reasonably expect to recover the capital cost of a computer [after allowance for tax, development grants, etc. (see Chapter 1)] in two years. It has been known for companies to recover their costs in less than 12 months, but one needs a pretty disastrous manual system to achieve such startling results! With improvements in stock level can also come savings in money tied up in work-in-progress. By working from analyses of customer ordering patterns, through the production line, to the vagaries of bought-out parts and materials, many companies have slashed the proportion of their assets tied up on the shop-floor.

Equipment A majority of small to medium-sized businesses have become 'computerised' when their accounting machine has become worn out. Sometimes, too frequently, the computer has been installed as a more sophisticated accounting machine and has been programmed only for the accounts office. Such an application is both short-sighted and wasteful, for there is potential for saving equipment in all parts of a business by transferring calculations and routines to a computer system.

9.2 Feasibility study

If, from the results of an analysis of the needs of the company, it seems that a computer would be a valuable addition to the company's assets, a feasibility study should be carried out to confirm that opinion. This is a step that many organisations feel they can omit. They have decided that a computer would help, so why not go and get one? Some firms that follow this course of action are very successful, will tell their story and will convince some others that the prophets of doom (like me!) who say that a feasibility study is essential are only trying to feather their own nests. The answer to that argument is that other companies which have not undertaken feasibility studies have had their fingers burned to the tune of hundreds of thousands of pounds. As they say ... 'Yer pays yer money and takes yer pick!'

A feasibility study should have the objectives of:
1   Establishing the aims and purposes of the computer system.
2   Reviewing problem areas.

3   Establishing applications areas.
4   Ensuring compatibility of any proposed solutions with future plans and company strategy.
5   Proposing alternative solutions.

These objectives should be written into the terms of reference of whoever is to carry out the study and should be thoroughly understood by the study team and the employing organisation. One useful parameter in establishing the scope of a study is the time required, and if a specialist is used, a company employing about 1,000 employees might expect to pay for about 10 days' work. Depending upon the approach taken this may cost nothing (in terms of additional budget) to £2,000 (1979 prices).

Basically there are four ways of commissioning the study:

1   Set up a working party within the company including representatives from all interested departments. The advantage of this approach is that there is comprehensive communication between staff at an early stage, a factor which can be of crucial importance during implementation. A disadvantage is that the expertise in analysis may not be available internally. Costs are, of course, minimal.

2   Invite manufacturers to carry out the study — or alternatively invite several manufacturers to carry out several studies and then compare the results. As an approach using external specialists this method will be quite inexpensive, but will inevitably result in the company needing (apparently) exactly what each manufacturer has to offer. In one particular case which comes to mind, a batch-oriented manufacturer laid heavy emphasis on the need for comprehensive reports, to be available in the boardroom at 9 o'clock each morning — a facility that his machine could provide more efficiently than any other. A real-time oriented manufacturer was much more concerned about the penalties of not meeting customer's delivery dates and proposed a sophisticated stock control system — which just happened to be his latest 'flavour of the month'.

Both were correct.
Both were wrong.

The company needed a compromise solution which would both give reports at a reasonable time and ensure an acceptable service level to customers.

3   Call in a 'Systems House' — one of the firms specialising in contract studies, systems analysis and programming (they advertise in computer journals and magazines, or may be found in Yellow Pages). Staff from such firms tend to be objective, competent and knowledgeable about business needs. They have, after all, seen it all before. If there is a weakness in their work it is that they may tend to have a few preferred solutions into which any firm is made to fit — but that is human nature and is unlikely to be any more marked in a systems house man than in anyone else.

Certainly they will probably be expensive in comparison with any other alternative, and since a company has no 'hold' on them negotiating for post-implementation work might be difficult.

4   Use the company's external auditors   Some of the country's best business systems analysts work for auditing firms, as do some of the most knowledgeable computer people. With their constant contact with companies getting into and out of financial tangles created by inexpert use of computers they can often give impartial and specialist advice. Not only that, but they have a vested interest in keeping companies alive. On the other hand, they are not noted for their entrepreneurial flair and may be more conservative than a company might like.

Whoever undertakes the study, one can expect it to divide naturally into three parts.

(a)   The investigation   Once the terms of reference mentioned earlier have been agreed by either a steering committee or the senior executive the analyst will want to study any previous material — it is *not* a good idea to withhold information and then compare notes later. The object of the exercise is to carry out a feasibility study, not test the analyst's powers. If he does not engender confidence, then don't let him do it, because if his conclusions agree with earlier ones you will probably disbelieve both! It is essential that the analyst is taken fully into the confidence of the firm. He must have freedom to go anywhere and see anyone, since one of his tasks is to establish a 'feel' for the company. He needs to assess whether the culture of the company is amenable to a computer installation (see Chapter 3), whether the channels of communication will need to change and whether the staff are capable of taking on their new roles.

These issues are independent of the purely technical issues of whether the company's *business* is amenable to computerisation and are just as important. This rather ill-defined stage will perhaps occupy a day or so, and will also be continuing whilst the analyst is gathering information about the business. He will first want to get a general picture of the existing system (volumes, time-scales, outputs, staffing, etc.) from the steering committee and/or the chief executive, and will follow up by interviewing staff at all levels. For some people, the interview schedule can be traumatic, for a good analyst will not only want to see specialists and departmental heads, but will also want to interview people 'at the coal face'.

Only by asking different people the same questions can fact be separated from opinion.

By the end of the interviews, the analyst will have a tome of information which has to be organised into a coherent report.

(b) The analysis Following interviews, analysts will bury themselves at home for a few days trying to establish some important requirements for the company's system from the plethora of 'absolutely crucial' in his notes.

At this point he will be pausing to ask: 'Will the company benefit from a computer?' If his answer is 'No', then his report should say so — *and the recommendation should be treated on the same basis as a 'Yes'.* (In other words, if the guy was a 'good bloke' during the interviews, he should still be a 'good bloke' if his recommendations are at variance with the chief executive's opinions.) Such a recommendation is rare — perhaps too rare — and after answering 'Yes' to the question, an analyst will then synthesise the type of system which he thinks will be most appropriate for the firm.

His thinking will include issues such as:

1. Form of management information system needed:
   — Database (see Chapter 6)
   — File sizes and structures
   — Management reports
2. Legal requirements:
   — Audit trails
   — VAT, etc.
   — Effect on employees
3. Procedures:
   — Customer and product (etc.) codes
   — 'Ownership' of data
   — Access rates
   — Exceptions
   — Volumes
   — Application areas, and their inter-relationships (See Chapters 2 and 8)

(c) The report The result of all his deliberations will be a report, presented to the chief executive for consideration by the steering group. *It must be expected that, in places, the report will be factually wrong!*

Even a saint of the type described in Chapter 3 will not have been able to separate every fact from the gigantic smoke-screen of opinion which envelopes every company (except yours!) and one of the first tasks of the steering group will be to discuss perceived errors with the analyst.

If the exercise is to be a success, it is important to remember that errors are initially 'perceived' and not 'proven'. Every department has *right* ways of doing things and every operator has his *own* way of doing things. Investigating perceived errors can be a useful way of finding out what actually happens.

With a 'corrected' version of the report, management should satisfy themselves that it contains:
1   The effects and potentials of continuing the existing systems.
2   An analysis of alternative solutions.
3   Proposals which appear, from the company's point of view, to be viable.

The proposals and their potential costs and potential benefits will need to be studied in some detail, since everyone is now in the area of speculation. However experienced the analyst might be, there will be factors peculiar to any company which could affect a final decision and which may be known only to a member of staff. And the performance of any specific computer cannot be guaranteed in unknown conditions.

If, as is usually the case, the final decision is to go ahead on the basis of the analyst's proposals, then tenders will be required from selected manufacturers.

9.3   Tenders

Buying a computer system entails buying (at least) three separate elements — hardware, software and communications — which can be permed in any way. (Hardware and software from one supplier, communications from another, or hardware and software from separate suppliers, communications from either hardware supplier, software supplier or from a separate supplier, etc.) From the feasibility study, one has a fair idea about how sophisticated each element has to be, and this can help to decide how to purchase. For example, a company with very specialised programming needs will probably benefit from going to a professional software house, thus treating hardware and software separately. For 'routine' business systems, packaged software which comes as part of the deal from either a manufacturer or OEM will probably be the best approach.

Some chief executives are nervous about using OEMs because they do not make the computer, but the reality of today's situation is that software is less reliable and more expensive than hardware — so if a 'special relationship' is to be established, there is a strong argument for establishing it with software suppliers in preference to hardware manufacturers.

One therefore has a choice between:
1   Manufacturers with software capabilities.

2   Manufacturers without software capabilities.
3   Software houses.
4   Systems houses.
5   Suppliers of refurbished equipment.
6   Batch bureaux.
7   Bureaux accepting remote job entry.
8   Time-sharing bureaux.
9   A combination of the above.

The real criterion, however, is whether the final system will do the job it is designed to do, and in this analysis the architecture of the computer (see Chapter 2), the flexibility of the programming language and the compatibility of these two components are obviously of greatest importance.

With guidance from the analyst, it is best to select three to four suppliers for each component (but trying to prevent a complex of alternative combinations which would require a computer to analyse) in a way which allows any alternative strategies to be explored, e.g. in-house minicomputer versus time-sharing bureau.

More tenders than this makes life very difficult, encourages suppliers (if they find out that you have asked 27 firms to quote for hardware) to treat a request as vexatious, wasting a lot of everybody's time and money. Fewer tenders make it difficult to assess the worth of those tendering. Remember that the tenders will be based upon the feasibility study, so that although it should be possible for those involved to form a clear idea of the hardware requirements (disk capacity, terminals, etc.), it will not be so easy to produce an accurate software tender. Be wary, therefore, of any tender that is very specific, because it means that the needs of your firm are probably going to be subjected to preprepared packages.

At the same time, be equally wary of software houses that say they are going to have to program your requirements from scratch. No firm is *that* different and there should be many subroutines already written which only need knitting together — with perhaps a few special items.

Suppliers should be given about a month to produce their tenders which should include:

1   An estimate for carrying out a detailed systems design. This does not mean that the feasibility study was inadequate, but new people coming into a company need to obtain the same 'feel' that the study analyst developed. They must then go into much more detail in every dimension to establish a system which will work. This part of the exercise could take several man-months.

2   An estimate for basic programming work, plus a further estimate (length of a piece of string variety) for any special quirks gleaned from

the feasibility study. For a small company planning to put its business requirements onto a minicomputer, the 1980 rate from a software house has been known to vary between £5,000 and £30,000.

3   Some fairly firm hardware costs. Based on the feasibility study, any self-respecting supplier of hardware or software should be able to say what type of machine is best suited to the firm's needs (mainframe, mini, micro, batch, teleprocessing, etc. — see Chapter 5) and what storage will be needed. (Watch out for suppliers who quote to your budget and not to your needs. It's a pound to a penny that their hardware will not do the job. Recently a very large hardware supplier, faced with a disclosed budget of £30,000 offered a system for £31,500 which patently could not meet the first and over-riding requirement for an information system. The additional hardware to meet the need would have cost between £8,000 and £15,000 — but that could come from next year's budget! Yet another company was offered a system for £23,000 (budget £20,000) which used a single 5M-byte fixed disk. The absolute minimum requirement for the company was 10M bytes with two spare removable disk packs. The total cost of the upgrade, including core, a new operating system and disk drives would have been over £10,000.)

Hardware figures should also include accurate costs for maintenance agreements and insurance, and should state security arrangements, accommodation requirements (including air conditioning and power supplies), training facilities — and delivery dates.

Most important — the supplier must include the names, addresses and phone numbers of up to six satisfied customers who are prepared to discuss their systems. Furthermore they should be customers who are:

a   Using the same (or similar) equipment to that which is being offered.

b   Similar in size and application to the potential purchaser. Where a computer is new on the market, this may be a difficult criterion to meet, and suppliers may need to make customers a more attractive offer to offset a lack of evidence about the viability of their systems (like free support and Maintenance).

4   Some company background, to prove that they are unlikely to go out of business whilst they are still needed. There should also be a copy of their normal contractual terms for perusal by the potential customer's legal advisers. Where separate contracts are signed for hardware, software and communications make sure that they all start on the same date. A favourite ploy none-too-scrupulous dealers is to argue that hardware is needed first for testing (say 1 January), then

software is implemented at Head Office (say 1 April) and communications are finally tested when the basic system is running (say 1 September). Getting out of those contracts without unnecessary cost is not easy, since each will probably have to be renewed for a minimum of 12 months.

5   And a timetable.

9.4   Proposal evaluation

By this time, most firms will be ready to choose the 'best supplier for our requirements' by weighing the proposals on the bathroom scales and giving the contract to the heaviest. Now is the time for mature and quiet reflection, comparing again what is *needed* with what is on offer.

There is no easy answer to the problem of selecting a supplier (or suppliers) and in more than one instance the decision will rest on the answer to the question 'Do I feel I can trust the person who presented the proposal to me?'

A few of the more objective criteria might be:
1   Can the equipment do the job:
    — Reliably?
    — To time?
    — With acceptable response times?
2   Is the system easy to use:
    — Is the operating system solid?
    — Is it easy?
    — Are the languages compatible?
3   Are suppliers compatible:
    — Can programs transfer to other machines?
    — Will they run on upgraded machines?
    — Will it be easy to cope with increased volumes, more applications?
4   Is it economically viable?

It should be possible to decide whether one can make a cost justification for the investment. This justification should take into account all 'hidden' costs such as supplies (paper, tapes, disks, etc.), ancillary equipment, telephone charges, etc., and hidden benefits (such as the ability to accommodate expansion at minimum extra cost, labour saving, etc.).

Perhaps it is appropriate at this stage to consider various payment options for the equipment. There are three choices available — outright purchase, rental and leasing. (Rental is not always popular with the manufacturers though from the user point of view there are advantages if the system is seen as a temporary 'stop gap' before moving to a more permanent solution.) Choice between purchase and leasing depends on tax position, cash flow situation and overall accounting policy towards capital equipment acquisition (see Chapter 1).

A lot of firms opt for outright purchase as the simplest and cheapest method (pundits of discounted cash flow techniques may disagree), but most small businesses work best on no-frills decisions, writing the whole cost of the machine off in the early years. Having paid for the equipment, make sure it is insured against the usual risks.

It is also worth noting that there may be a good market in 'used' or refurbished computers. Price savings are substantial and delivery periods short. Independent maintenance organisations exist to service this equipment, so there need be no worry on that score (other than perhaps over cost) and adequate basic software has usually been developed for these systems.

9.5 Detailed design

So, from the tenders, one supplier for each element has been chosen and now becomes part of the family. One of its staff may take up residence in the firm, with his own office and access to (your) secretarial services. He will be seen poking into corners where no man has trod before and, unless the entire staff are fully conversant with what he is doing, is ideally placed to create industrial unrest. In close cooperation with the steering group, the chief executive, the receptionist and any one else in the organisation, he will be preparing detailed plans for the flow of information and controls, assessing volumes and movements both now and in the future, investigating stock policy and coding systems, establishing reporting systems, etc. And at every stage he will be helping the steering group to separate fact from opinion.

He will also be in touch with the auditors to ensure that they are kept informed of developments.

When a computer is installed to control the business, it will inevitably affect every part of the company's activities, and a good business analyst will have been there first.

The design work will not only deal with procedures, but will also plan for staff training and familiarisation. The analyst will decide on the extent of parallel running, installation of clean power lines and telephones, and a million minor items without which the system will not be able to operate.

For a small company the analyst's involvement may be more limited than just described since he will undoubtedly have checklists of the logistic details which need to be considered, but if it is, be certain that the steering group is considering *every* aspect of implementation, and is carefully checking all the analyst's findings.

This is the last opportunity to check disasters. ('We forgot to order the stationery'; 'Where's the power-point?'; 'The floor won't take the weight'; 'I thought you were laying on the computer appreciation courses'.)

At the end of the detailed design stage, both parties should be satisfied that the systems will run, and suppliers can be left to get on with the programming — to a schedule.

There *must* be dates by which certain parts of the programs are guaranteed to be written *and documented*. Under *no circumstances* must undocumented programs be accepted or even entertained. Documentation is an unpleasant job for any programmer and one that is to be avoided like the plague. Without documentation programs are virtually unreadable, cannot be modified (except by the person who wrote them) and are, to all intents and purposes, *useless*. It cannot be stressed too strongly that documentation is a fundamental part of any program suite.

Equally fundamental is the need for programmers to keep to internationally agreed programming standards. It is tempting, and pleasing, for programmers to 'make the computer jump through hoops', but such programs are a nightmare to maintain. The suppliers should have it impressed upon them that what is wanted is programs that work well and can be easily modified — not clever, albeit superbly efficient, ciphers.

Chapter Ten

IMPLEMENTATION OF A COMPUTER SYSTEM

Chapter 9 has detailed many of the issues involved in selecting a computer system — hardware, software and communications. Other chapters will, hopefully, put flesh on those bones. This chapter looks very briefly at some of the issues involved in implementing a system. Briefly, not because it is seen as less important, but because many of the problems which arise during implementation could be avoided by applying some down-to-earth common sense. And how does one exhort people to use common sense?

The over-riding consideration is that *everyone* should be fully in the picture from the earliest possible date, i.e. just before the feasibility study, and that *all* views should be heard and considered. In this way many foolish mistakes can be avoided:
- The door's too narrow for the equipment.
- The printer is too near the telephone exchange (noise problem).
- Dust from the factory below gets in through the floorboards.
- 'Who can type?'
- There's no paper for the printer.
- The invoice numbers are wrongly coded.
- 'We stopped making 45-gallon barrels last month.'
- Customer codes are too long to fit on the new invoice forms.
- 'Where's the space for a separate shipping address?'

And so on.

10.1 Communications

In too many cases where nightmares have come true and dreams have not been realised, the blame has been directed towards 'communications'. Since the aim is for a smooth change from manual to computer systems, preparations cannot begin too early. Make sure that people are aware from the outset of the potential of new systems, allay fears (especially of redundancy) and ensure that training needs are identified (and the training given) in plenty of time.

There is also much to be gained by giving everyone the opportunity to make suggestions about the details of the proposed system — what type of terminal, where sited, display formats, etc. Many companies actually delegate this type of decision to a small group of the staff who will be using the terminal equipment. Not only does the exercise reduce the probability of disgruntled staff, unhappy with the kit they have to use, but it provides a very useful vehicle for training staff to use new equipment.

10.2 Planning and scheduling

To achieve a smooth changeover, there has to be some degree of planning to ensure that equipment and software are ready at about the same time. For very small installations it may be quite sufficient to accept the supplier's dates and arrange to train staff sometime before the equipment is delivered. Sometime during this period it will also be necessary to convert much of the manual data into computer format and prepare it on tape or disk for transfer to the new installation. This job itself can be quite daunting, and if for no other reason than to reduce it to manageable chunks, it is worth developing some form of planning network. At its simplest, the plan could have start and finish dates for each activity, perhaps shown as a bar chart (or Gantt chart). Items within the plan might include:

    Prepare computer room and terminal sites: power, air conditioning, lighting, noise levels.
    Identify security issues.
    Plan security procedures.
    Implement security procedures.
    Arrange for any hoists, furniture removing, etc.
    Agree delivery date for hardware.
    Agree delivery date for software.
    Select terminal equipment.
    Establish and implement any organisational changes (10.3)
    Train staff in the use of equipment, procedures, security, etc.
    Agree equipment acceptance trials.

Carry out equipment acceptance trials.
Agree software acceptance trials.
Carry out software acceptance trials.
Fix steering group (and other) progress meetings.
Arrange for data conversion: fixed, e.g. customer names and addresses, and variable, e.g. order quantity.
Carry out data conversion.
Verify accuracy of converted data.
Decide on the type of changeover to be used (see Section 10.4) and fix changeover period.
Establish evaluation criteria and timetable.

Of course, each of these headings will probably be broken down into smaller elements and the names of those responsible for meeting target dates added to them, together with the additional manpower and budgetary resources required. For example, data conversion may be undertaken in advance of installation by sending data to the supplier's premises to be coded by his staff. This may entail sending one's own staff to supervise the conversion.

If the Gantt chart gets complicated, then it is probably worth going to one of the more sophisticated planning systems such as PERT (Programme Evaluation and Review Technique) or CPM (Critical Path Method). Both techniques rely on creating a network showing the start and finish dates for each activity, together with the length of time it is expected to take. Some activities can be run in parallel, e.g. writing software and preparing the computer room, but others are interdependent, e.g. writing software and converting data, and must follow serially.

The ensuing network will have a 'critical path' where any slippage in time will delay implementation. Thus, by constantly (say weekly) reviewing the network, it is possible to keep a very close check on progress.

There are many good books on CPM and many computer manufacturers have applications programs that will create very sophisticated planning networks. It is highly likely that the supplier of your machine will be able to run a network for you. In fact, it is more than possible that he will have a network already prepared, which has been used for previous purchasers.

Physical environment

Often people get so deeply involved in the magic of hardware and software that they forget the mundane needs of their installation. Thus one finds that machines are put in rooms with no power-points (or just one), or the floor loading is inadequate, or the air-conditioning ducts fall directly underneath the disk pack, or, even worse, come up behind the printer and blow stationery round the room. Small points — but important.

There is a tendency (not unreasonable in a non-computer-oriented financial director) to try to put the machine in a room which is *just* large enough for it and an operator. Superficially this appears to be economical, but in reality it can be very expensive. Even though modern machines do not need many services (and probably no air-conditioning) they can still suffocate if they are not given adequate supplies of air. And from time to time the machine will break down and need repairing. This will certainly entail opening all the cabinets, pulling out circuit boards, and possibly wheeling oscilloscopes around. The engineer cannot work efficiently if he is cramped.

Looking to the future, it is more than likely that additional disk drives will be needed, more core may be added and a magnetic tape unit can be useful for daily logs. All will require more physical space and it is short-sighted not to plan for this potential expansion.

One final thought. Computers are heavy and bulky. Don't allocate a room on the third floor for a 1,000-lb unit, 5 ft long, if the lift will only carry 600 lb and is 4 ft wide!

People

The effect of computers on staff of all types has been discussed in some detail in Chapter 3. In this section on planning it is, however, worth re-emphasising that people cannot be 'planned' in the same cavalier fashion that one can deal with inanimate objects. Staff who object to being planned can ruin a CPM. There is no certain way of overcoming people problems — except by treating them as people and inviting them to become involved in plans.

Communications (see Section 10.1) form a basis for effective 'people planning'. However, 'people planning' is essential. One needs to establish whether additional staff will be required, whether they need special skills, whether existing staff need retraining. Each needs to be scheduled and training times fitted into the network.

It will also be necessary to fit in any computer appreciation seminars that may be needed. These can be especially useful for middle management who may feel that a computer will *(a)* solve all their problems or *(b)* create chaos. (A remarkably high proportion of the population lie at one or other of these poles.)

10.3 Organisation

One of the early decisions that needs to be taken is who is to control the installation. Traditionally, computers have been the responsibility of the finance department, possibly because they deal with numbers! It is difficult to justify the decision on more logical grounds, since every argument for it can equally well be applied to production or sales departments. Furthermore, the rather particular mentality which immersion in the financial world breeds may not be advantageous to either computer or end-user.

For instance, many batch systems have been installed in preference to on-line systems because they are:
1. Cheaper.
2. More easily controlled.
3. More conservative.
4. OK for journal entries.

Of course, they won't do the job required of them! If it is even remotely possible, someone should be in sole charge of the installation and should report directly to the chief executive. In this way each department's requests will be treated equally, and when the production department comes out into the real world it will not find that a majority of computer time is being devoted to payroll (a particularly pointless application anyway for the small company, since the major UK banks carry excellent payroll programs).

However, assuming that control of the new installation is given to the finance department, it will then be necessary to organise a 'computer department' to respond to the financial director.

Nobody wants to lose any benefits a computer might accrue by paying a small empire of computer specialists, but it will be necessary to have at least one person who is knowledgeable and who can carry the message to other departments. (If your finance man does not want the message to go outside his department, either forget the installation, or get rid of the man!) In the long run his salary will be cheaper than the chaos that a plethora of operating methods and internal bickering will create. He will also be able to encourage other staff in the finance department, and other departments, to learn about the machine and thereby devise additional ways of making it pay its way.

One thing that must always be remembered is that the 'Computer Department' is a *service* function to the business of the company (as is finance). Its place in the organisation must needs be defined such that it is always seen in that light, and its staff should be selected from people who view their role in that way. Positive control of the department to achieve defined business objectives will help to gain and maintain credibility for it.

Organisational effects may also be felt in other departments. The role of the storekeeper, for example, may change dramatically and where he has traditionally responded to the production department, he may now logically be attached to purchasing or sales. Order entry clerks might become part of the computer department (depending on the scope of their job).

Although changes in the organisation are by no means inevitable when a computer system is introduced, they should be considered as one of the likely repercussions.

Finally, if a company has more than one site and/or is considering the installation of more than one computer, it is absolutely essential that one person has central control over the entire computer services department. That is not to say that each site should not have some degree of autonomy over its destiny, but it must toe the line in a number of general respects such as:

   Data organisation (for sharing between sites)
   Program languages and suites
   Hardware (for compatibility and back-up)
   Standards

10.4 The changeover

With a fully trained staff, all equipment installed and tested, all software proved on test data, it is now time to implement the changeover. If the purchaser has total confidence in his supplier and the converted data, he can discontinue manual systems on Friday evening and start up the computer system on Monday morning. It is rumoured that companies have made the changeover in this way without any problems. But it is only a rumour. There are companies who have opted for a direct changeover who *claim* to have had no difficulty, but deeper investigation has shown that their claims are face-savers.

Aside from a direct changeover, there are three other recognised methods that people can choose between — each with its own advantages and disadvantages:

(a) Pilot system The data the computer system needs is collected for some weeks before commissioning. At installation the data is run and the results compared with manual results. This process tests the ability of software to deal with a wide range of data requirements and allows users to examine, at leisure, various report-generation techniques. It provides an invaluable form of 'on-the-job' training for users and allows people to make their mistakes in a 'risk-free' environment. However, this same freedom from risk also highlights one of the major weaknesses, for pilot running does not test the total system under real conditions.

(b) Restricted data The new system is used directly using a sub-set of the total data, e.g. a cost centre or a customer class. For that sub-set, it has the same disadvantages as a direct changeover, but if something does go wrong (as it will!) only a part of the business is affected and manual recovery procedures are readily available. Its advantages are that it tests the systems under real conditions, allows a gradual transfer of data — and staff — to the computer operations and, by having manual back-up always available, insures against any dramatic software bug, which may not show immediately. For instance, it has been known for a program to work perfectly on a data file of 25K bytes, but to fail miserably at 100K bytes. It should be said that this was not with a database management system (see Chapter 6).

(c) Parallel running Both computer and manual systems are run side by side. Results are compared at the end of each day and any differences are resolved. In this respect, parallel running is similar to a pilot system, but it has the advantage of immediacy. Parallel running is continued until more of the discrepancies can be attributed to the manual system than to the computer system or until there are no discrepancies. In many respects, parallel running is an ideal changeover system by virtue of the continuing cross-checking of both old and new systems, the opportunities it provides for identifying hitherto overlooked anomalies and its inherent safety. But it is expensive — in terms of both time and effort.

10.5 Evaluation

A post-implementation evaluation is an essential follow-up to any installation. It allows one to see if original objectives and anticipated benefits have been realised and if not, why not. It is the first available opportunity to compare actual costs with budget figures and provides the basis for future forecasts.

It is also a psychologically difficult thing to do. In the post-implementation euphoria (or despair) nobody will want to study results objectively or commit their findings to paper. If the installation is a palpable failure, there will be an inevitable desire to say as little as possible. If it has been an overwhelming success, everyone will know.

Yet the evaluation is essential, because it provides the base from which further developments will be built and the data from which benefits and costs can be measured.

There are three areas on which to concentrate:
1. *User departments* An easy survey to conduct if all has gone well, and one which may require the computer manager to act as

Devil's Advocate, trying to find holes in his system. If things have gone badly, then his courage and ability not to become defensive will be tested.

2 *Computer systems – hardware and software* Is the system doing what it should be doing:
   a   As efficiently as expected?
   b   With the anticipated volumes?
   c   As easily as promised?
   And if not, why not?
3 *Computer staff* Has recruitment (either internally or externally) been as successful as expected? Are they coping with the workload — or isn't there enough for them?

Further appraisals of the cost-effectiveness of the installation should follow at regular intervals, (say, every two years) to see if any changes are needed in the company, the computer department, or the equipment.

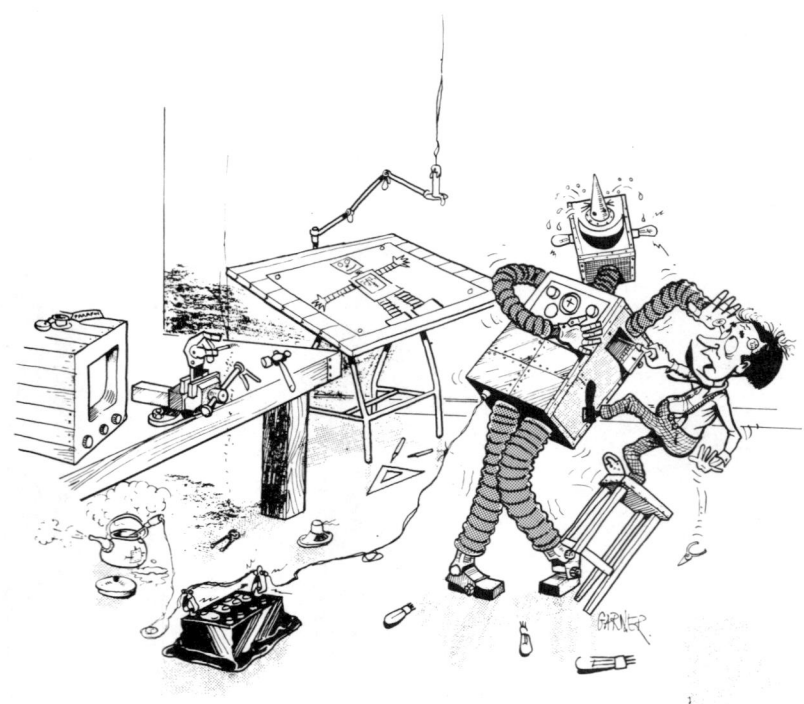

Chapter 11
INTRODUCING MICROCOMPUTERS

11.1 Background

It was in the late 1940s and early 1950s that the major technological advances were made which now give rise to our 'microprocessor revolution'. At that time scientists discovered that by treating the element germanium they could create within a single metal slice all the characteristics of a valve. From this beginning the whole field of semiconductor electronics developed, resulting very rapidly in 'valves' made not only from germanium but also from silicon.

Silicon proved to be a much more versatile source element than germanium and before long it was possible to create within a small slice of silicon all the characteristics of resistors, capacitors and valves. Where 'valves' were made from silicon a new device — the transistor — was born.

Such was the versatility of silicon as a source of semiconductor devices that engineers were soon producing complete circuits on a single silicon slice. In the early days these circuits were simple and reflected the logic requirements of electronic equipment. For example, they were able to sense whether signals were coming down two or three or more separate in-coming channels and only if a signal came from all channels at the same time would they allow a signal to be sent from the output (AND gate). These were the first of a whole field of integrated circuits which now cover amplifiers, logic circuits, calculator circuits, watches and even complete computers. In this last guise an integrated circuit, made from semiconductor materials (silicon), becomes a microprocessor or even a microcomputer (the difference will be explained later).

During the late 1950s and 1960s space exploration (as everyone knows) led to a desperate drive for smaller and even smaller components, and integrated circuits provided the obvious way forward. Enormous amounts of money were spent during that period finding ways of putting more and more circuitry onto small silicon slices. By the end of the 1960s more than 100 complete electronic circuits could be etched on a silicon slice no more than one quarter of an inch square. Ten years later more than 10,000 circuits can be etched on the same silicon slice! Thus microelectronics has come of age and the microcomputers and microprocessors of which we hear so much nowadays rely for their existence on semiconductor/integrated circuit/microelectronic technology (otherwise known as LSI — large-scale integration).

It is important to stress however, that microelectronic technology cannot actually do any more than traditional hardware technology; it simply does it better and in a much smaller space.

11.2 Features

Firmware

The functions of a microcomputer are no different from those of an 'ordinary' computer. In order to function as a computer any microcomputer still needs input and output devices and buffers, internal working storage and a central processor which is able to coordinate, control and monitor peripheral units and which also performs the arithmetic and logical processes demanded by the programme. The elements of a computer system as outlined in Section 7.2 and the functions of the central processing unit (Section 7.3) are still essentially the same — the technology has merely allowed us to put a complete central processing unit onto a quarter-inch square silicon chip — known as a microprocessor — and also allows us nowadays to put a complete computer system on the same size of silicon chip — a microcomputer.

In Chapter 7 the concept of addressing core locations was developed and earlier in Chapter 6 the idea of translating high-level computer languages into the binary notation used by computer hardware was discussed. In traditional computing technology (because the core storage of a computer relied on magnetised disks) it was impossible to retain any information in core once the power had been switched off.

However, electronic circuits exist which are able to retain a '1'-or '0' without power and once these circuits have been etched into a silicon chip we have an immediate means of storing data and programs irrespective of the condition of the power supply. The commonest example of this type of circuitry is that contained in pocket calculators where all the programs to perform additions, subtractions, multiplication and division and sometimes squares, square roots, standard deviations, etc., are held permanently within a silicon chip and cannot be affected in anyway by anything that we do to the calculator. This method of holding programs and data is known as *firmware*.

Other examples of the application of firmware are in television games and the form of electronic games that one sees in hotels and motorway service stations, etc.; small control circuits in equipment such as cameras and micrometers; and certain parts of computers where LSI circuits are used to contain what has previously been held as software.

The terminology in this area is still developing and although firmware can be used correctly to describe any microelectronic circuitry used to store software programs and/or data for certain computer purposes, different terms are sometimes used.

Read only memory

The core of a computer (as described in Chapter 7) needs to hold the operating system (software) programs and data. Where these are held in firmware the device is universally called an ROM (Read Only Memory). In fact, a microcomputer's Operating System is always held in ROM, as is the program language that it uses (normally BASIC). The actual construction of a microcomputer will be discussed later in Section 11.4 but in the meantime imagine the potential of a computer in which one simply unplugs one operating system and/or language compiler and plugs in another, more powerful one, when it becomes available.

11.3 What makes microcomputers different?

Although microcomputers do nothing different from ordinary computers, the way in which they do it makes them exceptionally powerful and gives rise to the vast range of applications to which they can be directed.

Microcomputers (and the microprocessor that forms a part of a microcomputer) are cheap, compact and reliable.

Cheapness In present-day values the first commercial computer available in the UK (Ferranti's Mark I Star) cost about £1 million. The cheapest available microcomputer (at the time of writing) costs about £150 — but a direst cost comparison cannot be made because even the simplest microcomputer is more powerful than the first machine. In comparison with modern computers using 'conventional' hardware, a microcomputer is some 1,000 times cheaper for the same processing capability. To give a specific example, one can buy a central processing unit for a microcomputer, i.e. a microprocessor, for about £8.

In the areas of special-purpose computing, control activities and even in the domestic market of television games, etc., such cheapness opens up applications that have never previously been economically viable.

Compactness Microprocessors are now being fitted in micrometers, cameras and people's hearts. Every day new applications are appearing which capitalise on the smallness of microcomputers.

Each year the amount of circuitry that can be fitted onto a 'standard sized' chip is doubling. This means that by 1984 the experts expect that a single silicon chip only 8 mm square will contain the equivalent of 100,000 active components. For comparison the Mark 1 Star needed some 3,000 cubic feet for a tenth of the number of components, i.e. a room the size of a large living room.

Such power in such a tiny space means that the computer can be put alongside — or even inside — the equipment it is controlling, thus opening a completely new dimension to machine control. Conversely, given a particular amount of space the amount of computing power that can be packed into that volume is now quite vast in terms of storage capacity, e.g. ROM. Microelectronic circuits can now store as much information as the experts think the human brain can handle in a space about four times that of the human brain. By 1984 it should be possible to pack sufficient electronics to match human memory capacity in a space smaller than that presently occupied by our brain.

Reliability Only about 50 per cent of the microprocessor units manufactured pass initial inspection and up to 30 per cent of these fail the final rigorous test. Those that finally get onto the market are perfect and seldom fail in use. In fact the 'mean time between failures' of a modern microelectronic circuit is approximately 50 years — significantly longer than the life of the equipment in which it will be fitted. Even in the most adverse temperature conditions, microcomputers will keep going without complaint. In fact a recent publication by the UK Department of Industry *(Microelectronics – the New Technology)* says of the Ferranti F100 Microprocessor: 'It is millions of times more reliable than the Star and it functions happily at any temperature from −55 degrees C to +125 degrees C'. So put a microcomputer in a freezer or near a blast furnace and it will still perform to its full capability over its entire life.

Already computers in control applications on aircraft and in process plant have clocked many thousands of hours of service without fault.

11.4 Producing a chip

Silicon integrated circuits are made out of a slice of silicon about three or four inches in diameter and about 0.015 inches thick cut from a single crystal of what is known as 'P type' silicon. On this single slice thousands of integrated circuits are built up layer by layer.

Circuitry is designed in the normal way by engineers and circuit diagrams are drawn to a very high degree of accuracy using computer-aided design techniques and graph plotters. The initial art work for the layers can be 300 times the final size of the microcircuit and each layer pattern is photographically reduced to the actual circuit size before being repeated over and over again on a larger photograph until it covers an area equal to the silicon slice on which it is to be printed. Typically each 4-inch diameter slice will contain 1,500-2,000 complete microcircuits. Remember that a microcircuit may well be the complete central processing unit of a computer, itself containing several thousand circuits.

During the production process the slice is first oxidised to form a film over its surface which then acts as an electrical insulator. The regions to be 'doped' in the first layer of the circuit are outlined by means of a mask and the surface is given a photosensitive coating. After the mask has been exposed to light, photosensitive material at the masked regions remains soluble and can be removed whereas the material 'fixed' by the light stays as a protective shield for the oxide film during subsequent etching processes. The next stage is to etch, with acid, those areas where 'windows' are opened to the underlying silicon, for doping treatment. The slice is then put into a furnace in an atmosphere containing the dopant (sometimes arsenic) until diffusion is completed. (The length of time in the furnace depends upon the type of electrical component which the chip is being made to simulate.) Normally the furnace atmosphere will also contain an oxidising agent which will form a barrier over the treated parts as the process comes to an end.

The above sequence is repeated with each mask until all the devices in the circuit have been formed. Naturally the process has to be very accurately controlled. If any mask is even a fraction out of position (and typically a quarter of a millionth of a metre is a maximum allowable tolerance) the chip will be ruined.

After the final doping more 'windows' are etched through the oxide film to open up contact points to the devices and a thin film of aluminium is placed on the entire surface of the slice including the contact points to provide a form of in-built printed circuit.

Every device on the slice is tested and those which fail are rejected (up to 50 per cent of those on the slice in fact) finally each surviving chip is built into its 'package' which has to be large enough to carry the pins which will connect the unit to the outside world.

Although the process sounds long and involved the fact that many thousands of chips are being produced each time a slice is put in the furnace means that the unit cost is extremely low. Obviously it will vary depending upon the complexity of the circuit and the closeness of each component to each other on the slice. Many fairly complicated integrated circuits, e.g. a complete audio amplifier, will retail in the United States for only a couple of dollars and in the UK for about £2.

One of the most widely used microprocessors in the world can be picked up at any reputable dealer for about £8.

11.5 The developing microprocessor

The first microprocessor (Intel's 4004) appeared on the market in 1971, and although a tremendous breakthrough at the time, now appears to be clumsy and of limited capability. This microprocessor contained a limited number of flip-flops, arithmetic registers and logic circuits and could deal with variables of no more than 4 bits (binary digits). Later, as techniques for etching improved and manufacturers were able to pack more components onto the quarter-inch square chip of silicon, they were able to extend the length of the variable accepted by 8 bits (which resulted in the Intel 8008). (Although 8 bits equal one byte in mainframe terminology, it is more commonly called a *word* by micro afficionados!) The 8-bit word gave the processor much more power and accuracy, but reduced the number of flip-flops and the associated registers on the chips. By 1974, however, the era of Large Scale Integrated Circuits (LSI's) was fully upon us and it was possible to pack enough circuitry onto a chip to be able to create a genuine computer out of the pieces.

Today there is a wide and increasing range of microprocessor configurations produced by manufacturers constantly striving to increase the number of components on a chip and at the same time reduce its cost. At the time of writing an Intel 8080 microprocessor (the successor of the 8008) is *retailing* for under £8, and quantity purchases of tested microprocessors cost less than £2 per chip. (Right now, costs in the UK are almost double the costs in the USA for nearly all computer components, from chips to minicomputers.)

Recently the first 16-bit processors were announced by the two major suppliers in the game (Intel's 8086) and Motorola (68000) and by the early 1980s it is expected that all the major producers will have joined these two — plus Texas Instruments (TMS 9900), Ferranti (F100-L) and Digital (LSI 11) — with 16-bit processors.

Should one wait before buying? No — because it will be some years before anything on the market is not obsolete before it gets there, and 8-bit processors can be turned into fairly powerful machines — powerful enough to undertake most of the applications listed in Section 11.7. But '16-bit word' processors will bring advantages. For one thing they will allow more working memory to be accessed directly. This will permit bigger configurations and increase the speed of the computer. Further, they will improve the accuracy of the arithmetic registers. (The Commodore PET microcomputer presently calculates 9 x 9 as 81.0000001. Not far out, but it looks a little strange in a listing of squares of numbers.)

By 1985 we expect to have 32-bit word microprocessors — which is the standard used for most mainframe computers. It is, therefore, quite possible that by 1985, microprocessors costing less than £10 at present-day prices will have the power and capabilities of an IBM 370 at over £1 million.

And now the disclaimer. That is not a valid comparison, because the microprocessor needs working storage, languages, input/output devices and on-line storage. Present estimates puts the total cost of such a system at some £5,000 — still cheap. But there are snags, largely in the areas of software, security and communications that need to be overcome before the microprocessor directly replaces the mainframe. In the meantime, more and more microprocessor power is being installed *within* mainframes and minicomputers, the most notable being Digital's LSI11 which can virtually replace their PDP11 series hardware.

Elsewhere, manufacturers are concentrating more on working storage rather than processing power.

Working memory

To be strictly logical, this section should precede the former, because working memory is *all* flip-flop and the development of denser packing on chips results most immediately in more working memory on a single chip. In 1972 it was 1K words (of 4 bits); by 1974 it was 4K words (of 8 bits); by 1976 1K words (of 8 bits); and in 1978 it became 64K words (of 8 bits).

Exactly 10 years earlier, a mainframe with 64K of core was a big machine. Now a single chip contains that amount of random access memory (now called RAM) with two or more chips in a computer — though presently most microcomputers are using 16K RAM chips and limiting working storage to 32K because of the limitations of 8-bit words mentioned earlier.

There are variations in RAM technology which result in slightly faster or slower reading and writing time but to the user these can be thought of as details for the expert. Worth mentioning, however, is the difference between 'static' RAM (which is a jargon term for flip-flop RAM) and 'dynamic' RAM, which does not use flip-flops but relies on creating small capacitors which can be charged (1) or uncharged (0). The packing density of dynamic RAM can be much greater than for static RAM and it is significantly cheaper to produce as one might expect.

With RAM one can store programs, data and even compilers in the same way one would on a minicomputer or mainframe. Many mainframes and mini's are now using RAM as their 'core' storage and one manufacturer recently advertised increments in 'core' of 32K bytes for under £2,000. (Although that sounds cheap in minicomputer terms, it is really rather expensive for circuitry based on a single chip costing under £5!)

In the retail outlets such as Tandy (Radio Shack in the USA) 4K static RAM is on sale at £9.95, with an access time of under 500 nsec (1 nsec is a nanosecond — 0.000000001 seconds!)

11.6 Applications

With so much of the power of a 'traditional' computer and the advantages of cheapness, reliability and small size, microcomputers open up applications which have never before been possible. It is in fact difficult to imagine any field of activity in which the microcomputer could not have a significant impact.

We have to be careful, however, to recognise that in order to achieve their potential, microcomputers have got to be programmed and in order to be programmed we have to thoroughly understand the principles on which we want the equipment to operate. In other cases we have to be sure that microcomputers are not introduced simply because they happen to be 'the flavour of the month'. For example, in some control applications they offer nothing that cannot be achieved at the present time; however they may be able to provide it either at a lower cost (for new installations) or to a higher degree of reliability (see Section 11.7).

In product/production/process control situations there is no doubt that the microcomputer will have a very significant effect and nowhere more than in the application of robotics in manufacturing plant.

In medicine the microcomputer is *expected* to revolutionise the aids available to doctors, the sick and the handicapped.

In the educational sector systems that talk and listen to the user's response are already available and will develop rapidly in both scope and complexity over the next five years. (Texas Instruments 'Speak and Spell' is a fine example of an aid in this area — though at the time of writing it only speaks in American. An English language version is promised!)

The development of voice recognition facilities on a wide scale will have a far-reaching impact on design offices and as microcomputers increase in power at very low cost it will be possible to devise programming languages that can be used by 'ordinary people' probably using voice recognition.

The list of existing and potential applications that are economically viable is virtually endless — the reason being that there is little in the field of volume industrial and commercial endeavour which cannot be done more competitively by applying microprocessor technology. The key word in that sentence is *volume* because the cost of writing software needs to be spread over many identical applications if it is to show a useful return. And preparing programs is at least as difficult for microcomputers as it is for 'conventional' computers.

These considerations lead us to a list of applications embracing both existing products and opening the door to new types of product.

Enhancement of existing products

Calculators — of all varieties, both pocket and desk-top.
Cameras — control of aperture, focus, flash and film.
Cash registers — totals, change calculations, stock numbers.
Cash dispensers — and other banking terminals.
Communications equipment.
Control systems:
    Of any sort:
        Aircraft
        Continuous plant
        Missiles
        Navigation
Computer peripherals.
Domestic appliances:
    Cookers and ovens
    Dishwashers
    Sewing machines
    Television tuning
    Toasters

    Vacuum cleaners
Educational aids:
    'Speak and Spell'
    Arithmetic tables practice
    History tutor, etc.
Lifts — otherwise known as elevators.
Meters — for taxi's, domestic gas or petrol.
Time clocks in general.
Navigation equipment — compasses, direction-finders.
Security devices.
Smoke detectors.
Typewriters — for erasing mistakes and proportional spacing.
Watches and clocks — for dates, stopwatch, etc.
Vehicles and components — ignition, fuel-saving, etc.

New types of product

Computers — small domestic variety, e.g. TRS-80.
Educational aids.
Electronic toys (including TV games).
Electronic instruments.
Facsimile transmitters.
Navigation equipment — using satellite transmissions.
Telemetry — long-distance monitoring using fibre optics.
    Apart from the generalised applications just mentioned, we can pick out some of the more recognisable applications areas of conventional computers and look to changes wrought by the features of microcomputers discussed earlier. In particular, the low cost of microcomputer hardware and the possibility of spreading software costs across large numbers of users, creates especially attractive possibilities for data processing in any small business sector, e.g.:
    General practitioners
    Dentists
    Employment exchanges
    Estate agents
    Pharmacists
    Consulting engineers
    Accountants

Control applications

By far the greatest impact is likely to be in the area of laboratory equipment and plant control, where limited progress has been made to date because of the physical size, and cost, of the necessary hardware.

Laboratory analysers, for example, costing £2,000-£5,000 cannot be economically controlled by a computer costing £10,000 — even if it is capable of controlling 10 at a time (not that many laboratories have 10 analysers). However, individual control for under £100 is a different matter altogether.

Instrument control loops can cheaply and easily be monitored and controlled by microcomputers — just so long as they 'fail-safe' — which may be exceedingly difficult to achieve.

In a control application, the microcomputer can only perform the controlling operation. Fed with signals from the process, it can create signals which will open or close valves, adjust potentiometers, etc., 'in accordance with certain specified rules'. If the rules are not known, the process cannot be controlled. If the rules are known, the task of programming the microcomputer is still not an easy one.

- What happens if one of the input signals goes outside its expected range?
- What happens if the telemetry lines are broken?
- What happens if one of the sensors in the process stream goes on the blink?
- What happens if a valve sticks?
- What happens if services (steam, compressed air, etc.) fall below their specifications?
- What happens if someone attempts deliberate sabotage?

Those questions are, of course, as valid before a microcomputer is introduced as after. But in the 'before' situation, humans are monitoring the process and (one hopes) 'fail-safe'. Can one be sure that a microcomputer system will 'fail-safe' under each and every circumstance? The answer is that one cannot — even with the very best software — and in every computer-controlled system known to the writer, activity outside the norm transfers control to humans. In many instances, micros are not even used to control the process but to monitor it, producing only readings on which operators adjust the control parameters.

There are still advantages to be gained from using micros, however, since 'inferred' readings can be plotted in addition to actuals. For instance, in beer-making, there comes a stage when one wants to control the alcohol content of the product, but the only direct readings available are those of refractive index, density, temperature, colour and pH value. Using traditional techniques, the operator must calculate approximate alcohol content or work from 'experience'. A microcomputer can continuously calculate alcohol content and present it directly to the operator, who then adjusts the temperature, water input, etc., appropriately.

To sum up, if one can assume that microcomputers are to be used to

control the process, one is presented with the choice of letting it:
1. Control steady-state conditions only, handing over to human operators in any emergency or 'off-spec' conditions.
2. Control emergency conditions only, leaving operators to adjust for steady-state conditions. (I can see no merit in this approach, though it does have its advocates who say that the humans are kept busy.)
3. Control all conditions — no human intervention needed.

At the present time, option (1) seems to be the preferred route, though it does raise questions about how operators are to be employed during smooth-running periods, whilst still maintaining maximum alertness for instant action in the event of a crisis. A compromise used on some major installations is to submit small parts of plant to microcomputer control, with each part of the process linked through a human operator. In this way, it is hoped that the operator will feel he is gainfully employed and is alert enough to deal with emergencies. Frankly, it would seem that such an approach is more likely to make the operator feel he is being 'conned' into doing a non-job, and in doing the job he is likely to tire and be unable to give his best in the event of an emergency.

A more attractive proposition would seem to be that being developed in some US organisations where the microcontroller can also act as a tutor to the operator, giving him regular 'dry-runs' with emergency procedures, using the same equipment he will be operating in a real emergency.

Or perhaps one tries to combine the roles of maintenance engineer and operator.

The very nature of a computer means that it can act as its own fault-finder, using built-in symptom/fault matrices, or hierarchical search strategies to isolate faulty units. The low cost of hardware means that the maintenance policy will certainly be one of replacement rather than repair, and such replacements should be easy to achieve.

In the final analysis, though, the game is too new to be able to give solutions with any firm sense of confidence. In truth, the outcome will undoubtedly be one of 'horses for courses' depending on:
1. The process — and its volatility.
2. Safety.
3. The equipment and measuring devices used.
4. The quality of staff available.
5. Job satisfaction and the remuneration package offered to employees.
6. Costs.

11.7 Business applications

Almost weekly some new advance is made in the application of microcomputers to data processing. There were no serious contenders in this marketplace in 1976 and only 1 or 2 in 1978. By 1980 the numbers look like increasing to over 100 and heaven help the would-be purchaser in 1985. Already microcomputer systems are as powerful in data processing applications as many existing small business systems in both hardware and software terms except that many of the facilities implemented on small business systems as software appear in a microcomputer as firmware. Thus they are that much more reliable in unfriendly environments (such as the secretary's office).

A typical microcomputer considered for business applications will now contain 64K of memory — which will be totally available to the user since all its operating systems will be held in ROM. It will accept up to seven remote terminals — though some will accept up to over 200 — and will have available to it as much applications programing software and storage capacity as a standard SBS.

At this point any reader can go back to earlier chapters about the selection of computer systems because everything which was said there about traditional computing is now becoming valid for microcomputers. The most important features are, as always, the quality of the operating software and the applications programs. By and large hardware — wherever it comes from — will be adequate. Certainly microcomputers tend to be slower than mainframe computers because of the way they are put together and only the newest integrated circuit technology will allow a CPU to contain more than 64K bytes of core storage (to be absolutely accurate one should really say random access memory — RAM — since 'core' is no longer a valid concept).

A word of caution is, however, worth sounding here because many of the firms developing microcomputer hardware and to a lesser extent software are staffed by 'enthusiastic amateurs' (in the nicest possible sense of the term!) Many of these small firms are extremely helpful and exceptionally knowledgeable about the manufacture and processes of microelectronic circuitry, but do not have the design background in data processing that has been developed over the years in the major computer hardware and software houses. In particular, a number of the newly available business packages are lamentably short on security features and some do not show the grasp of business concepts that one would expect from a comprehensive applications package. Having said that, do not take it as a generalisation of all business packages, but more as a warning to be more careful about selection.

No doubt within twelve months of writing that paragraph the situation will have changed rapidly and it will no longer be valid.

A majority of microprocessors still only allow applications

programs written in BASIC but increasing numbers of the more expensive hardware are containing, within ROM, compilers for COBOL and RPG. Others have these languages plus FORTRAN, PASCAL and PILOT available as software stored on disk. Thus the line between a microcomputer used for data processing and a minicomputer is becoming very blurred indeed and it is probably best for any would-be buyer to ignore the difference and concentrate entirely on the objectives which he wishes the system to achieve within a given budget.

11.8 Sources of help

Microcomputing is progressing at such a rate that the only means of keeping up-to-date is through journals and personal contact. The following short list of journals and contacts may be of help.

Journals

Electronics Weekly
Creative Computing
Personal Computing
Personal Computer World
Practical Computing
Computing Today

Organisations

Electrical Research Association
Cleeve Road, Leatherhead, Surrey KT22 7SA

National Computing Centre
Oxford Road, Manchester M1 7ED

PA Management Consultants
Bowater House East, 68 Knightsbridge, London SW1X 7LJ

PACTEL (associate company of PA Management Consultants)
(Address as above)

Department of Industry (Electronic Applications Division)
Dean Bradley House, 52 Horseferry Road, London SW1P 2AG

Appendix One
THE BASIC LANGUAGE

A1.1 Introduction

Of the fifty or so computer languages available to users only about six are in widespread use, and of these BASIC is perhaps the simplest to learn and most widely available on all types of computer, including microcomputers.

BASIC is essentially a conversational language, designed for use with terminal systems and by non-specialists. In its original form it was developed under a National Science Foundation grant to the US Navy's Dartmouth College, in order to provide a high-level language for beginners. The name BASIC reputedly means *B*eginners *A*ll-purpose *S*ymbolic *I*nstruction *C*ode, and, as it says, it is intended as a general-purpose language. At the time of its development (mid-1960s), FORTRAN was the major language for scientific work — an efficient language with extensive *fo*rmula *tra*nslation (hence the name) properties, but weak in terms of input and output control. The commercial world was (and still is) using COBOL, which has powerful input/output facilities, is written in words, e.g. SALES MULTIPLIED BY PRICE, but tends to be tedious and in places confusing for a beginner.

Since the early 1970s many new languages have been developed for specific purposes, e.g. RPG for report writing, and as general-purpose languages, e.g. APL and PL/1. However, many of these have been developed to provide almost limitless flexibility, and are not for the beginner, or casual user.

The purpose of including an Appendix on BASIC is to give 'rabbits' an opportunity to understand the concepts of applications programming without hiding the wood within the trees. By the time the reader reaches the end of this Appendix, he should also be able to flow-chart and write some simple programs.

First, it is important to separate systems analysis, design and flow charting from programming — we can only write a program when we know what is wanted, and have expressed it as a set of decisions.

'If income is greater than £x deduct tax at a%.
If income is less than £z deduct tax at b%.
Otherwise, deduct tax at c%.'

If the decisions are wrong, the answers produced by the program will be wrong — but the program itself may be perfect, in that it performs every step in the calculation correctly.

In any systems design there is always a grey area where systems analysts leave the charting to programmers, and it is often in this very detailed flow charting that 'It's the computer' problems often arise, e.g. bills for £0.00 that can only be satisfied by Bank Giro transfers of £0.00!

In developing the concepts of the BASIC language it will be assumed initially that there are no flow-charting difficulties. They will be introduced later.

Stage 2 in getting to grips with a computer language is to realise that the programmer, as well as being himself, has to play the parts of the computer and of the user; answering questions of the type:
- What do I (computer) do with new information from the user? And how do I tell him I'm ready for it?
- How do I (user) tell the computer what I want it to do?
- What do we (computer and user) do if things go wrong?

A1.2   Statements and expressions

As with all languages, BASIC controls the computer through a series of statements: statements that demand information of the user, that respond to decisions, that repeat operations, that produce output.

Unfortunately BASIC statements are not identical on different machines (particularly when it comes to file handling) but the dialect that has been used here has been selected for its generality and programs using only the expressions explained in this chapter should run on most machines.

Relationships

Forming a relationship within the BASIC language through equations is very similar to school algebra and somewhere between 'O' level and 'A' level mathematics should be considered as the minimum acceptable level of numeracy for a potential user of BASIC. Anyone reading this section without difficulty should be able to program — anyone

	Ordinary	BASIC	Reason for difference
Add	+	+	—
Subtract	−	−	—
Multiply	×	*	Letter x is overused
Divide	÷	/	No character on typewriter keyboard
Less than	<	<	—
Greater than	>	>	—
Equal to	=	=	—
Less than or equal to	≤	< =	No single character on keyboard
Greater than or equal to	≥	> =	No single character on keyboard
Not equal to	≠	< >	No single character on keyboard
Raise to the power of		↑ or **	No ordinary character to express this relationship

Figure A1.1

experiencing severe difficulty with this section would be well-advised not to read any further in this chapter (except, perhaps, the final section on cost/benefit).

By and large the expressions available to the BASIC user are the normal arithmetic operators (add, subtract, multiply, etc.), but some of the characters used are slightly special. A comparison is given in Figure A1.1.

Brackets are used in exactly the same way to separate parts of an equation to ensure that calculations are carried out in the correct order. For example

$$A = B/C + D$$

could mean:

$$A = B/(C + D) \qquad (1)$$
$$A = (B/C) + D \qquad (2)$$

Without brackets, BASIC would assume (2), since multiplications and divisions take precedence over addition and subtraction. Exponentiation (raised to the power of . . .) takes precedence over either.

The examples below should illustrate how relationships are formed, using BASIC language statements:

$$Y = A*(X \uparrow X) + (B*X) + C \quad \text{(quadratic equation)} \tag{3}$$

$$C = P*A + (1 - P)*B \quad (P = \text{probability}) \tag{4}$$

Naming variables

A limitation of BASIC in comparison with other languages is that the 'variable names' used are limited. Thus in example (4) above, we have to use C rather than COST — which would be much more meaningful.

There is some freedom to extend 'variable names' by using numbers: C0, C1, C2, C3, etc., as far as C9, but anyone writing in BASIC needs to keep a record of the 'names' used, and what they are used for. There is still, however, a maximum number of variables which BASIC can handle, i.e. $26 \times 10 = 260$.

Arrays

To handle more variables, BASIC allows 'array' or 'matrix' variable names which, in effect, use the same name for a range of variables. Far from being confusing (as it might appear at first sight), the facility is extremely helpful when dealing with (for instance):
1 Sales territories.
2 Batch numbers.
3 Product sales/sales territory.
4 Discount rate/customer type.

Any individual value in an array (or matrix) is called an array (or matrix) element, and is referred to by its position in the array (or matrix). Thus the fourth sales territory is denoted by T(4) and the seventh batch as B(7) and each will have its own value. For the examples just listed, we might have arrays (and matrices) of:
1 Sales territories: T(1), T(2), T(3), . . ., etc.
2 Batches: B(1), B(2), B(3), . . ., etc.
3 Product sales/sales territory: S(P,T)
4 Discount rate/customer type: D(R,C)

which may be used in conjunction with a table such as:

Batch no.	1	2	3	4
No. in batch	2,164	2,165	2,166	2,167

$\left.\begin{array}{l} B(3) = 2,166 \\ B(1) = 2,164 \end{array}\right\}$ Array names and their values

or, by product sales/territory

	Territory					
	1	2	3	4	5	6
Product	Scot	NW	Mid	SW	S	SE
1 Throat lozenges	2,160	2,204	1,963	1,079	567	5,123
2 Cough syrup	284	216	304	297	379	501
3 Nasal spray	513	512	597	601	497	304
4 Linctus	1,076	1,317	1,017	1,539	1,728	2,016
5 Eye drops	216	214	301	504	749	1,026

If we call the matrix S, then cough syrup sold in the Midlands would be S(2,3) = 304. The 1,728 bottles of linctus sold in the Southern area would be element S(4,5).

Within a program, arrays are not normally written in numeric terms, but algebraically, so that the 'subscripts' can take on any value, at the whim of the user. Thus we would find B(N), where N can take any of the range of values 1 to 4 (using the first example); or S(P,T) where P could take values 1 to 5 and T the values 1 to 6. In this way, values for N, P, T, etc., can be either defined or calculated elsewhere in a program and then used to pick out values from the array.

It is difficult to show examples of how this might be done at this point, without using commands which have not yet been explained. As the section progresses, examples of the use of arrays will be introduced to illustrate their application.

To complete this section, let's just list a few possible combinations of equations which use the facilities so far described:

$$A(X,Y) = B(X) * C(Y)$$
$$P = (A1 * P1) + (A2 * P2) + (A3 * P3)$$
$$P = (A(N) * P(N)) + P$$
$$Z = ((A * B) + (C/D1)) \uparrow X(N)$$

'Alpha' variable names

Finally, mention should be made of one other form of variable name. The ones used so far are designed for use with numbers (26.471, etc.), but users often want to use alphabetic characters (customer names for example). To achieve this in a limited way, most BASIC interpreters allow users to put words of up to six characters into an ordinary variable, e.g. B1 = JONES. For longer names a special 'dollar' notation is used, which will usually allow words of up to 72 characters (the length of a terminal line) e.g. A$ = FREDERICK.A. JONES. (Note that spaces between words are not allowed.)

Functions

Many BASIC dialects contain a number of functions that simplify some of the more frequently used calculations. Unfortunately, there is no common list of functions, but those which follow have been found in several different versions, and should be capable of being used with relative freedom.

    SIN(X)   Calculates the sine of X (in radians).
    COS(X) Calculates the cosine of X (in radians).
    TAN(X) Calculates the tangent of X (in radians).
    EXP(X) Calculates e to the power X.
    LOG(X) Calculates the natural logarithm of X.
    ABS(X) Calculates the absolute value, i.e. ignores + or - signs, of X.
    INT(X)   Calculates the integer value of X by ignoring any decimal places.
    SQR(X) Calculates the square root of X.

In all cases, X may be either a single variable or an expression, e.g.

    A = EXP(B)

    X = SQR (B ↑ 2 - 4*A*C)

Again, the use of functions will be expanded through examples.

Input/output

Now that we have dealt with the elements of the BASIC language, we can concentrate on producing programs that will solve problems. The first requirement is to make the computer provide the user with information (which requires a programmer to play the part of the computer), whilst the second is to obtain information from the user.

    These functions are controlled by the statements PRINT and INPUT, respectively. Within a program they will frequently be followed by the variable name of whatever is to be input or output. For example two lines in a program:

```
INPUT A
PRINT A
```

would require the user to input *any* number (27,360, - 24.6, etc.) which would be held in the computer as variable A. The second line prints the value to the user (who, throughout the rest of this section, we will assume is sitting at a terminal). At his terminal, he would see:

```
?  -24.6
-24.6
```

(Note that the characters printed by the computer have been underlined.)

PRINT can also be extended to print complete lines of text in order to let a user know what is required of him, by putting it within quotation marks:

```
PRINT "ENTER PRICE PER POUND"
INPUT A
PRINT "PRICE/POUND = £", A
```

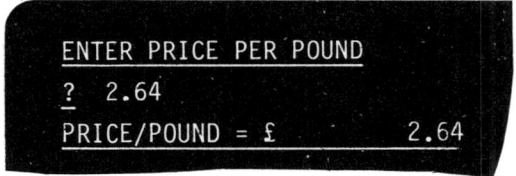

```
ENTER PRICE PER POUND
?  2.64
PRICE/POUND = £         2.64
```

Note that the user only enters the figures — not the "£" sign, which is printed from within the quotes of the PRINT statement. Note also that on the third line of this simple program, the 'Literals' (within quotes) are separated from the name (A) by a comma.

It is essential to separate different parts of a print line by either a comma or a semi-colon. A comma leaves a big gap on the line, a semi-colon closes the gap.

In a similar way several names can be put on an INPUT line by using commas or spaces (*not* semi-colons), and printing can occur in any way the programmer chooses.

```
PRINT "ENTER NO. SOLD, PRICE & DISCOUNT RATE"
INPUT N, P, D
PRINT "PRICE = £"; P; "; NO. SOLD = "; N
```

```
ENTER NO. SOLD, PRICE & DISCOUNT RATE
?  23, 2.64, 5
PRICE = £2.64, NO.SOLD = 23
```

By using a special form of variable name, it is also possible to ask the user to input alphabetic characters. The form of names (as explained above) requires a dollar sign to follow the normal character. For example:

```
PRINT "ENTER CUSTOMER NAME & ACCOUNT NO."
INPUT A$, A
```

```
ENTER CUSTOMER NO. & ACCOUNT NO.
?  F.BLOGGS, 21674
```

The ability to use alphabetic characters is called *string handling*, and many versions of BASIC allow one to manipulate parts of strings, for example by picking out the 'B' of BLOGGS in order to compile an alphabetic list of customers. This facility will be mentioned again later.

Most BASIC's also have a facility which allows users to input their data on the same line as the request. It will have been noticed that the input in the previous examples has always come on the line after the demand, and that the line starts with a computer-generated question mark. (In fact, the INPUT command always generates a question mark, and if a user is being asked a question there is no necessity to insert one in the 'literals'.)

To suppress the line-feed, however, just add a semi-colon after the print statement.

```
PRINT "WHAT IS YOUR NAME";
INPUT A$,B$
PRINT "HELLO"; A$
```

```
WHAT IS YOUR NAME?    JOE BLOGGS
HELLO JOE
```

Unconditional branches

In the introduction, brief mention was made of the need to obey decisions, and the simplest decision is to instruct the computer to go to a different part of the program. The command is GO TO *n*, where *n* is a number representing the line in the program to which control should be transferred. For example:

    GO TO 20
    GO TO 45

In order to do this, the line in question must have a number on it (obviously!) and one could imagine a program which went:

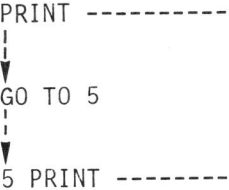

Line numbers

There is, however, a rule in BASIC which has so far been ignored. This says that *every line must have a line number*. So the very first example should read:

    1 INPUT A
    2 PRINT A

The output is not altered:

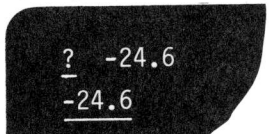

BASIC executes programs in line number order (unless there is a GO TO command), but it does not need the numbers to be consecutive. Thus

    1 INPUT A
    7 PRINT A
    10 INPUT B

would be perfectly acceptable. This freedom is exploited by most programmers who allow space for errors by deliberately omitting certain line numbers, producing a convention in which lines are numbered in tens, for example:

```
10 PRINT "WHAT IS YOUR NAME";
20 INPUT A$
30 PRINT "HELLO"; A$
40 GO TO 70
```

The last line here (40) is the unconditional branch. Unconditional branches are usually only used when the program gets complicated and the programmer has to dig himself out of a hole, or when the user is allowed only a certain range of inputs and fails to choose one of them. In this instance the GO TO command would be used to make him choose again (as shown in a later example).

Conditional branches

A much more widely used form of branch is the conditional branch which operates only if certain conditions are fulfilled. For example, if a particular credit code is located, the program may branch to another part of the program (in order to print a demand, say):

```
70   PRINT "ENTER CREDIT CODE";
80   INPUT C
90   IF C = -1 GO TO 200
100  ----
```

Line 90 represents the conditional branch, which always takes one of the following forms:

IF (relationship) GO TO (line number)

IF (relationship) THEN (line number)

One of the strengths of the language is that the 'relationship' can take many different forms, from simple comparisons (as above) to complex equations. Some examples should help to illustrate the range:

```
30  IF X = 2     THEN 180
70  IF Z < 5     THEN 190
200 IF A >= 6    THEN 250
65  IF C>A*B     THEN 42
90  IF D<3*(A/B + C) THEN 80
```

The relationship can even include a string of letters, e.g.

```
75  IF X$ = "YES" GO TO 400
```

This form is particularly useful if 'X$' is the answer to a direct question which the computer, i.e. the program, poses to a user, e.g.

```
200 PRINT "IS EMPLOYEE MARRIED";
210 INPUT A$
220 IF A$ = "YES" GO TO 1000
230 IF A$ = "Y" GO TO 1000
240 IF A$ = "NO" GO TO 2000
250 IF A$ = "N" GO TO 2000
260 IF A$ = "HELP" GO TO 5000
270 PRINT "PLEASE ANSWER 'YES' OR 'NO'"
280 PRINT "IF YOU NEED ASSISTANCE, TYPE 'HELP'"
290 GO TO 210
300
```

To the user this part-program might appear as:

```
IS EMPLOYEE MARRIED?    DON'T KNOW
PLEASE ANSWER 'YES' OR 'NO'
IF YOU NEED ASSISTANCE, TYPE 'HELP'? YES
```

What has happened is that the computer has compared the user's answer of 'DON'T KNOW' with 'YES', and found that it does not match. The next check (and that on line 250) allows the user to take a short cut by putting in only the first letter of the correct answer, but again there is no match, and the branch to line 1000 does not occur. Similarly there is no branch to line 2000 — or line 5000.

The program, therefore, continues at line 270 by printing a message which gives all the acceptable alternatives — YES, NO and HELP. The GO TO statement on line 290 is a useful way of making a user go round the same loop again and again until he gets it right, and here it transfers control to the INPUT statement on line 210.

It is a little unfortunate that the statement automatically prints a "?"; which makes the printed line "IF YOU NEED ASSISTANCE, TYPE HELP?" look strange. (The semi-colon on line 280 puts the "?" on the same line of print, as explained earlier.)

The user's new answer 'YES' is valid, and control is immediately transferred to line 1000. Other places where the facility is of considerable value include:
1   In selecting a name, for example, when finding the sales of a particular salesman.
2   For restricting access to part of a program, when the user cannot give a particular 'password'.

Loops

Computing started because people wanted the same calculation repeated for different values of one or more of the variables, in order to find maximum or minimum values, or just to plot a complex graph. For example, if we wish to calculate and plot a graph of the thickness of a coat of paint (T) depending on the area it is spread over (A), we simply need to perform the equations $T = V/A$ (V is, of course, the volume of paint) for many values of A. The command that allows us to do this most easily consists of two parts, as shown in the sample program below:

```
10 PRINT "WHAT VOLUME OF PAINT IS TO BE USED (LITRES)";
20 INPUT V

30 FOR A = 1 TO 5            ⎤
40 T = V/A                   ⎥  LOOP
50 PRINT A; "T = "; T; "MM"  ⎥  FORMED
60 NEXT A                    ⎦
```

which would appear at the terminal as:

```
WHAT VOLUME OF PAINT IS TO BE USED (LITRES)?    5
1    T =    5.0000 MM
2    T =    2.5000 MM
3    T =    1.6666 MM
4    T =    1.2500 MM
5    T =    1.0000 MM
```

The LOOP command comprises a FOR... statement at the beginning and a NEXT... statement at the end. The program goes round the loop as often as is necessary to make the named variable reach its maximum value. (In the trivial example we have just done, the loop is repeated five times for A = 1, A = 2, A = 3, A = 4 and A = 5.)

The command is much more powerful than this, however, since the start and finish values can themselves be variable, and the increment need not be 1, e.g.

```
FOR I = A TO B STEP C
NEXT I
```

means that the first value of I is A (which must have been defined or calculated earlier in the program), the last value is B (similarly defined or calculated) and the step-size is C (likewise).

The easiest way to illustrate its use is by an example. Imagine a situation where a production manager wishes to assess the effect on the cost of an item if one of the bought-out parts increases in price. In the program, the following representations have been used:

A for INITIAL COST OF PRODUCT
B for COST OF ONE COMPONENT
C for COST OF ONE COMPONENT
D for COST OF COMPONENT UNDER REVIEW
F for COST (AFTER INCREASE IN D) OF PRODUCT
G for % INCREASE IN COST OF PRODUCT

Quite arbitrarily it has been assumed that there is program before this calculation, which has resulted in this sequence starting at line 500.

Note that values for A, B, C and D have to be given to the computer before the main calculation can be performed. There are many ways of doing this — for the moment we will assume that they have to be input each time by the user.

Note also that F and G have been introduced as the results of the calculation. If the INITIAL COST variable (A) had been used, its value would have been destroyed at line 580 and it would then have been impossible to calculate the following line.

```
500 PRINT "ENTER INITIAL VALUES FOR THE COST OF EACH COMPONENT"
510 INPUT B, C, D
520 PRINT "WHAT ARE MIN. & MAX. % CHANGES";
530 INPUT L, M
540 PRINT "WHAT INCREMENTAL CHANGE";
550 INPUT N
560 A = B + C + D
570 FOR P = L TO M STEP N
580 F = B + C + D*(1 + P/100)
590 G = (F/A - 1)*100
600 PRINT P, F, G
610 NEXT P
```

```
ENTER INITIAL VALUES FOR THE COST OF EACH COMPONENT
? 5, 7, 13
WHAT ARE MIN. & MAX. % CHANGES? 1, 5
WHAT INCREMENTAL CHANGE? 0.5
 1             25.13           0.52
 1.5           25.195          0.78
 2             25.26           1.04
 2.5           25.325          1.3
 3             25.39           1.56
 3.5           25.455          1.82
 4             25.52           2.08
 4.5           25.585          2.34
 5             25.65           2.6
```

Decisions based on, for example, increases of more than 2 per cent in finished product costs can therefore directly, and easily, be related to bought-out part costs using a very short 'loop' program. By changing the range (M and L in the program) or the increment (N) the calculation may be made more or less specific at will. It requires very little extra programming to change the values of the other bought-out parts, and test their effect on the total costs. In fact, by 'nesting' loops (one within another) it is possible to produce a table which shows the effect on total cost of incremental changes in each bought-out part in turn. For example:

> Increasing D from between 1% & 5% for B and C + 1%
> Increasing D from between 1% & 5% for B and C + 1.5%
> Increasing D from between 1% & 5% for B and C + 2%
> etc.
> Increasing D from between 1% & 5% for B + 1% and C
> Increasing D from between 1% & 5% for B + 1.5% and C
> etc., etc.

With 10 different values of B, C and D, the program would produce a table of 1,000 elements.

For 100 different values, e.g. increments of 0.1 per cent between 0 and 10 per cent, the table would contain 1,000,000 values.

The program below is all that is needed:

```
500 PRINT "ENTER INITIAL VALUES FOR THE COST OF EACH COMPONENT"
510 INPUT B, C, D
520 PRINT "WHAT ARE MIN. & MAX. % CHANGES & INCREMENT";
530 INPUT L, M, N
540 A = B + C + D
550 FOR R = L TO M STEP N
560 FOR Q = L TO M STEP N
570 FOR P = L TO M STEP N
580 F = B*(1 + R/100) + C*(1 + Q/100) + D*(1 + P/100)
590 G = (F/A - 1)*100
600 PRINT R; Q; P; F; G
610 NEXT P
620 NEXT Q
630 NEXT R
```

The points to note in the coding we have just shown are:

1 The loops are 'nested' — if a line were drawn down the left-hand margin joining each FOR to its respective NEXT, the lines would not

cross. By way of contrast, the loops shown below are *not* legal, because of the 'cross' at line 260.

```
200 FOR I = 1 TO 10
210 FOR J = 1 TO 5
230 A = B + C/D
240 FOR K = 1 TO 3
250 X = A*3.14/S
260 NEXT J
270 NEXT K
280 NEXT I
```

2 Line 580 (the calculation) will be completed for the full range of values of P whilst Q and R retain their original value. When the range is complete, Q will be incremented by the first step (N), and again the calculations will be performed for the full range of P; when Q will go to its second-value. Only when Q has gone through all its values from L to M will R increment — when the whole process starts again. Thus 14 lines of program can easily produce a table 1,000,000 lines long!

3 A combination of commas and semi-colons have been used on line 600 to spread out the values on the page. Clearly, nobody is going to sit and watch 1,000,000 lines of paper pass before his eyes and we would introduce cut-off points for the print line using conditional branches (IF. . . THEN. . .).

For instance, we might only wish to print values IF the percentage increase in total cost is greater than 5 per cent. A GO TO statement could then be used to jump to the end of the loop, since all higher values within the loop would give even larger percentage increases.

The following lines, added at the appropriate place in the program would do the job adequately, but will still leave some redundant data:

```
544 PRINT "ENTER LIMITING VALUES OF % INCREASE";
546 INPUT H
595 IF G<H GO TO 610
605 GO TO 620
```

If the calculations used in this example seem trivial, remember that B, C and D may themselves be the result of a complex of equations, and that A might only be a sub-assembly.

Data statements

So far it has been assumed that all data used by a program has been input by the user via his terminal. In nearly every application, however, up to 90 per cent of data is essentially fixed, and it only wastes the user's time to input it. With some applications, particularly commercial ones, all data will have been prepared in advance and have been stored on data files. In the latter case, file-handling routines, specific to the computer's operating system, will be used and because every one is different, file handling will not be discussed in any great detail in this Appendix.

In the former case, two statements READ and DATA are used to input fixed data to the program. The READ statement has the same format, and effect, as INPUT except that the program looks, not to the user, for data, but to the data statement:

```
210 READ A, B, C, D
220 DATA 210, 3.6, -4.2, 11
```

would result in

```
A = 210, B = 3.6, C = -4.2, D = 11
```

As an example let us take the case of three products, being sold at £5, £10 and £15 by 5 salesmen. We need simple totals for the value earned by each salesman.

Note that, by convention, data statements come at the end of the program:

```
10   PRINT "PROGRAM TO CALCULATE TOTAL SALES VALUE"
20   FOR I = 1 TO 3
30   READ P(I)
40   NEXT I
50   FOR I = 1 TO 3
60   FOR J = 1 TO 5
70   READ S(I,J)
80   NEXT J
90   NEXT I
100  FOR J = 1 TO 5
110  S = 0
120  FOR I = 1 TO 3
130  S = S + (P(I)*S(I,J))
```

```
140 NEXT I
150 PRINT "TOTAL SALES FOR SALESMAN"; J; "=£"; S
160 NEXT J
170 DATA 5, 10, 15
180 DATA 25, 50, 75, 100, 50, 64, 70, 62, 80
190 DATA 77, 206, 194, 203, 301, 253
200 END
```

```
PROGRAM TO CALCULATE TOTAL SALES VALUE
TOTAL SALES FOR SALESMAN 1 = £3855
TOTAL SALES FOR SALESMAN 2 = £3860
TOTAL SALES FOR SALESMAN 3
```

(All the printing comes from the computer, so underlinings have been omitted.)

The program first uses an array and a loop to obtain prices from the DATA statement in line 170. Then nested FOR-NEXT loops read the number of items sold from DATA statements in lines 180 and 190.

To obtain a total, a new variable 'S' is used, which is first set to zero, then has individual sales values added to it. In terms of school mathematics the equation $S = S + X$ is absurd, but if we remember that, in computer terms, the letter S denotes the name of a variable, which is being made successively larger, the statement makes sense.

The program finally prints total sales for each salesman.

Subroutines

Within some programs it is possible to identify separate 'modules' which can be calculated separately from the main program, but which need to be executed before the program can proceed past a particular point. Such modules are called subroutines. As will be seen in Section A1.3., programs should be split into subroutines wherever possible. It facilitates changes and reduces fault-finding problems.

To transfer control to a module, the command GOSUB is used, and to return control to the program, the command RETURN.

The program that follows uses a single subroutine to calculate 'present worth' in a discounted cash flow analysis. Line 260 transfers control to the subroutine which starts at line 650. The RETURN on line 700 transfers control back to the main program *which continues at Line 270.* Control is again transferred to the subroutine at lines 400 and 540.

The program actually calculates the DCF rate of return (and prints the solution at line 510) for a maximum of 10 periods (A). There are ways of increasing the maximum number of values which the array (A) can hold, but since these have not yet been discussed, this example only deals with a limited number of periods.

Note how lines 520 and 220 automatically allow the user to repeat his calculations, but if his first cash flow value is "END", the program stops.

```
100   PRINT "PROGRAM TO FIND DCF RATE OF RETURN OF";
110   PRINT "CASH FLOW SERIES."
120   PRINT "UP TO 10 CASH FLOWS MAY BE USED"
130   PRINT "------------------"
140   PRINT
150   PRINT "CASH FLOWS, IN AS +, OUT AS -"
160   FOR I = 1 TO 10
170   INPUT A(I)
180   IF A(I) = "END" THEN 220
190   NEXT I
200   PRINT "ONLY 10 CASH FLOWS ALLOWED"
210   GO TO 150
220   IF I = 1 THEN 640
230   I = I - 1
240   PRINT I; "VALUES INPUT"
250   R = 0
260   GOSUB 650
270   A = R
280   F1 = S
290   IF S<0 THEN 320
300   I1 = 10
310   GO TO 330
320   I1 = -10
330   R = A + I1
```

```
340   IF R>-90 THEN 370
350   PRINT "RATE LESS THAN -90%'
360   GO TO 150
370   IF R<1000 THEN 400
380   PRINT "RATE GREATER THAN 1000%"
390   GO TO 150
400   GOSUB 650
410   B = R
420   F2 = S
430   IF S<>0 THEN 460
440   A = B
450   GO TO 510
460   IF F1*F2<0 THEN 500
470   A = B
480   F1 = F2
490   GO TO 330
500   IF ABS(B - A)>0.0001 THEN 530
510   PRINT "DCF RATE OF RETURN -"; A
520   GO TO 150
530   R = (A + B)/2
540   GOSUB 650
550   C = R
560   F3 = S
570   IF F1*F3>0 THEN 610
580   B = C
590   F2 = F3
600   GO TO 500
610   A = C
620   F1 = F3
630   GO TO 500
640   END
650   S = 0
660   R1 = 1 + R/100
```

```
670  FOR J = 1 TO I
680  S = S = A(J)/R1↑(J-1)
690  NEXT J
700  RETURN
```

```
CASH FLOWS, IN AS +, OUT AS -
? -1000, 500, 400, 1200, "END"
5 VALUES INPUT
DCF RATE OF RETURN -56.2330
CASH FLOWS, IN AS +, OUT AS -
? -1546, 560, 490, 300, 700, 200, "END"
6 VALUES INPUT
DCF RATE OF RETURN -15.2472
CASH FLOWS, IN AS +, OUT AS -
? "END"
```

(This time the USER'S responses have been underlined.)

A1.3 Designing simple programs

The commands and functions in Section A1.2 will allow users to carry out a wide range of programming jobs. Section A1.4 will outline some of the more advanced features which are also widely available.

It is of little value being able to write a program unless it produces the right answers, and the object of this section is to outline one method of designing simple programs. Since it is written for users, it will not be exploring any of the more sophisticated methods of producing efficient programs. It will not even consider program efficiency since the user's time is generally much more valuable than computer time, and core space is unlikely to be a problem.

For a user designing programs for his own purposes, it is also not helpful to use any of the database techniques which, in emphasising data integrity, can restrict the programming method. Such techniques will, of course, be known to, and used by, professional programmers.

Elsewhere, mention is made of the need to produce 'secure interfaces', meaning that programs should be written to be capable of dealing with absurd data. Again such interfacing is not necessary for users writing their own programs — they will soon discover that the data they are using is inconsistent.

Experience has shown that a pragmatic approach to programming is as cost-effective as any, particularly where the 'programmer' is highly paid. Wherever possible, such programs should be written without flow-charts or other planning aids. In many cases it may be possible to produce a program without recording the variable names used.

The only check which is always necessary is that a calculation be done manually, against which the program result is compared. Only in this way will a user discover if he has made an error.

If some preparation is needed, then the following seven-step plan is suggested as a routine which will reduce the potential for error, and increase the speed with which a program can be brought to working efficiency:

1 Split the task into self-contained modules.
2 Treat each module separately.
3 Draft the equations and the logic of each step.
4 Produce an outline flow-chart.
5 Prepare some data and calculate the module manually, making a note of any problems that arise. Check the logic and equations — if necessary create more 'sub-modules'.
6 Write the program, noting the name used for each variable.
7 Run the program, check that the answers agree with the correct ones! Repair as necessary!

Step 1

The concept that every task consists of a system of sub-tasks has been extensively developed by computer specialists, by production specialists, by systems engineers, etc., and it seems reasonable to use their work in a simple way to produce simple programs.

For example, in one company, an accountant wanted to forecast his firm's expenses for the coming year. He was concerned about the effects of staff numbers, inflation, average number of miles travelled in company cars, nights away and average cost of hotels, estimates in increases in public transport costs, time spent overseas and currency exchange rates, etc. One way of showing his needs as a system would be as shown in Figure A1.2.

Step 2

Each element in the system can be treated separately, with provision for changing the inputs specific to that module.

For the purpose of this section, let us take CAR COSTS and follow the steps needed to prepare this module, which will then become a

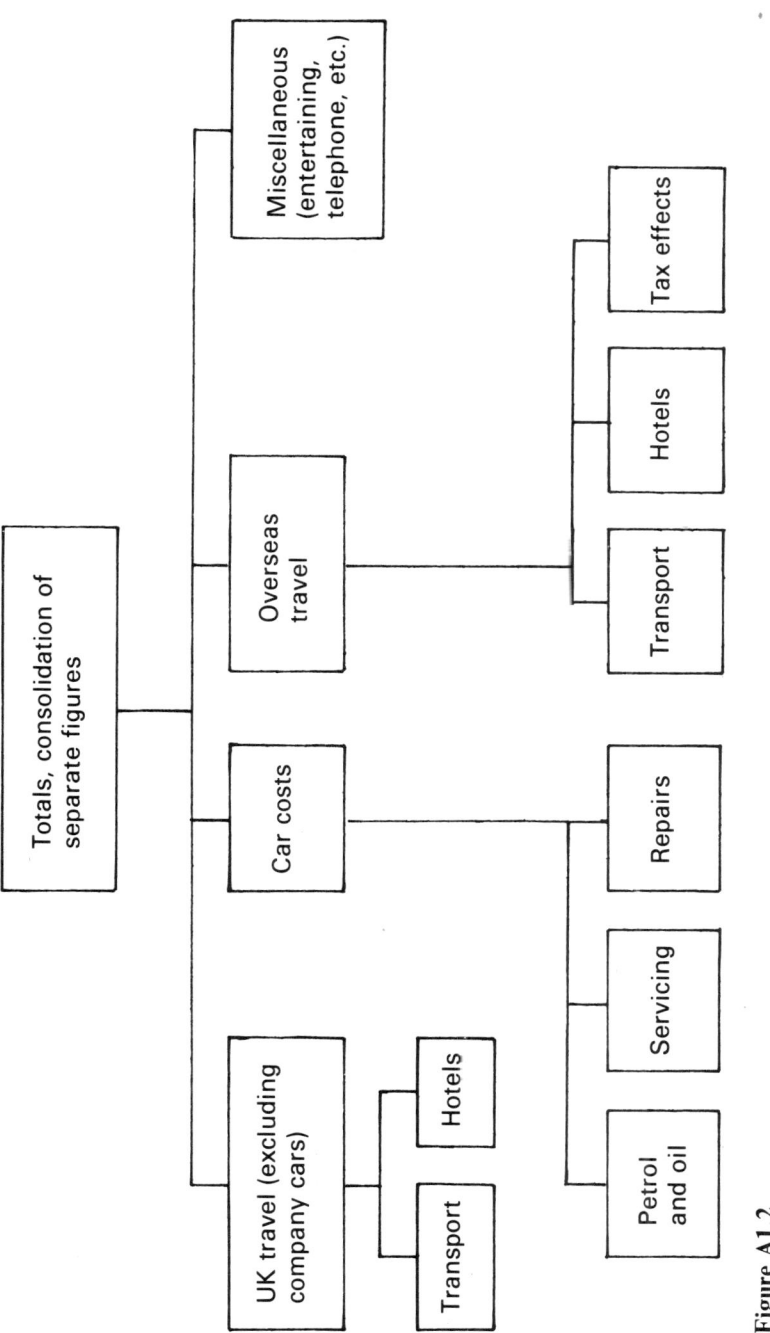

Figure A1.2

subroutine in the final program. Because CAR COSTS itself comprises three parts, there is a possibility that the subroutine will itself call other subroutines.

Step 3

1 Petrol and oil The information needed to perform petrol and oil cost calculations is:

Cost/gallon of petrol	C1
Cost/gallon of oil	C2
Average mileage/employee	G1
Average miles/gallon (petrol)	M1
Average miles/pint (oil)	M2
Number of employees	E

Some variables are relatively static and could be read from data, e.g. M1 and M2. The others are likely to form part of the accountant's analysis: C1, C2, E, G1. However, it is also likely that he would prefer to input changes in percentage terms over last year's actual figures. Hence C1, C2, E and G1 can also be read from data. Other variables, say P1, P2, P3 and P4, will be used to represent the percentage increase. The equations are therefore:

$$T1 = G1*(1+P4/100)*E*(1+P3/100)*C1*(P1/100+1)/M1$$
$$T2 = G1*(1+P4/100)*E*(1+P3/100)*C2*(1+P2/100)/(M2*8)$$

2 Servicing Use last year's figures for cost of servicing (C3) and allow for inflation. If the average mileage is less than 25,000 miles per annum, then assume one service every 6,000 miles. If the average mileage is more than 25,000 miles per annum, then assume one service every 5,000 miles. The equations are:

$$T3 = G1*(1+P4/100)*E*(1+P3/100)*C3*(1+I1/100)/K1$$
$$K1 = 6000 \text{ IF } G1*(1+P4/100) < \text{ OR } = 25000$$
$$K1 = 5000 \text{ IF } G1*(1+P4/100) > 25000$$

3 Repairs Use last year's figures for average cost of repairs person (C4) and allow for inflation. Add a further 10 per cent if the average mileage/person is greater than 20,000. The equations are:

$$T4 = E*(1+P3/100)*C4*(1+I1/100)*K2$$
$$K2 = 1 \text{ IF } G1*(1+P4/100) < \text{ OR } = 20000$$
$$K2 = 1.1 \text{ IF } G1*(1+P4/100) > 20000$$

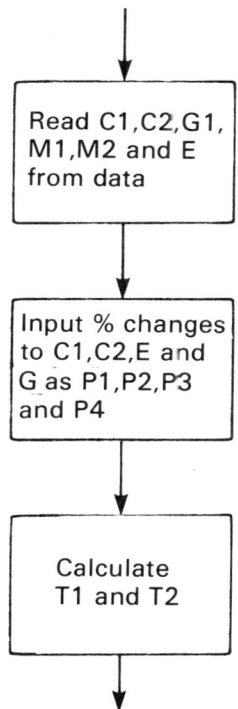

Figure A1.3 *Petrol and oil*

Step 4

Flow-charts are used to illustrate the logic of a task, and are probably best demonstrated by example (see Figures A1.3 — A1.6). Only two symbols need be remembered.
1   A square, which is used to show a calculation.
2   A diamond, which is used to show a conditional branch.

Obviously, flow-charts can get much more complicated, and even professional programmers are divided about their value in really complex logical relationships, preferring to rely on their own expertise, or other techniques. For user-programmers, they are still extremely useful.

Step 5

The next step is to check the flow-charted logic and equations using real figures.

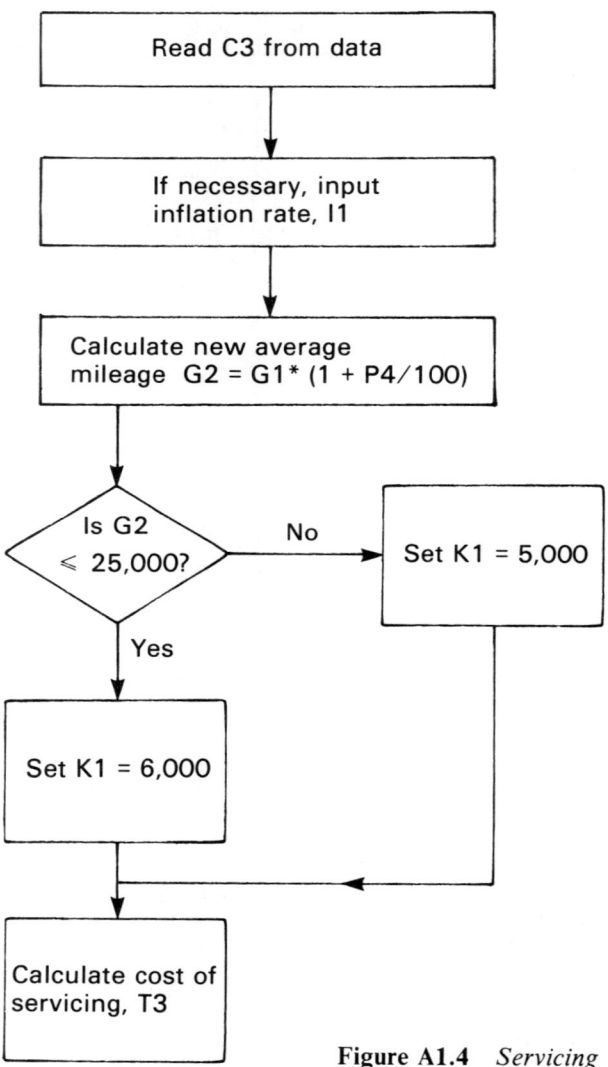

Figure A1.4 *Servicing*

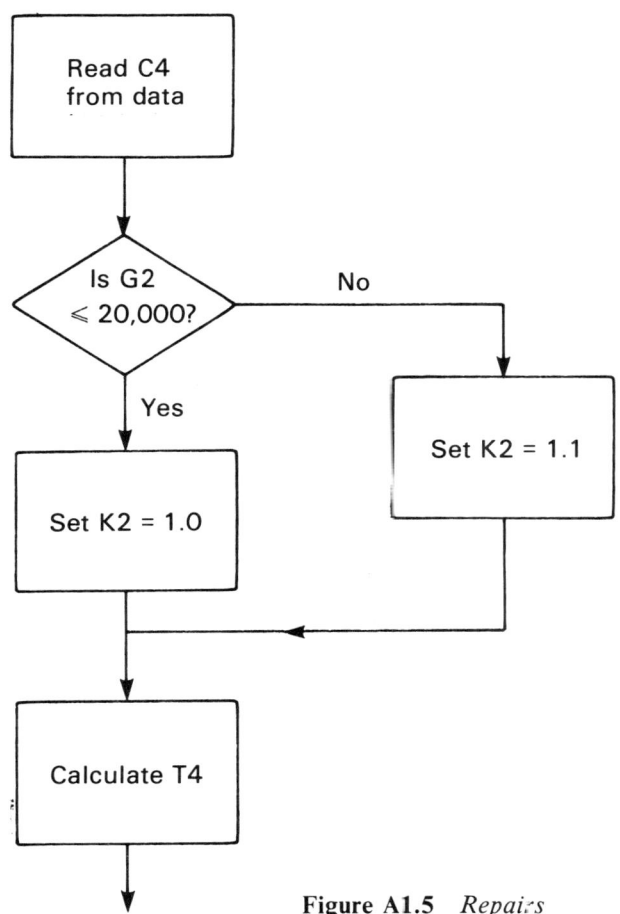

Figure A1.5 *Repairs*

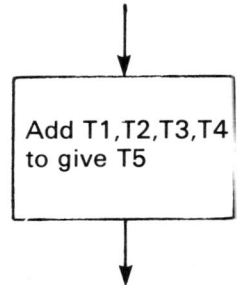

Figure A1.6 *Car costs*

(a) *Petrol and oil*

C1	= 0.8		P1	= 10
C2	= 4.0		P2	= 10
G1	= 22,000		P3	= -10
M1	= 30		P4	= 0
M2	= 2,000		E	= 120

Then, by calculation,

$T1 = 69{,}696.0$ and $T2 = 1{,}306.8$

(b) *Servicing*

$C3 = 35 \qquad I1 = 10$

Then, by calculation, $G2 = 22{,}000$ and therefore $K1 = 6{,}000$, so

$T3 = 15{,}246.0$

(c) *Repairs*

$C4 = 127$

Then, by calculation, $G2 = 22{,}000$ and therefore $K2 = 1.1$, so

$T4 = 16{,}596.36$

(d) *Car costs*

By calculation

$T5 = 102{,}845.16$

Step 6

As one would expect, no unforeseen problems arose whilst calculating car costs manually, and it is now possible to prepare a program from the flow-charts and equations given above:

```
1000   PRINT "- - - - - - - - - - - - - - "
1010   READ C1, C2, G1, M1, M2, E
1020   PRINT "ENTER % CHANGES FOR PETROL COSTS, OIL COSTS"
1030   PRINT "NO. OF EMPLOYEES & MILES TRAVELLED"
```

```
1040  INPUT P1, P2, P3, P4
1050  G2 = G1*(1+P4/100)
1060  T1 = G2*E*(1+P3/100)*C1*(1+P1/100)/M1
1070  T2 = G2*E*(1+P3/100)*C2*(1+P2/100)/(M2*8)
1080  READ C3
1090  PRINT "WHAT INFLATION RATE (P.A.)";
1100  INPUT I1
1110  IF G2<25000 GO TO 1140
1120  K1 = 5000
1130  GO TO 1150
1140  K1 = 6000
1150  T3 = G2*E*(1+P3/100)*C3*(1+I1)/K1
1160  READ C4
1170  IF G2<=20000 THEN 1200
1180  K2 = 1.1
1190  GO TO 1210
1200  K2 = 1.0
1210  T4 = E*(1+P3/100)*C4*(1+I1/100)*K2
1220  T5 = T1+T2+T3+T4
1230  PRINT "CAR COSTS", "P", "O", "S", "R"
1240  PRINT T5, T1; T2; T3; T4
1250  DATA 0.8, 4.0, 22000, 30, 2000, 120
1260  DATA 35
1270  DATA 127
1280  END
```

Step 7

For this step one needs a computer. The following printout has been copied from a terminal, though the layout has been stylised in the transfer to the printed page (specifically the PRINT lines at 230 and 240 do not lie as accurately as shown here). In this illustration it is the *user's* activity which has been underlined.

```
ENTER % CHANGES FOR PETROL COSTS, OIL COSTS
NUMBER OF EMPLOYEES AND MILES TRAVELLED
? 10, 10, -10, 0
WHAT INFLATION RATE (P.A.)? 10
CAR COSTS    P         O        S          R
102845.16   69696.0   1306.8   15246.0   16596.36


HALT AT 1280
```

The module is ready for use or incorporation in the rest of the program, as a subroutine, which is why its line numbers were started at line 1000. As a subroutine line 1280 would need to read

    1280 RETURN

We can imagine that the main program might read:

```
  ⋮
 60  ----------
 70  GOSUB 1000
 80  GOSUB 2000     (for overseas travel)
  ⋮
```

A1.4 Further BASIC commands

Section A1.2 outlined the major BASIC expressions and commands. There are many others, some specific to particular computers, others more general in nature. Listed here are some of the more common ones, in alphabetical order, with an explanation of their use.

DIM

Earlier, in Section A1.2, the number of cash-flow periods in a DCF calculation was arbitrarily limited to 10. The reason was that BASIC normally allows up to 10 values for an array variable, but does not reserve space for addition values.

The DIM statement, placed at the beginning of the program, creates space for however many values are required, e.g. DIM A(20) will create space for 20 values in array A, and DIM B(10,30) will create a 10 × 30 matrix, named B.

In order for the DCF calculation to be extended over the normal number of pay-back periods, a line would be needed before line 100,

```
90  DIM A(50)
```

and line 160 would be changed to

```
160  FOR I = 1 TO 50
```

PRINTUSING

Several programmes have already been written in which column headings have been printed, with successive values beneath them. Section A1.3 showed the output from a program which printed

```
CAR COSTS     P     0     S     R
```

as headings, followed by numerical values and it was mentioned that the layout at the terminal would not have been as neat as appeared on the printed page. The reason is that the normal separators ";" and "," leave a specific number of blanks between the end of one variable and the beginning of the next. Thus long numbers will displace the rest of the line to the right and numbers will not always lie below their headings.

The PRINTUSING statement allows neat report formats. It consists of two parts, a PRINTUSING command in place of the normal PRINT command, and a second line (usually placed at the end of a program) which sets the layout. The layout line to be used at any one time is shown in the PRINTUSING statement. Thus:

```
100  PRINTUSING 1000, A, B
```

would use line 1000 as a 'model' for printing values A and B.

Although some BASIC interpreters allow users to put all sorts of variable names in PRINTUSING statements, it is normally safer to create a simple variable first and print that, e.g.

```
210  PRINTUSING 999, A(I), B(I,J), C
```

uses line 999 as the layout (or format) and prints whatever values of the arrays A and B are appropriate for the values of I and J existing at the time, e.g.

```
200   FOR I = 1 TO N STEP 0.5
210   FOR J = X TO Y STEP Z
230   PRINTUSING 999, A(I), B(I,J), Z
240   NEXT J
250   NEXT I
```

Line 999 has a special format, and is identified as such by putting a colon (:) immediately after the line number, i.e. 999:. What follows on the line is printed at the terminal EXACTLY as it is formatted. Thus the car costs example in the previous section:

```
1230   PRINT "CAR COSTS", "P", "O", "S", "R"
```

could be replaced by the two lines

```
1230   PRINTUSING 1500
1500:  CAR COSTS         P        O        S        R
```

When the program is run, the terminal would receive line 1500 from the first character after the colon(:).

Another special character (#) is used if the *values* of variables [A(1), etc.] are to be printed. The character is placed on the line where the value is required, and as many characters as are needed for the value are used. For example to print A where A has the value 237.17, the combination below could be used:

```
300   PRINTUSING 500, A
500:  - - - - - - A = ###.## - - - - -
```

(the "-" is intended to denote a blank). At the terminal would appear

The # character specifies where the variable is to be printed, and how many places it is allowed. Thus, for the above example:

```
500:A = ###.#
```

(only one place after the decimal point, and no spaces after the colon) would produce:

```
A = 237.1
```

If too few spaces are allowed before the decimal point, the system will normally print an asterisk (*) to show that it cannot fit a sensible answer into the space provided.

    500: A = ##.##   (for A = 237.17)

```
A = *
```

The example in the previous section could therefore be modified to produce a neat report as follows:

```
1230  PRINTUSING 1500
1240  PRINTUSING 1510, T5, T1, T2, T3, T4

1500: CAR COSTS        P          O        S         R
1510:   #######.##   #####.##  #####.##  #####.##  #####.##
```

The output would then be:

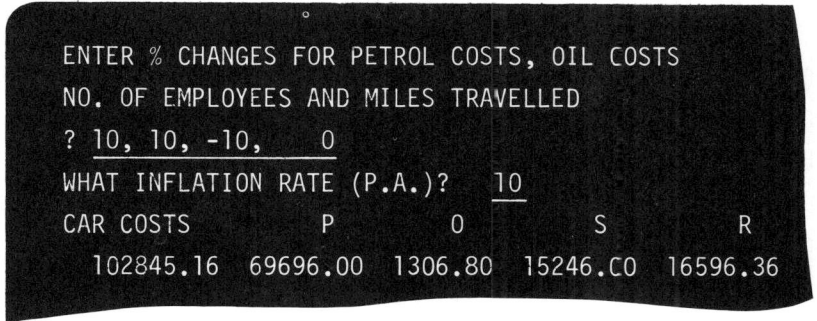

```
ENTER % CHANGES FOR PETROL COSTS, OIL COSTS
NO. OF EMPLOYEES AND MILES TRAVELLED
? 10, 10, -10,   0
WHAT INFLATION RATE (P.A.)?   10
CAR COSTS        P          O          S         R
   102845.16  69696.00   1306.80   15246.C0  16596.36
```

Note that the decimal point comes precisely under the letters, as set in lines 1500 and 1510.

REM

Programs that are to be stored should have within them some indication of what they are for and should contain an explanation of each new module. Thus the program developed in Section A1.3 has three modules, and it would be helpful to others looking at the program to show where and what they are.

The REM command allows REMARKS to be inserted, without affecting the program in any way. Thus useful additions to the program might be:

```
1003    REM THIS PROGRAM CALCULATES CAR COSTS
1006    REM PETROL & OIL COSTS ARE CALCULATED FIRST
1008    REM C1 = PETROL/GALL, C2 = OIL/GALL, G1 = MILES P.A.
1009    REM M1 = M.P.G., M2 = OIL MILES/PINT, E = EMPLOYEES
1075    REM SERVICING COST (C3 = LAST YEAR'S AVERAGE)
1155    REM REPAIRS (C4 = LAST YEAR'S AVERAGE)
1290    REM FOR MORE INFO. ABOUT OTHER PROGRAMS IN
1300    REM THE SUITE, CONTACT J. BLOGGS (X2716)
```

Sample program

The commands described in Section A1.2 were illustrated by the program of Section A1.3. The following program uses all of those commands and illustrates the use of the additional commands described in this section.

```
10     REM THIS PROGRAM CALCULATES THE FUNDAMENTAL FREQUENCY
20     REM OF A CIRCULAR CLAMPED SLAB OF METAL DENSITY = D;
30     REM POISSONS RATIO = P; YOUNGS MODULUS = Y*10↑11
40     DIM R(19), F(19)
50     PRINTUSING 1000
60     PRINTUSING 1010
70     PRINT
80     READ D, P, Y
90     PRINT "ENTER THICKNESS OF SLAB IN CM.";
100    INPUT T
110    IF T = "END" GO TO 240
120    GOSUB 250
130    REM FORMAT AND OUTPUT
```

```
140  PRINT
150  PRINTUSING 1020
160  PRINTUSING 1030
170  FOR I = 1 TO 19
180  PRINTUSING 1040, R(I), F(I)
190  NEXT I
200  PRINT
210  PRINTUSING 1020
220  PRINT
230  GO TO 90
240  END
250  REM SUBROUTINE CALCULATES FUND. FREQ. FOR RANGE OF
260  REM RADII FROM 1 TO 10 IN STEPS OF 1, AND FROM
270  REM 10 TO 100 IN STEPS OF 10
280  N = 1
290  FOR X = 1 TO 100 STEP N
300  IF X<10 THEN 320
310  N = 10
320  R(X) = X
330  F1 = (0.467*T/X↑2)
340  F2 = SQR(Y*(10↑11)/(D*(1-P↑2)))
350  F(X) = F1*F2
360  NEXT X
370  RETURN
1000:            FUNDAMENTAL FREQUENCIES
1010:            ----------  ----------
1020: ****************************************
1030:            RADIUS     FUND.FREQ.
1040:
```

This would produce (user's response underlined) the output depicted overleaf.

```
         FUNDAMENTAL FREQUENCIES
         ----------- -----------

ENTER THICKNESS OF SLAB IN CM.?   0.703
****************************
              RADIUS       FUND. FREQ.
                1          174269.0000
                2           43567.2000
                3           19363.2000
                4           10891.8000
                5            6970.7500
                6            4840.8000
                7            3556.5000
                8            2722.9500
                9            2151.4600
               10            1742.6900
               20             435.6720
               30             193.632
               40             108.918
```

A1.5 Test facilities

BASIC can be implemented in two forms, a 'compiler' version and an 'interpreter' version (see Chapter 6 for an explanation of the terms). Compiler BASIC's have to be tested in the same way as other high-level languages such as FORTRAN and COBOL. However, BASIC was conceived as an interpreter language, and for the purposes of this section it will be assumed that a user has access to such a BASIC.

The first point to note is that by using an interpreter it is impossible to write a line of BASIC that violates the language's syntax. Any mistakes will be identified by the interpreter and a diagnostic message printed. Sometimes the message will not be too helpful in identifying the mistake and the user has to examine the line in detail to locate it. For example, in the sample program given at the end of the previous section, the user might have written

```
340  F2 = SQR(Y*(10↑11)/(D*(1-P↑2)
```

which might have generated a message such as

```
340  BAD FORMULA
```

Close examination of the line shows that a closing bracket ")" has been omitted. Other messages may be much more explicit:

```
375  FOR WITHOUT NEXT
```

indicates that a FOR loop has been opened, but not closed.

After a program is syntactically correct, comes the moment of truth when it is run. The first errors to come to light will be logical errors which prevent the program from completing — typically the program contains a GO TO which creates a loop with no escape:

```
10  INPUT X
20  Y = X↑2
30  PRINT Y
40  GO TO 10
50  END
```

Or, more expensive if the computer is not stopped quickly,

```
10  INPUT X
20  Y = X↑2
30  Z = (Y↑2) - (4*Y) + 6
40  GO TO 20
50  PRINT X; Y; Z
60  END
```

Interpretive BASIC gives users the facility of stopping the program by hitting a specified key on the terminal and examining the value of each variable. Thus programs can be stopped at any line and the values compared with those expected from test data. Frequently BASIC interpreters allow users to execute programs a line at a time, helping to locate any 'bugs'. Lines that are found to be causing trouble may be corrected immediately, others may be added or deleted at will. Even variables which have been given the wrong values can be corrected, and the program restarted at the same point or some other. Testing a program can therefore be quick and relatively painless.

A1.6 Cost/benefit of user programming

The example developed in Section A1.3 took no more than 3 hours to design, program and test. It is now available at any time for any user in the company where it was produced. The total cost was 3 hours of the accountant's time plus a minimal computer cost on their in-house machine. Even using bureaux the computer cost will probably be less than £5 per hour using BASIC. When it is used in the future, each run will take less than 30 seconds from start to finish, and will not cost more than £1.

The benefits are, as always, much more difficult to assess. What is the value of predicting budget increases? How can it be measured? What is the effect of not predicting budgets accurately?

Such questions are best left to the manager who prepares budget figures, and whose own ability to judge trends may improve as a result of better understanding the sensitivity of the total budget to individual items.

An exactly similar analysis can be carried out in the sales office, warehouse, production area, laboratory, or design office.

One design engineer, introduced to BASIC for the first time, wrote a program which calculated friction losses in a pipe. This is a calculation which he carries out many times a day and immediately before attending the seminar (at which he learned BASIC) he had been presented with a problem which required him to make over 1,000 calculations. He estimated they would have taken him 3 to 4 days to complete manually (6-8 minutes/calculation).

Within 2 hours the program had been written and the problem solved — saving him at least $3\frac{1}{2}$ days of his time, guaranteeing the accuracy of the calculations, and forever ridding him of the need to repeat the calculation manually.

Cost/benefit predictions have never been easy to make, nor can they always be justified retrospectively. The examples just given are not, therefore, intended to prove that writing simple BASIC programs will *always* produce benefits which heavily outweigh costs. However, as inexpensive microcomputers become universally available for this type of program, 'costs' will reduce and 'benefits' might increase.

At the time of writing, Commodore, Radio Shack (Tandy in the UK) and others are offering low cost microcomputers which will allow users to develop DIY programs for a total capital outlay of only a few week's salary. These systems (as explained in more detail in Chapter 11 devoted to microprocessors) will also support comprehensive commercial suites, but it is not being suggested that 'users' should prepare programs of that complexity. Rather it would seem that the benefits a user might expect to gain will come from the sort of short program discussed in this Appendix.

Appendix Two
UK SOURCES OF INFORMATION

Anyone wanting further information about computers can either read one or more of the computer magazines or journals (there are dozens) or directly approach a consultancy organisation. Those listed below have been chosen because they were well placed to direct enquirers to other organisations which can give direct assistance (in some cases, the organisations below may be able to help — particularly in the area of training).

British Computer Society
20 Portland Place, London W1N 4HU
Tel: 01-637 0471

Computing Services Association
109 Kingsway, London WC2B 6PU
Tel: 01-405 2172

National Computing Centre
Oxford Road, Manchester M1 7ED
Tel: 061-228 6333

Manpower Services Commission Training Services Division
95 Wigmore Street, London W1
Tel: 01-486 6688

Industrial Training Boards
(Contact that for your particular industry)

Department of Industry (Electronic Applications Division)
Dean Bradley House, Horseferry Road, London SW1P 2AG
Tel: 01-212 7676

British Institute of Management
Management House, Parker Street, London WC2B 5PT
Tel: 01-405 3456

and, of course, the company by which the writer is now employed:

BIS Applied Systems Ltd
York House, 199 Westminster Bridge Rd, London SE1 7UT
Tel: 01-633 0866

Appendix Three
COMPUTER MANUFACTURERS

The list that follows is intended merely as an introduction to some of the bigger names and their computer systems — and even they change their addresses from time to time! The computers listed against each supplier tend to be those offered for normal business operations, and some of the bigger systems, e.g. the CDC Cyber, have been omitted as being too large for the average firm.

Allied Business Systems
(Multibus)
1 Berkeley Street, London W1X 6NN

Burroughs Machines Ltd
(B80, B800 and B8000 series)
Heathrow House, Bath Road, Cromford, Middlesex
Tel: 01-759 6522

Computer Technology Ltd
(Modular One)
Eaton Road, Hemel Hempstead, Herts
Tel: 0422 3272

Data General Ltd
(CS and Nova series)
Westway House, 320 Ruislip, Greenford, Middlesex
Tel: 01-578 9231

Digital Equipment Corporation
(DEC 10, DEC 20; PDP8, PDP11 [family]; LSI 11 [family])
Fountain House, Butts Centre, Reading RG1 7QN.
Tel: 0734 583555

Hewlett Packard Ltd
(HP2000, HP3000)
King Street Lane, Winnersh, Berkshire, RG11 5AR
Tel: 0734 784774

Honeywell Information Systems
(H116 and H26 series; Level 62, Level 6)
Honeywell House, Great West Road, Brentford, Middlesex

IBM United Kingdom Ltd
(Series/1, System/32, System/34, IBM 360 series, IBM 370 series)
(General Systems Division), 28 The Quadrant, Richmond, Surrey TW9 1BW
Tel: 01-940 9545

International Computers Ltd
(ICL 1800 series, ICL 2800 series, System 10)
ICL House, Putney, London SW15
Tel: 01-788-7272

NCR Ltd.,
(8100 series, 8200 series)
206 Marylebone Road, London NW1 6LY
Tel: 01-723 7070

Nixdorf Computers Ltd
(Nixdorf 8800 series)
Hounslow Centre, 1 Lampton Road, Hounslow, Middlesex
Tel: 01-572 3111

Philips Data System
(P312, P330 and P410)
Elektra House, Bergholt Road, Colchester, Essex CO4 5BE
Tel: 0206 5115

Sperry Univac
(BC/7 series)
Sperry Univac Centre, Brentfields, London NW10 8LS
Tel: 01-965 0511

For more details about the computers systems mentioned in this Appendix, the processor they use, maximum core storage, peripherals etc., see *Guide to Small Business Systems* (ISBN 0 906481 00 7) edited by I. St. J. Hugo and published by Computer Guides Ltd (Tel: 01-359 7480). This comprehensive guide is published annually, so try to get 'this year's' copy.

Appendix Four
GUIDE TO UK MICROCOMPUTERS

The following list of microcomputers has been compiled to give some idea of the marketplace in 1980. However the range is constantly growing and it should not be taken as comprehensive. Up-to-date information is available from a number of sources and anyone wanting to either extend this list or get more details about any of the microcomputers mentioned here would do well to look back at Appendices 2 and 3.

Minicomputer	Micro-processor	Primary supplier(s)	RAM	Backing storage	Main languages	Approx. price (Jan 1980)	Notes
Apple	6502	Microsense (TEL. 0442 41191) and many dealers throughout the UK	16K-64K	Floppy disk and cassette	BASIC PASCAL Assembler	£1,000	
Attache	8080	Several suppliers throughout UK	16K-64K	Floppy disk	BASIC	£1,750 to £5,000+	Several business packages available: S100 bus
Billings	Z80A	Mitech Data Systems (TEL. 04862 23131)	64K	Floppy and hard disks	BASIC COBOL FORTRAN Assembler	£4,300	
Commodore PET	6502	Vast range of suppliers	8K-32K	Cassette and floppy disk	BASIC Assembler	£500 to £2,500	IEEE interface
Compelec Series 1	Z80	Compelec (TEL. 01-580 6296)	32K-64K	Floppy and cartridge disks	BASIC COBOL PASCAL FORTRAN IV Assembler	£5,000 up	Several business and word-processing packages
Compucolor	Z80	Abacus (TEL. 01-580 8841) & other distributors	8K-32K	Cassette and floppy disk	BASIC	£1,400	
Compucorp 610	Z80	Several dealers in the UK	Up to 60K	Floppy disk	BASIC Assembler	£4,000 up	Business packages & test editor

(Continued)

Minicomputer	Micro-processor	Primary supplier(s)	RAM	Backing storage	Main languages	Approx. price (Jan 1980)	Notes
Computer Centre Maxi	Z80	Computer Centre (TEL. 02514 29607)	16K	Floppy disk	BASIC ALGOL COBOL FORTRAN	£900	
Computer Workshop S1 to S3		Many dealers in UK	12K(S3)-40K(S1)	Cassette and floppy disk	BASIC Assembler	£1,300 (S3) to £5,000+(S1)	
Cromemco Z2	Z80	Comart (TEL. 0480 215005), Microcentre & many others	16K-512K	Floppy disk	BASIC FORTRAN COBOL Assembler	£360 to £3,700	Several other configurations available between Z2 & System 3/64 RS232 interface
Cromemco S3/64	Z80	As above	64K	Floppy and cartridge disks	BASIC FORTRAN IV COBOL Assembler	£3,270	Multichannel analogue interface (S100) Multi-user system
DSC-2	Z80	Modata (TEL. 0892 39591)	32K-64K	Floppy and rigid disks (up to 28Mb)	BASIC FORTRAN COBOL TEXT PROCESSOR	£4,500	RS232 interface
Dyle House Business Computing System 2000	Z80A	Dyle House Ltd (TEL. 01.529 2436)	About 64K	Floppy disk	BUSINESS BASIC	On request	Many business packages

Equinox	WD	Equinox Computer (TEL. 01-739 2387)	48K-256K	Floppy and hard disks	BASIC LISP PASCAL Macro Assembler TEXT PROCESSOR	£5,000 to £40,000+	Multi-user system
Euroc	8080A	Eurocalc (TEL. 01-405 3113)	64K	Floppy disk	BUSINESS BASIC	£8,000	Various business packages included
Exidy Sorcerer	Z80	Factor One	16K-32K	Cassette and floppy disk	BASIC Assembler EDITOR	£1,200	
Heath WH89	Z80	Heath Schlumberger (TEL. 0452 29451)	16K-48K	Disk	BASIC Assembler FORTRAN	£1,600	RS232 interface
Imsai			32K-64K	Floppy disk		£4,500	
Luxor ABC80	Z80	CCS Microsales	35K-40K	Cassette and floppy disk	BASIC Assembler	£800	60 compatible I/O interfaces
Megamicro	8080/Z80	Bytronix (TEL. 0252 726814)	64K	Floppy disk	BASIC COBOL PASCAL FORTRAN		Many business packages
Microstar		Microsolve (TEL. 01-951 0218)	64K	Floppy disk	RPG	£5,000+	Various business packages, multi-user RS232 interface

(Continued)

223

Minicomputer	Micro-processor	Primary supplier(s)	RAM	Backing storage	Main languages	Approx. price (Jan 1980)	Notes
Midwest Scientific Instruments	M6800	Strumech (TEL. 05433 4321)	16K-64K	Cassette, floppy and hard disks	BASIC EDITOR Assembler TEXT PROCESSOR	£1,100 to £12,000+	
Pegasus	Z80	London Computer Store (TEL. 01-388 5721)	48K-64K	Floppy disk	BASIC COBOL FORTRAN Assembler	£2,700	S100 bus
North Star Horizon	Z80A	Many UK distributors	16K-56K	Floppy disk	BASIC FORTRAN COBOL PILOT PASCAL	Under £1,000 to £2,500	S100 bus
Pertec	Z80A	Compelec (TEL. 01-580 6296)	32K-64K	Floppy disk	BASIC FORTRAN COBOL	£3,000-£5,000	Similar to Altair
Powerhouse 2	Z80A	Powerhouse (TEL. 0442 42002)	16K-32K	Cassette and floppy disks	BASIC	£1,200 up	Aimed at scientific use, e.g. real-time process control, RS232 interface
Processor Technology Sol	8080	Several distributors including Comart (TEL. 0480 215005)	16K	Cassette and floppy disk	BASIC Assembler	£5,000	S100 bus

Rair Black Box	Z80	Rair (TEL. 01-836 4663) and other distributors	32K-64K	Floppy and hard disks	BASIC FORTRAN IV COBOL	£2,300 up
Research Machines 380Z	Z80	Research Machines Ltd	4K-56K	Floppy disk	BASIC Assembler TEXT EDITOR FORTRAN COBOL ALGOL	£830 to £3,500 — Widely used in educational sector
SDS	8080	Airamco (TEL. 0294 65530)	32K-46K	Floppy disk	BASIC FORTRAN COBOL	£3,750 up — RS232 interface
Semel 1	Z80	Semel (TEL. 0822 5439)	4K-64K	Cassette and floppy disk	BASIC Assembler FORTRAN COBOL	£2,000 — Light-pen option
Solid State Technology Athena 8200	8085	Butel-Comco (TEL. 0703 39890)	1.2Gb	Cassette, floppy and hard disks	All major languages	£3,000 up — Multi-user, multi-tasking
Sord M100	Z80	Midas Computer Services (TEL. 0903 814523)	16K-48K	Cassette and floppy disk	BASIC	£730 up — S100 bus
TRS-80	Z80	All Tandy outlets & many other dealers	4K-64K	Cassette and floppy disk	BASIC	£500 to £5,000
Vector Graphics	Z80	Several distributors	48K	Disks	BASIC	£2,300

Appendix Five
GLOSSARY

This glossary has been compiled from the comments of a number of people who have read this book and who previously knew nothing about computers. It does not purport to be a complete glossary of all computing jargon you may come across — nor will some of the definitions necessarily coincide with those in some other glossaries. The reason for this is that, for an allegedly exact science, computer experts use words very loosely. And I have to say that I have seen some terms defined wrongly in other glossaries (confusion between time sharing and real time is a typical case in point). On other occasions my interpretation of a term may simply be different from another compiler's.

This glossary is wholly pragmatic. For a more complete — and wholly readable — glossary I would recommend the one published in *Practical Computing* in 1979.

Acoustic coupler Equipment used to connect terminals to the telephone system for onward connection to a computer. It is usually used in conjunction with a time-sharing system.

Address The location in the storage area of a computer in which any given variable is held.

Answer-back drum A small magnetic drum, fitted to a terminal, that carries an identification code — the code is read by the computer at log-on time.

Arithmetic processing unit (APU) The area within the central processing unit in which calculations are performed.

Assembler Computers will only work in binary numbers — which are difficult to write programs in. Assembler is a language, peculiar to a given computer, which is easier to deal with. It uses normal words and symbols, but (usually) still requires programmers to access core addresses directly.

Backing store Sometimes used to mean any method of storing programs and data other than within the computer's core. More usefully it is applied to storage held 'off-line', and not immediately accessible to the computer without human intervention (such as mounting a magnetic tape or disk).

Back-up files Spare copies of files for use if current files are damaged, corrupted or destroyed.

BASIC A high-level programming language developed for use by beginners. It is widely used by time-sharing bureaux and universally by microcomputers. BASIC purports to stand for Beginner's All-purpose Symbolic Instruction Code.

Batch processing The execution of one job at a time (in contrast to time sharing). See Chapter 5 for a full explanation.

Binary The number system that contains only two digits — 0 (zero) and 1 (one). Computers can only use binary and have a special code (see *EBCDIC*) for converting the usual decimal numbers and alphabetic characters to binary digits — bits.

Bipolar A manufacturing process for producing integrated circuits. It contrasts with MOS (*q.v.*).

Bit A binary digit — a zero or one used to represent numbers in the binary system.

Boot-strapping Derived from the expression 'Pulling yourself up by your boot-straps'. This term is used to describe the way computers start themselves up.

Buffer A small area in the core of a computer used to hold incoming and outgoing data — a sort of 'waiting-room'. Also applied to similar holding areas when data is transferred between tapes and disks, or any other device.

Byte A group of eight bits; used to represent any alphanumeric or special character.

Cartridge disks A form of disk used to store large amounts of data, often up to 250 Mbytes per cartridge pack.

Central processing unit (CPU) The part of the computer that stores programs and data during execution. It also holds the operating software which controls execution and does the sums.

Character A single letter of the alphabet or any special symbol such as * , ! or @ .

Chip Common parlance for any integrated circuit, but particularly reserved for a microprocessor.

COBOL A high-level language used in commercial applications. Derived from Common Business Oriented Language.

Compiler A form of program that converts complete high-level-language programs into machine code (binary code). See also *Interpreter*. Compiler languages include COBOL, FORTRAN and RPG.

Core The internal storage of a computer. Originally constructed from ferrite ring (hence 'core'), it now consists of modern semi-conductor devices.

Database An integrated system of data files that enables all programs to access the same data and which allows logical enquiries to be made.

DBMS Database management systems.

Disk The primary means of storing data for rapid access by the CPU.

Disk drive The device that contains disks and moves them to allow access to the data on the disk.

Dumping The process of transferring files to off-line storage for security.

EBCDIC The code used world-wide to represent characters. It stands for Extended Binary Coded Decimal Interchange Code.

Editor A utility program that facilitates the editing of files by users.

EPROM — Erasable programmable read only memory Like PROM and ROM, but the data can be removed by irradiating an EPROM with ultra-violet light.

Executive Another name for the operating software of a computer system.

Field Originally any single data value on a punched card, e.g. Price, Account No. or Quantity. The term is often applied to any piece of data that is meaningful in its own right.

File A set of data stored on a disk or magnetic tape, referenced by a single name, e.g. Stock. The data can be either numeric (Stock records) or a program (Re-order level calculations).

Firmware ROM (*q.v.*) which has been programmed with an operating system, compiler, interpreter, or applications program.

Floppy disk A form of disk used to store relatively small amounts of data (typically 110K bytes). Physically a floppy disk is similar to a 45 rpm record, but is more flexible.

FORTRAN A high-level language developed for scientific applications. It stands for FORmula TRANslation.

Hardware Any equipment used by, or in conjunction with, a computer installation — including the computer itself.

Head crash Term used to describe the accidental loss of files held on disks caused by the 'head' touching the disk's surface — either directly or because of dust.

Housekeeping Computer operations designed to help the efficiency of the system.

Integrated circuit (IC) A generic term used to describe any circuitry that can be put onto a small slice of silicon by suitably treating the silicon. It can be a simple logic gate, an amplifier or a complete computer (then known as a microcomputer).

Interpreter A form of computer program that converts high-level-language programs *line-by-line* into machine code (binary code). See also *Compiler*.

Interrupt handler A computer can be quietly minding its own business crunching numbers when an 'outsider' suddenly demands attention. The interrupt handler deals with the interruption, decides whether it should take priority over existing activities and handles the consequences.

K A measure of storage capacity — 1K = 1,024. For example, a storage capacity of 64K bytes.

Large scale integration (LSI) Term used to describe the production of large numbers of circuits on a single chip.

Load module (or program) An 'object module' (*q.v.*) with core addresses added, making it 'non-relocatable'.

Lock-out bit A binary digit used to enhance the security of a CPU.

Log-on code The code by which a user identifies himself to the computer.

MOS A type of integrated circuit design, determined by the production method. It stands for Metal Oxide Semiconductor and contrasts with the other common form of manufacturing — bipolar (*q.v.*).

Machine code The final, binary version of any source program after compilation.

Mainframe Term used to describe the very largest computers. It is usually reserved for complete systems costing in excess of £100,000. Typical mainframes include IBM370, DEC10, ICL1900 and CDC6600.

Management information system (MIS) A total system of files and high-level programming languages (usually linked with a database) which allows management to ask almost anything about anything.

Mega (M) A million (10^6).

Memory Same as core.

Microcomputer A complete computer made from integrated circuits. It will include a microprocessor, RAM, ROM and miscellaneous other integrated circuits (ICs). Some commercial microcomputers among over 60 on the market at the time of writing are Apple, PET, TRS-80, and 380Z.

Microprocessor A central processing unit implemented in 'chip' technology.

Minicomputer Originally this referred to a small computer that was much less powerful than a mainframe (*q.v.*). Nowadays, definition in these terms is impossible since many minicomputers are more powerful than the mainframes of the early 1970s. My definition of a minicomputer is reserved for complete hardware systems costing less than £100,000.

Modem A MOdulator-DEModulator that puts the signal from a terminal onto a carrier wave acceptable to the Post Office circuits and *vice-versa*. It is used to connect computers to terminals via the telephone network.

Monitor Another name for the operating system (*q.v.*).

Multiplexor A device for transferring code from several low-speed channels to a single high-speed channel — and *vice-versa*.

Multiprogramming A method of using the CPU so as to allow several programs to be executed simultaneously.

Nibble A term introduced as a joke to describe the 4-bit words used by early microprocessors. (Half a Byte!)

Object module (or program) The machine code output from a compiler. Whilst the term is sometimes used to describe the executable form of the program, it is normally reserved for the version that is stored on a disk and which does not have assigned addresses. See *Load module*.

OEM Original equipment manufacturer.

On-line Strictly speaking, anything that is connected directly to the CPU. Often applied to terminals and storage.

OS — Operating system The program or programs that control all the facilities and activities of a computer system.

Overlay Using an area of core several times during the execution of a single program suite. Doing so obliterates any existing program using the overlaid part of core.

Parity A means of checking that any single bit within a byte has not been corrupted. The normal technique is to add an extra bit which is set to 1 or 0 in order to ensure an odd or even number of 1's.

Peripherals Anything except the CPU. However, on-line terminals are usually excluded from the class of peripherals.

Processor See *CPU*.

Program A collection of instructions written in a language the computer can deal with (either high-level, assembler or machine-code), which enables the computer to perform some function.

PROM — Programmable read-only memory Like *ROM* (*q.v.*) but it can be programmed by the user with a special piece of equipment called a 'PROM-blaster'.

RAM — Random access memory An integrated circuit designed to act as the core storage of a computer. It can contain and store data, but will lose the data if, for example, the power is switched off.

Random access A means of storing data such that each item (or field) can be located directly.

Read only executive An executive that cannot be altered (written to) by the user.

Read only memory See *ROM*.

Real time A computer system that operates synchronously with actual events. The system 'works' only when external events demand it. Despite common usage, it is not the same as *time sharing*.

Record A single line of program or a single line of data file (usually the latter). The length of a data record is not defined.

Remote terminals *(a)* Terminals that are not in the same building as the computer; *(b)* any terminal connected to a time-sharing system.

Resident executive That part of the executive (operating software) that is in the core (CPU) at a given time. Many executives are wholly resident permanently.

ROM — Read only memory An integrated circuit designed to store data (or instructions) in the same way that 'core' holds data. But it does not lose the data if, for example, the power is switched off. Once set up, ROM data cannot be altered. Sometimes ROM is used to denote 'relocatable object module' (see *Object module*).

RPG   A high-level language originally designed to make report-writing easy to program and now a fully fledged programming language. RPG stands for 'report program generator'.

SBS — Small business system   A package of hardware and software designed to carry out all the business control and recording functions needed by a company. SBSs are normally implemented on minicomputers.

Software   A generic term used to describe all forms of computer program — operating, applications or database. Contrasts with *hardware* and *firmware*.

Source program   Any program written in a high-level language, before it is compiled.

Statement   A single instruction in a source (high-level) program.

Supervisor   Another name for the operating system.

Teleprocessing   A method of linking terminals to the computer.

Terminals   Devices that allow on-line keyboard access to a CPU and visual or hard-copy output. Sometimes also used to describe card readers that are remote from the computer premises.

Time sharing   A means of allowing several users to use core in turn in such a way that it appears to the user that he has sole use of the computer. Typically each user can have up to 0.1 sec of CPU at a go.

ULA — Uncommited logic array   Many logic circuits start with a standard layout which is then 'programmed' to the users' requirements. The circuit, before 'programming', is a ULA.

Utilities   Machine-code programs held within a computer's operating system which can be called into the object modules of source programs to perform standard functions such as sorting.

VDU   See *Visual display unit*.

Virtual memory (or storage)   In the early 1970s when 'core' was still expensive, some manufacturers devised ways of treating disk storage as though it were 'in core'. This effectively increases core memory. The first virtual memory computer was built in the 1950s — the Manchester Atlas.

VRC — Visible record computer An obsolete form of accounting machine which has a computer CPU but which holds its data on magnetic ledger cards.

Visual display unit (VDU) A terminal that displays the computer's output on a screen. Sometimes reserved for terminals with visual output which are not 'remote'.

Word The number of bits which the computer handles as a unit. When the number is 8, a word is equivalent to a 'byte'.

Appendix Six
BIBLIOGRAPHY

Barden, W., *How to Buy and Use Minicomputers and Microcomputers*, Prentice Hall (1977).

Bartel, T. C., *Digital Computer Fundamentals*, McGraw-Hill (1972).

Healey, M., *Minicomputers and Microprocessors*, Hodder and Stoughton (1976).

Distributed Data Processing: A Management Guide, Digital Equipment Corporation (1977).

Hardcastle (Editor), *Trends in Distributed Systems*, National Computing Centre (1978).

Galley, J. N., *The Board and Computer Management*, Business Books (1978).

Sanders, D. H., *Computers and Management in a Changing Society*, McGraw-Hill (1974).

Schoeffler, J. P., and Temple, R. H., *Minicomputers: Hardware, Software and Applications*, IEEE Press [Wiley Interscience (Distributors)], (1972).

Smith, C. L., *Digital Computers Process Control*, Intext Educational.

Weizenbaum, J., *Computer Power and Human Reason*, Freeman, (1976).

There are literally hundreds of potentially useful references. This short list will provide reference to many more.

The following journals/magazines are amongst those worth perusing: *Computing, Computer Weekly, Which Computer?* and *Which Wordprocessor?*

INDEX

Access, prevention of unauthorised, 47-8
Accounting systems, diagrams of, 128-9
Addresses:
   journals etc., 174, 236
   of manufacturers, 217-19
   sources of information, 215-16
Advice, where and how to obtain, 174
   see also Addresses
Analysis using Small Business Systems, 130-31
Applications:
   batch operation, appropriate and inappropriate, 67-8
   business (of microcomputers), 173-4
   can it be done?, 11
     and what can be done, 14-15, 18-20
   circuit work, 15-16
   electronic engineering, 15-16
   for control functions, 170-2
   for finance, 11-12
   glossary of terms, 226-33
   in business, 11-12
   multiprogramming, appropriate and inappropriate, 71
   needs, beware of changing, 14
   office management, 13
   of microcomputers, 168-72
   of Small Business Systems, 132-4
   production control, 12-13
   real time, appropriate, 76-7
   remote job entry, appropriate and inappropriate, 68-9
   research and development, control of, 12
   sales control, 13-14
   software, 88-93
   stock control, 16-18
   teleprocessing, appropriate and inappropriate, 73-4
   time sharing, appropriate and inappropriate, 75-6
Architectural requirements to house, 104-5
Arithmetic processing unit, 105
ASC 11, 115
Audit, need for continuous, 60

BASIC (language), 177-214
   approach to subject, 177-8
   commands, explanation of additional, 206-12
   DIM, 206-7

PRINTUSING, 207-10
  sample program, 210-12
  expressions, *see* Statements *below in this entry*
  origin of term, 177
  programs, designing simple, 197-206
  statements and expressions, 178-97
    'Alpha' explained, 181-2
    arrays, 180-1
    conditional branches, 186-8
    data statements, 193-4
    functions, 182
    input and output, 182-4
    line numbers, 185-6
    loops, 188-92
    output and input, 182-4
    relationships, 178-80
    sub-routines, 194-6
    unconditional branches, 185
    variables, naming of, 180
  test facilities, 212-14
Batch operating, 65-8, 77
Bibliography, 234-5
Binary codes, 106-9
Breakdowns, 59-60
Budget variances, 2
Buildings to house computers, 104-5
Business analysts, 26-7
Business applications, 11-12
Bytes, 123-4

Cassettes, 119
Central processing units, 105-113
Chip, microcomputerised, 165-6
Circuits for electronics, 15-16
COBOL explained, 177-8
Commercial bureau, security measures peculiar to, 53-4
Computer system, what constitutes a, 3-4
Computers, *see* Addresses; Advice, where and how to obtain; Applications; Financial aspects; Glossary of terms; Hardware; Implementation; Language; Microcomputers; Operating configurations; People; Security; Selection of system; Software
Control applications of microcomputers, 170-2
Core configuration, 109-13

Database Management Systems (DBMS), 2, 93-9

Data processing, safety measures as to, 51-3
Data store, security precautions for, 61-2
DBMS, *see* Database Management Systems
Decimal interchange code, 108-9
Decision-making, using computer for, 139
Denary and binary codes contrasted, 107-9
Design criteria in selecting a system, 148-9
Development areas, government assistance in, 4
DIM statement, 206-7
Disks, 116-18

EBCDIC (code), 108-9
Editing software, 87
Electronic engineering, 15-16
Environmental needs, 153-4
Evaluation after implementation, 157-8
Extended binary code, 108-9

Feasibility studies, 140-4
File management, software, 85-6
Files, safeguarding content of, 46-7
Finance, institutional use for, 11-12
Financial aspects, 1-8
  advantages, 1-3
  capital outlay, 4-5
  cost control, 2-3
  hardware, 3-6
  insurance, 5
  maintenance costs, 5
  need, not budget, criterion, 4
  pitfalls to avoid, 1
  program capability, 6-7
  security aspects, 8
  software, 6-7
  staffing needs, 7-8
  write-off period, 5
Fire precautions, 55-6
Firmware (microcomputers), 162-3
FORTRAN explained, 177
Fraud, guarding against, 54

Glossary of terms, 226-33

Hardware:
  architectural needs, 104-5
  ASCII (code), 115-16
  binary codes, 106-9

cassettes, 119
central processing units, 105-113
components, 105-13
computer system, what comprises?, 103-5
core configuration, 109-113
disks, 116-18
EBCDIC (code), 108-9
for Small Business Systems, 123-5
functions explained, 105-6
historical background, 101-3
input devices, 103, 113-16
magnetic tape, 118-19
modern developments, 106
output devices, 104, 113-16
peripherals, 113-16
punch cards, 119
requirements, 3-6
security precautions and, 61-2
storage devices, 103, 116-19
Hiring, 4

Implementation of computer systems, 151-8
changeover, effecting the, 156-7
environmental needs, 153-4
evaluation following, 157-8
foolish mistakes, avoiding, 151
organisational needs, 155-6
planning stage, 152-3
scheduling project, 152-3
Information:
about computers, where and how to obtain, 174
prevention of leaks in, 48
retrieved (using Small Business Systems), 135
sources of obtaining, on computers, 215-16
Input devices, 104, 113-16
Installation, security of, *see* Security
Insurance factor, 5
Interpreters (of language), 83
Inventory, *see* Stock Control
Involvement, ensuring proper, 40-1

Job descriptions, how computer effects, 55
Journals on computers, 174, 236

Language, 11, 30
glossary of terms in common usage, 226-33
software, 79-83

see also BASIC language
Language compilers, 82-3
Leasing, 4
Ledgers and Small Business Systems, 133

Magazines devoted to computers, 174, 236
Magnetic tape, 118-19
Manager, computer, finding the right, 27-8
Management, computer use by, 35-9
Meanings of terms in common usage, 226-33
Memory:
enquiry of, in Small Business Systems, 130-1
in microcomputers, 163
in microprocesses, 167-8
security measures concerning, 57-8
Microcomputers:
applications of, 168-72
to business, 173-4
approach to subject, 161-2
are they special?, 163-5
chip, producing a, 165-6
compactness, 164
control usage through, 170-2
developments taking place, 169-72
features of, 162-3
firmware, 162-3
help, where and how to obtain, 174
microprocessors, 166-8
names of varieties of, 220-5
reliability, 164
suppliers of, by make, 220-5
types manufactured, 220-5
Microprocessor, development of, 166-8
Minicomputers:
names, types and suppliers of, 220-5
programmers for, 33-4
Multiprogramming, 70-1, 77

Office, the computer in the, 13
Operating configurations, 65-77
batch operation, 65-8
suitability or otherwise, 77
comprehensive system, 76
multiprogramming, 69-71
suitability or otherwise, 77
realtime, 76-7
suitability or otherwise, 77
remote job entry process, 68-9
suitability or otherwise, 77

239

teleprocessing, 72-4
  suitability or otherwise, 77
time sharing, 74-6
  suitability or otherwise, 77
Operations staff requirements, 32-3, 154
Order processing by Small Business Systems, 132-3
Organisations dealing with advice, 174
Output devices, 104, 113-16

People and the computer, 23-42
  attitudes, understanding work force, 23-5
  manager, finding the right, 27-8
  operations staff required, 32-3
  programmers, 29-30
    costs involved, 31
    distinguished from analysts, 29-30
    for minicomputers, 33-4
    selection of, 31-2
    —, for minicomputers, 34
    systems, 32
    training of, 30-1
  specialisms, 25-34
    business analysts, 26-7
    systems analysts, 25-6
  users, 34-42
    involvement, creating the right atmosphere in, 40-1
    management, 35-9
    training for, 42
    work force, 39-40
Peripherals, 104, 113-16
Planning the implementation of a system, 152-3
Preventive measures, *see* Security
PRINTUSING statement, 207-10
Problem-solving by computer, 138
Process control, *see* Robotic systems
Production control techniques, 12-13
Production scheduling with Small Business Systems, 133
Programmers, *see under* People
Programs:
  maintenance of software, 92-3
  multi systems, 70-1
  sample of using steps in, 210-12
  security of, 61-2
  see also BASIC language
Program speeds, 6-7
Publications devoted to computers, 174, 235

Punch cards, 119

Real-time configuration, 76-7
Remote job entry system, 68-9, 77
Research and development controls, 12
RPG system, 177

Safeguards, *see* Security
Sales, control aspects for, 13-14
Screen display software, 87-8
Screen formats (Small Business Systems), 127-8
Security, 45-63
  audit, need for continuous, 60
  data processing, is it adequate?, 51-3
  definition in computer context, 45
  fire risks, 55-6
  job descriptions, effect on, 55
  protection safeguards, 54-63
    against breakdown, 59-60
    for data, 61-2
    for memories, 57-8
    fraud, 54
    of installation, 55-7
    of people, 54-5
    of programs, 61-2
    of software, 58-9
    using hardware for, 61-2
    using software for, 62-3
  threats to, 46-50
    access, preventing unauthorised, 47-8
    as to file content, 46-7
    installation, 48-50
    leaking information, 48
    peculiar to commercial bureaux, 53-4
  training aspects, 54-5
Selection of the system, 137-58
  as a decision-maker, 139
  benefits, 139
  design criteria, 148-9
  feasibility study, 140-4
  inventory levels, 139-40
  need, identifying the, 138
  problem solving, 138
  staff reductions, unlikely to produce, 139
  suppliers, evaluating the proposals of, 147-8
  tendering when buying, 144-7
Silicon chip, microcomputerised, 165-6
Small Business Systems, 5

accounting system (diagrammatically), 128
advantages, 126
analysis procedure, 130-1
applications of, list of typical, 132-4
approach to subject, 121-3
considerations, 13; questions to ask about, 125
hardware, 123-5
inquiry of retained memories, 130-1
restrictions in operating, 126-7
screen formats, 127-8
software, 125-31
   applications of, 131-4
stock directory (diagrammatically), 129
suppliers, list of, 134-5
utilities, available, 131
Software:
   applications, 88-93
      in Small Business Systems, 132-4
      packages, 88-9
      program maintenance, 92-3
      when custom-built, 90-2
   approach to subject, 79
   database, 93-9
   for Small Business Systems, 125-31
      applications of, 131-4
   languages, 79-83
   operating techniques, 93-8
      editing, 87
      file management, 85-6
      operating system costs, 88
      screen displays, 87-8
      utilities, 87
      virtual memory, 84
   requirements, 6-7
   security precautions and, 58-9, 62-3
Staff, will computer result in reduction of ?, 139
   see also Operations staff; People
Stock control, 16-18
   by Small Business Systems, 129, 133
   inventory levels of, 139-40
Storage (hardware) devices, 103, 116-19
   see also Data storage; Memories
Suppliers of Small Business Systems, 134-5
   evaluating proposals of, 147-8
Systems analysts, 25-6

Teleprocessing, 72-4, 77
Tenders to purchase a system, 144-7
Terms, glossary of, 226-33
Time-sharing configuration, 74-6, 77
Training:
   in security matters, 54-5
   of programmers, 30-2
   of users, 42

Uses see Applications
Utilities available with Small Business Systems, 131

Work force and use of computer, 39-40